THE IMPACT OF LUIS PALAU ON GLOBAL EVANGELISM

10 1/25/21 3,00

THE IMPACT OF LUIS PALAU ON GLOBAL EVANGELISM

AN EVALUATION OF HIS THEOLOGY AND STRATEGY

Hongnak Koo

The Impact of Luis Palau on Global Evangelism

Published in the United States by Credo House Publishers,
a division of Credo Communications, LLC, Grand Rapids, Michigan;
www.credocommunications.net

Published in partnership with Luis Palau Association.
LPA's mission is to proclaim the gospel, mobilize the church,
and equip the next generation.

To respond to the message of this book, for more information about the ministry, and for details on how to order additional copies of *The Impact of Luis Palau on Global Evangelism*, please contact us at

Luis Palau Association
PO Box 50
Portland, Oregon 97207
Phone: 503.614.1500
Fax: 503.614.1599
Email: info@palau.org
www.palau.org

ISBN-10: 1-935391-50-X
ISBN-13: 978-0-935391-50-0

Cover design by Katie Bredemeier
Interior design and composition by Frank Gutbrod

Printed in the United States of America

First Edition

To Jesus, my Savior and Lord,
to Sangsim, my beloved wife,
and to Sophia, Gloria, Grace, and Eunice,
my dear daughters, precious gifts from God.

To Greg & Ann!

You have blessed
my life for so many
years! The Lord bless +
encourage you always!

Ps 37:4

CONTENTS

LIST OF ABBREVIATIONS

BGEA	Billy Graham Evangelistic Association
CONELA	Confraternity of Evangelicals in Latin America
ICIE	International Conference for Itinerant Evangelists
LCWE	Lausanne Committee for World Evangelization
LPA	Luis Palau Association
	(LPEA changed its name to LPA in 2005)
LPEA	Luis Palau Evangelistic Association
MARC	Missions Advanced Research and Communications Center
OC	One Challenge International
QPR	Queen's Park Rangers (Football Stadium)
SEPAL	*Servicio Evangelizador Para America Latina*
WCC	World Council of Churches
WEA	World Evangelical Alliance
WEF	World Evangelical Fellowship
IFMA	Interdenominational Foreign Mission Association
EFMA	Evangelical Foreign Missions Association
NGA	Next Generation Alliance

PREFACE

Evangelism has been my heart's desire and passion ever since I was converted. The gospel gave me the reason, purpose, and direction for my life. Along the pathway of my spiritual journey, however, I sometimes forget God's love and the despair in people's lives without Christ. It has been a privilege for me to write this book on evangelist Luis Palau. His passion for the gospel and compassion for lost people have rekindled my heart with the love of Christ.

I am indebted to many individuals for the completion of this dissertation. First of all, my sincere gratitude goes to two professors of evangelism, Dr. Roy Fish and Dr. Malcolm McDow. Through their lives and teachings, they have provided invaluable lessons to me. I also would like to express my gratitude to Dr. John Moldovan, who recommended this topic and guided me through the process of writing. Without his valuable insights, this work could not have been completed.

Many thanks go out to the staff at Luis Palau Association for this research. Without their cooperation and support, this book could not have been accomplished. I am particularly grateful to Kathy Chastain, Media Coordinator for LPA, who arranged interviews with key staff of LPA and provided valuable information and materials that were essential to this work. I also want to express my gratitude to David Jones, Vice President of Corporate Affairs and CFO for LPA, for his encouragement and help in the process of publication. I am also grateful to Mindi Fires, who encouraged me through prayer and who proofread my original manuscript. In addition, I must express my utmost appreciation to the congregation at Midland Korean Baptist Church, which I serve as pastor. Without their understanding, support, and prayer I could not have finished this dissertation.

Finally, I owe a debt of gratitude to my wife, Sangsim, and to my dear daughters, Sophia, Gloria, Grace, and Eunice. Their presence, love, and prayer have sustained and enabled me to finish what I started. Most of all, glory be to God, who loved me, saved me, and called me as His servant for His kingdom.

Hongnak Koo
Midland, Texas
September 2010

FOREWORD

It is a great honor to be asked to write the foreword for a book about Luis Palau. Hundreds of articles and brief pieces have been written about Luis, some of them very extensive, but a comprehensive biography has not been written about him since 1980. This present book meets a critical need.

With the winding down of the preaching ministry of Billy Graham, numerous evangelicals have been rather gloomy in their predictions about the future of mass crusade evangelism. Historically this has happened before; but God has a way of surprising the pessimistic forecasters by raising up another whose mass evangelism crusade ministries impact entire cities and draw hundreds of thousands to witness it happening. Luis Palau, an Argentinean evangelist who speaks flawless English, has signaled another positive sign for crusade evangelism's future.

This book introduces us to a man who next to Mr. Graham stands taller in the ministry of crusade evangelism than any of his contemporaries. Palau is certainly a man who is deserving of first-rate biographical study. Through various aspects of the media, along with his crusades, he has preached the gospel to over one billion people. Over one million have made commitments to Christ through his ministry. This book makes Luis Palau come alive and will cause one to think they know him personally or at least to wish they did. It answers the question, "How does it happen that God puts His hand on a South American, who, on the surface does not appear to be anything extraordinary, and yet God uses him as an instrument through which He shakes cities all across the world." In answering this question, the author leaves us a book which is both factual and tremendously inspiring.

Few evangelists have ever handled the tense areas faced by a vocational evangelist any better than Palau. He understands well the relationship between evangelism and social concern as well as the imperative of a workable program of discipleship for those who make commitments through his ministry. Having come to his defense in these areas, it must be said that the real driving force in Palau's ministry has been his urgency in sharing the message of Jesus. This is unquestionably his highest priority.

This book gives us page after page on which one will find no dullness. Thank you, Luis, for coming our way through a book which should be read by hundreds of thousands of readers.

Dr. Roy J. Fish
Southwestern Baptist Theological Seminary

INTRODUCTION

Throughout church history, Jesus' Great Commission has been carried out by godly individuals who had both passion for the message of the gospel and compassion for the lost people of the world. It has been especially during the last couple of centuries that God has raised up great evangelists as His witnesses. Christians are familiar with names like John Wesley, George Whitefield, Jonathan Edwards, Charles G. Finney, D. L. Moody, Wilbur Chapman, R. A. Torrey, Billy Sunday, and Billy Graham.

Each of these men had his unique calling, personality, theology, and strategy.[1] Building upon the theology and methods of their predecessors, they also developed their own theological emphases and approaches. Their ministries were not without flaws, but they obeyed the Lord's Great Commission and advanced the kingdom of God on Earth with excellence. Through their faithful service, they not only impacted their own worlds but left a tremendous legacy for evangelists in succeeding generations.

Because they often traveled from place to place to preach the gospel, these men were called itinerant evangelists, and due to the fact that their audience involved a large number of people their evangelistic efforts were often classified as "mass evangelism."[2] Even though the term is fairly new, this form of proclamation of the gospel goes back to the first century. Jesus not only shared the message of the gospel individually but also proclaimed the good news to the masses. This practice was followed by His apostles after His death and resurrection.[3]

Mass evangelism has played an important role from the beginning of the Christian faith and has continued to be an effective tool for communicating the message of the gospel to large bodies of people throughout the centuries. In the words of Alvin Reid, "Mass evangelism has endured as a timeless method ordained by God in Scripture and used with incredible effectiveness throughout history."[4]

Despite the strategic role of evangelists and the effectiveness of mass evangelism in Christian history, many pessimistic concerns have arisen among Christians. These negative outlooks compelled this researcher to probe the ministry of Luis Palau, one of the most successful evangelists in the world today.

Current Challenges to Evangelists and Mass Evangelism

Throughout Christian history, evangelists have been God's spokespersons, bringing sinners to salvation by proclaiming the message of the gospel. Yet there have to varying degrees been skeptical voices. According to the observation of Edward Murphy, resistance to the idea of mass evangelism "runs all the way from cool indifference to hot opposition."[5]

Delos Miles, for example, records Arthur C. Archibald's statement, made in 1946, which expressed his pessimistic outlook on mass evangelistic campaigns and itinerant evangelists: "Revivals and the vogue of itinerant evangelists were essentially a nineteenth century product. They grew out of the camp-meeting custom and the ways of pioneer preachers. On the whole, they served their day and generation well. But that day has passed."[6]

This view was expressed more than sixty years ago, but uncertainty about mass evangelism seems widespread still today. In his 1995 discussion of the contemporary situation, evangelist Kelly Green expresses the following:

> As we enter the final few years of the second millennium, some are arguing that mass evangelism's days are numbered. Critics argue that rapidly changing culture, particularly in North America, has made this approach irrelevant. The fast-

> paced 1990s do in fact provide many more options for people to spend their time than did the 1950s. Furthermore, lost people do not attend religious meetings as readily as they did in the 1950s. The televangelist scandals have helped bring the public's opinion of evangelists to what may be an all-time low.[7]

The outlook for mass evangelism is even more in question since the renowned and respected evangelist Billy Graham, who preached to more people than any other in human history,[8] is fading from the public scene.[9] Accordingly, as Michael Cassidy states, "Anxiety about mass evangelism is real, deep and widespread."[10]

On the one hand, this hopeless perception stems from changing circumstances, including a lack of interest in religion and spiritual matters due to increasing secularism and materialism. On the other hand, however, the gloomy outlook originates from criticisms related to mass evangelism itself. In fact, scholars have over time debated the validity of mass evangelism.[11] Leighton Ford, for example, commented on the clashing debates surrounding mass evangelism in his day:

> In the contemporary debate on "mass evangelism" proponents may pinpoint certain results—the stirring of an indifferent community, the power of a united witness to the common Christ, the encouragement of Christians, the undoubted conversions of outsiders and nominal Christians, the numerical strengthening of the churches. Critics may focus on alleged weaknesses—that evangelistic campaigns are based on questionable emotional, financial, and organizational techniques, create an artificial context for decision, lack social involvement, postpone genuine involvement in mission, fail to produce lasting results, stress superficial "appeals" as signs of commitment, present a distorted message, and transfer evangelistic responsibility from the church to a specialist.[12]

Although this statement was made in 1966, the current situation is not much different.[13] How do Christians respond to the seeming ineffectiveness of mass evangelism, as well as to other, related criticisms?

As Mathews asks, "Are these concerns compelling enough to require creative adjustments in its application or serious enough to disqualify its use altogether?"[14] The bottom line question is whether mass evangelism can still be used as an effective method for the evangelization of the world or whether it will be a thing of the past, as some have predicted.

There have been strong voices among scholars demanding new approaches in mass evangelism. Church growth expert Win Arn asks, "Can the 'method' of mass evangelism be more effective in reaching people for Jesus Christ and incorporating them into His Body? Yes and no. Apparently not, if we continue doing it the same old way."[15] Henry Schmidt also made this remark,

> With the exception of Billy Graham crusades, they [campaigns] no longer capture people's attention (crowds) and the support (churches) as they did in an earlier era in North America. This does not invalidate their legitimacy or necessity, but *it does call for some revamping and retooling for greater effectiveness* [emphasis mine].[16]

In fact, unless there is a breakthrough, the future does not seem bright. If this is indeed the case, what would be the answer to the current pessimistic perception? Is there any hope for mass evangelism in the future? If there is, who would provide a new role model and guidelines for mass evangelism? This research seeks to find some plausible answers in the evangelistic ministry of Luis Palau.

Luis Palau as a Role Model for Evangelists

Luis Palau, an Argentinean-born evangelist, has recently sent a positive signal for the future of mass evangelism. According to a recent survey by *Christianity Today*, in answer to the question "Are city-wide crusades a thing of the past?" 62 percent of participants in the survey said no. One of the main reasons for such a positive outlook for mass evangelism centered around reports from Luis Palau's evangelistic campaigns in 2007: Approximately 400,000 people attended his festival in Monterrey, Mexico, and 140,000 people his two-day festival in Tampa Bay.[17]

Through his evangelistic campaigns, Luis Palau has proclaimed the gospel of Jesus Christ to more than 25 million people in seventy-two nations. Furthermore, he has reached more than 1 billion people worldwide through various evangelistic events and media, including radio, television, print, and the Internet, leading more than 1 million people to make a registered decision for Jesus Christ.[18] He has authored more than fifty books and booklets, as well as numerous articles on various issues involving Christian faith and life.[19] His radio broadcasts, both in English and in Spanish, are heard daily over three thousand radio outlets, reaching forty-eight countries. Palau also has counseled around the world with many leaders in business and politics. His evangelistic ministry has impacted countless individuals, ranging from a president even to a terrorist.

Palau's evangelistic ministry has been acknowledged by many over the past couple of decades. In his discussion of current situations in mass evangelism, Green states: "In our own day, Billy Graham and Luis Palau are among the most prominent of a whole host of itinerant evangelists who are proclaiming the Gospel throughout the world in large crusades, cooperative revival meetings, or single church evangelistic emphases."[20] William Morrow also acknowledges Palau's effective ministry in the midst of growing concern about the future of mass evangelism. Referring to Palau's "festivals," which represent a contemporary expression of evangelistic campaigns, he states, "These festivals have shown signs of promise in reaching areas where traditional campaign evangelism may not be effective."[21]

Furthermore, the media has called Luis Palau "Evangelist to Three Worlds,"[22] "the Billy Graham of Latin America,"[23] and "the Next Billy Graham."[24] According to the poll by *The Church Report,* he was even voted the seventh most influential Christian in America in 2004.[25] Despite such honorable designations and flattering praises, Palau's impact on evangelism has not been studied comprehensively.[26] Although there have been some studies focusing on his ministry, their scope is limited to certain times and places.[27] More comprehensive academic research on Luis Palau and his evangelistic ministry is needed.

The Role of the Evangelist Is Not Obsolete

The purpose of this research is to assert that Luis Palau's evangelistic ministry demonstrates the strategic role of evangelists and the viability and effectiveness of mass evangelism for world evangelization. Through his evangelistic ministry Palau has shown that the role of evangelist is not obsolete and that mass evangelism is not outdated, as some argue; rather, evangelists have a strategic place in today's world in terms of fulfilling the Great Commission, and mass evangelism, when used in a relevant way, as dictated by rapidly changing circumstances, is still effective and powerful.

This researcher will examine various aspects of Palau's evangelistic efforts, including his life, theology, strategy, and fruits, providing answers to the following questions: Who influenced Palau to be an evangelist? What are the core theological and philosophical convictions on evangelism that drive him to passionately pursue evangelism? And what strategies does he utilize to accomplish the task of evangelism in a rapidly changing world?

The answers to these questions are indispensable in understanding Palau's impact on contemporary global evangelism. By investigating the fruit of his ministry around the world and examining his theology and strategy pertinent to his evangelistic ministry, one will ascertain the positive and contributing role of evangelists and mass evangelism for world evangelization. In the final analysis, an integrative conclusion will be drawn, analyzing all of the aspects enumerated above, along with suggestions for future applications for mass evangelism.

Preliminary Definitions

Definition of Evangelism

Before discussing Luis Palau's impact on global evangelism, it is necessary to define the meanings of evangelism and mass evangelism. As evangelism has emerged as one of the crucial issues of the Christian faith and Church, numerous definitions have come to light.[28] This research will not attempt to discuss the whole range of different meanings of evangelism or definitions that have been posited.[29] Rather, a brief working definition for the purpose of clarification and development of the thesis will be offered.

One such designation is the 1918 Anglican definition of evangelism: "To evangelize is so to present Christ Jesus in the power of the Holy Spirit, that men shall come to put their trust in God through Him, to accept Him as their Saviour, and serve Him as their King in the fellowship of His Church."[30] Due to its simplicity and clarity, this definition has been adopted and quoted widely. George Hunter III lists six reasons, to follow, for its "enduring strength and unchallenged status":

1. It implies the necessity, within God's redemptive design, of the human initiative of Christians toward prechristian [*sic*] people.
2. It affirms the roles of Jesus Christ as both Savior and Lord.
3. It affirms the Trinitarian understanding of God and the respective roles of the three Persons in evangelism.
4. It understands the Church to play a central role within evangelism.
5. It views the new Christian's response as including both faith and service.
6. The definition's total thrust actually supports the ministry of evangelism, i.e., it is for it![31]

Throughout this study, the writer will use the term "evangelism" as defined in this 1918 Anglican definition.[32]

Definition of Mass Evangelism

Mass evangelism is one type of evangelism. As noted by Robert Lynn Asa, it is hard to find any consensus of definition for mass evangelism.[33] Some have even raised the question of the legitimacy of the term.[34] Leighton Ford and Hollis Green, for example, have advocated that mass evangelism cannot be totally differentiated from personal evangelism since individuals make decisions for Christ even though the gospel is preached to the masses.[35]

Their observation on the inseparable nature of mass evangelism and personal evangelism is accurate. The term "mass evangelism," however, is neither "misleading,"[36] as Leighton Ford calls it, nor "a misnomer,"[37] as Hollis Green claims. Since mass evangelism is definitely a different approach from personal one-on-one sharing of the gospel, it is legitimate to separate the two methods into different categories.[38]

It is also true that mass evangelism has often been associated and confused with revivals.[39] As a matter of fact, many famous evangelists in the past, such as Wesley, Whitefield, Finney, and Moody, had been great revivalists as well. However, mass evangelism and revival should be differentiated, since revival aims to awaken the spirituality of believers, while evangelism seeks to reach unbelievers with the gospel.[40]

Furthermore, although mass evangelism has typically been identified with citywide evangelistic campaigns,[41] it cannot be confined to campaigns. Although the most common method of mass evangelism has been the evangelistic campaign, other effective methods have been used as well, especially since mass communication has become possible through various means of mass media.

Thus, as William Morrow states, "Other methods of mass evangelism might include the use of mass media like the *Jesus Film*, a Gospel radio program, or a television program. Still, additional methods include festivals,[42] felt-needs clinics, dramas, and musicals."[43] Luis Palau agrees with the view that mass evangelism cannot be limited to evangelistic campaigns. In his article "The Future of Mass Evangelism," Palau articulates this idea:

> From the standpoint of mass evangelism, the 1980s could be the most exciting and significant period in the history of the Christian church. Why do I say this? Because mass evangelism implies not merely mass rallies in stadiums, bullrings and football fields; it also includes radio, television, films, videotapes, cassettes, and other forms of mass communication.[44]

Throughout this analysis, the term "mass evangelism" will be used in a broad and general sense, referring to any forms of evangelism that involve a large number of people as audiences of the gospel message. Finally, as a matter of terminology, this researcher will use the term "evangelistic campaign" instead of "evangelistic crusade" or "crusade evangelism," unless they are used in original quotations; the word "crusade" carries a negative historical connotation related to the Crusades against Islam during the Middle Ages.

Overview of Literature

Primary sources for this research will be Luis Palau's published books, articles, sermons, interviews with news reporters, and electronic media such as CDs and DVDs. The writer will also refer to ministry reports and articles published by Luis Palau Association (LPA).[45] Other sources will include Ph.D. dissertations, D.Min. projects, and books and articles written by others. Various Internet websites and media sources, such as TV, radio, and newspapers, will also be cited.

Primary Sources

A prolific writer, Luis Palau has published more than fifty books and booklets, along with numerous articles.[46] Through his writings he has dealt with various aspects of the Christian life, from new birth to maturity. The topics are in fact so broad, diverse, and interrelated that they cannot be categorized in a simple way. Beyond the focus of his writing on evangelism, many of his works address various other issues related to the Christian life, such as discipleship, Christian counseling, and apologetics.[47]

Concerning discipleship, Palau deals with topics such as holiness, spiritual renewal and growth, and prayer. In the area of Christian counseling, topics are related to family issues like dating, marriage, sex, divorce, education of children, and so on. In addition, some of Palau's books and articles discuss psychological and social problems, including grief, loneliness, suicide, and alcoholism. Perhaps apologetics is the most recent area Palau has begun to explore. Many of his previous writings are apologetic in nature, but from the late 1990s he has debated with intellectual fervor against atheism and agnosticism.[48]

Among Palau's many books, several are of particular importance for this study. His autobiography, *Luis Palau: Calling America and the*

Nations to Christ,[49] is helpful for understanding his life and ministry as an evangelist. With regard to understanding his theology and philosophy of evangelism, two books are outstanding. *The Only Hope for America*,[50] coauthored with Mike Umlandt, provides valuable insights into Palau's passion and convictions on evangelism, as well as his theology and philosophy.

The other, *Telling the Story*,[51] was coauthored with Timothy Robnett, the director of Next Generation Alliance (NGA). Today, NGA is part of the Palau Association's Alliance Ministries, a coalition of organizations that have evangelism as their primary mission. Since *Telling the Story* is addressed primarily to vocational itinerant evangelists, it is helpful for distilling Palau's theology and philosophy on the works of itinerant evangelists and mass evangelism.

For the analysis of Palau's preaching, *Our God Reigns*[52] will be useful, along with additional sermons recorded in other books and journals and on CDs. Besides these, Luis Palau has published many books, articles, and essays on evangelism and the Christian life. These will be referred to as needed in this research. In addition, certain of his recorded speeches at evangelism conferences have special value in assessing various issues in this research.

Secondary Sources

In addition to Palau's own writings are several useful works by other authors. Susan Holton and David L. Jones coauthored *Spirit Aflame: Luis Palau's Mission to London.*[53] This may be the single most significant work detailing Palau's strategy for evangelistic campaigns. It describes the preparation, process, and results of Palau's campaigns in London in 1983 and 1984. Other seminal works include three in-depth studies featuring Palau's evangelistic campaigns and their results. These independent works are recommended by Palau himself to refute a criticism that people's decisions to follow Christ made at evangelistic campaigns do not last long.[54]

Like *Spirit Aflame*, two of these works are studies on Palau's campaigns in London in 1983 and 1984. Roy Pointer, who served on the Executive Committee for these campaigns, authored *Crusade Evangelism.*[55] In this study Pointer describes the fruit of Palau's campaigns in London, along with criticisms and suggestions for future campaigns. His assessment is objective and well balanced, dealing with both negative and positive aspects of the London campaigns.

Peter Brierley authored two separate studies of these campaigns, *Mission to London: Phase 1, Who Responded?* and *Mission to London: Phase 2, Who Went Forward?*[56] These are two separate studies of *Mission to London*, 1983–1984. Finally, Henry J. Schmidt wrote "Crusade Decisions: Counting and Accounting for Lost Sheep,"[57] a follow-up study of Palau's Central California Campaign held in Fresno, California, September 21–28, 1986.

There are some other D.Min. projects, as well as one dissertation in Doctor of Theology that deal with Palau's evangelistic ministry. Scott Bauer wrote his D.Min. project, "Crusade Evangelism," in 1995.[58] The background of this project is Palau's 1994 campaign in San Fernando Valley, California. Based on his active personal involvement in the campaign, as well as his research conducted before, during, and after the event, Bauer provides valuable insights for Palau's campaign evangelism from the perspective of a participating local church.

William A. Giovannetti titled his D.Min. project "A Strategy for Linking Crusade Evangelism with Church Planting."[59] As is evident in the title, Giovannetti tries to connect two methods of evangelism, urban evangelistic crusade and church planting, to point out their complementary nature and the effectiveness of linking the two methods. Even though his rationale for the project is insightful and practical, its scope is limited to Palau's evangelistic campaigns in connection with church planting.

Kevin T. McBride wrote another D.Min. project on Luis Palau's statewide evangelistic campaign in Maine in 1999.[60] The goal of his paper was to evaluate the immediate and long-term impacts of the evangelistic campaign on the churches and communities of Maine. McBride discusses and supports the idea of unity and cooperation among the local churches for evangelistic purposes. After addressing the historical disunity among the churches in Maine and discussing the biblical and historical backgrounds for unity among Christians, he presents Palau's campaign in Maine as the case study for his thesis.

This project provides another valuable viewpoint from a participating church from one of Palau's campaigns. It is limited to a single campaign and does not deal with other aspects of Palau's evangelistic endeavors.

Finally, Michael Lee McGinnis titled his doctoral dissertation "A Church Growth Analysis of Mass-cooperative Evangelism."[61] Chapter 5 of his critique presents and evaluates Palau's evangelistic campaign in Rosario, Argentina, in 1975. Regrettably, the "Rosario Plan" that McGinnis presents as a case study is not part of the main thrust of his dissertation and does not contribute much to the formation of his main thesis, as evidenced in his concluding remark on this chapter, "Rosario can serve as an example but not as an absolute."[62]

Although many other books, articles, and news reports address Luis Palau's evangelistic ministry, most of them are mere reports rather than critical analyses and assessments of his ministry. Furthermore, their scope is limited to particular times and places, and they do not lend themselves to intense study of Luis Palau's ministry from a variety of perspectives.

Research Method

This research will utilize the available primary and secondary sources, including books, articles, news reports, electronic media, and websites. First, the biographical books written by Luis Palau and others will provide the foundational information for the discussion on his life as an evangelist. Analysis of his evangelistic theology and philosophy will be achieved by examining his books and various writings, with special attention given to his lectures and speeches presented at evangelistic conferences.

For Palau's evangelistic strategy, the writer will rely on Palau's own writings, along with various ministry reports and articles published by LPA. In addition, selected media recordings will be useful for the analysis of Palau's message, delivery, and style of evangelistic preaching. Finally, his evangelistic fruit around the world will be examined by looking into his biography and various reports from LPA. To enhance the objectivity of the research, news reports from both Christian and secular media, as well as observations from third parties (if available and helpful), will be referenced and compared.

This researcher has also conducted interviews with Luis Palau and some of his staff working for the Luis Palau Association. This has helped to clarify some of the issues related to Palau's theology, philosophy, and evangelistic strategy. Interviews with staff concerning their particular areas of expertise have contributed much to the delineation of strategies pertinent to Palau's evangelistic campaigns, use of mass media, and equipping of next-generation evangelists.

Significance of Research

Luis Palau's impact on evangelism encompasses virtually every continent and includes many countries but has not been studied thoroughly. By exploring his theology and strategy of evangelism, along with the fruits of his ministry, this research will contribute to the academic field of evangelism and help those striving to share the gospel to do so more effectively. At least three groups of people will benefit from this study.

First, this work will serve as a groundbreaker for scholars in evangelism who want to do future research on Luis Palau and his influence. It will also serve as a case study for successful contemporary mass evangelism, despite growing negativism among scholars concerning the future of mass evangelism. It is hoped that this work may persuade them to believe that mass evangelism, far from being obsolete, is not only still valid but useful as one of the most effective evangelistic methods.

Second, contemporary and future evangelists can take away valuable lessons. They will discover Palau's theology and strategy of evangelism and be enabled to implement them in their own evangelistic ministries. The innovative evangelistic approaches employed by Luis Palau will equip them as evangelists both practically and theoretically, inspiring them to proclaim the good news of Jesus Christ to the multitudes.

Finally, local church leaders and congregations will acquire an enhanced understanding of itinerant evangelists and evangelistic campaigns. They will discover the benefits of working with evangelists and the necessary preparations for evangelistic campaigns in their own churches and areas, while avoiding unnecessary confusion and conflict. Consequently, they will be able to partner with evangelists to host successful evangelistic campaigns and thus grow their local bodies, carrying out the Great Commission more effectively.

Endnotes

1 For an overview of the prominent preachers during the last three centuries (18th–20th), see Malcolm McDow & Alvin L. Reid, *FireFall: How God Has Shaped History Through Revivals* (Nashville, TN: Broadman & Holman Publishers, 1997), 183–273.

2 See "Preliminary Definitions" later in this chapter for the discussion of definitions of the terms "evangelism" and "mass evangelism."

3 Cf. The New Testament contains numerous examples of mass evangelism. Ed Mathews, for instance, gives some examples of mass evangelism in the first century: "Jesus proclaimed the kingdom to 'large crowds,' Matthew 4:25. On one occasion, when He saw the 'crowds,' He went up on a hillside and preached what is called the Sermon on the Mount, Matthew 5:1. Later, such 'large crowds' gathered around Him that He got into a boat and spoke to them, Matthew 13:1–9. At various times throughout His ministry, 'great crowds' followed Him and listened to His words, John 6:2.... Peter spoke to thousands on the day of Pentecost, Acts 2:41. 'Crowds' heard Philip in Samaria, Acts 8:6. Paul and Barnabas spoke to a 'great number' of Jews and Gentiles in Antioch of Pisidia, Acts 13:44, Iconium, Acts 14:1, and Lystra, Acts 14:18. Paul and Silas spoke to 'large numbers' of Jews and God-fearing Greeks in Thessalonica, Acts 17:4, and Athens, Acts 17:17, 22–32." Ed Mathews, "Mass Evangelism: Problems and Potentials," *Journal of Applied Missiology* 4, no. 1 (1993): 440. Others also confirm the use of mass evangelism for spreading the gospel in the early Church. For more detailed discussion on biblical basis of mass evangelism, see William Brad Morrow, "Mass Evangelism and Its Effect on Church Planting: A Filipino Case Study" (Ph.D. diss., Southern Baptist Theological Seminary, 2003), 28–33.

4 Alvin Reid, *Introduction to Evangelism* (Nashville, TN: Broadman & Holman Publishers), 266. For the discussion on the history of mass evangelism from the second century to Reformation era, see Morrow, "Mass Evangelism and Church Planting," 33–37.

5 Edward F. Murphy, "Mass Evangelism Is Not Obsolete," *Christianity Today*, 28 February 1975, 6.

6 Delos Miles, *Introduction to Evangelism* (Nashville, TN: Broadman Press, 1983), 287. According to Miles, Archibald's assumption might be true in some denominations. However, evangelistic revival meetings are still vibrant in many denominations, such as Southern Baptists, the Nazarenes, the Free Will Baptists,

and most of the independent churches in America and Canada. Cf. Arthur C. Archibald, *New Testament Evangelism* (Philadelphia: The Judson Press, 1946), 21. For similar pessimistic prospect on mass evangelism, see also Oswald J. Smith, *The New Evangelism* (Toronto: The Peoples Church, 1932), 10–11.

7 Kelly Green, "Mass Evangelism for the 90s: A New Look at an Old Approach," in *Evangelism for a Changing World*, eds. Timothy Beougher & Alvin Reid (Wheaton, IL: Harold Shaw Publishers, 1995), 143.

8 According to Billy Graham Evangelistic Association (BGEA) [online], Billy Graham has preached the gospel to nearly 215 million people in more than 185 countries around the world; accessed 25 November 2007; available from http://www.billygraham.org/mediaRelations/bios.asp?p=1; Internet.

9 "Just As We Were," *Christianity Today*, 5 July 2007, 54. According to a recent survey by *Christianity Today*, 38 percent of participants in the survey said yes to the question, "Are city-wide crusades a thing of the past?" One of the reasons for such an answer was "Billy Graham appears to be the last of a noble but dying breed."

10 Michael Cassidy, "Limitations of Mass Evangelism and Its Potentialities," *International Review of Mission* 65 (April 1976): 203.

11 For a series of criticism and debate on the validity of mass evangelism, see Morrow, "Mass Evangelism and Church Planting," 1–4, 24–26; Leighton Ford, *The Christian Persuader* (New York: Harper and Row Publishers, 1966), 81–91; Cassidy, "Limitations and Its Potentialities," 204–10; Win Arn, "Mass Evangelism: the Bottom Line" in *Pastor's Church Growth Handbook* (Pasadena, CA: Church Growth Press, 1979), 95–105; John Mark Terry, *Evangelism: A Concise History* (Nashville, TN: Broadman & Holman Publishers, 1994), 170.

12 Ford, *Christian Persuader*, 85.

13 For instance, Kirk Hadaway claims, "There is no evidence that mass evangelistic events help churches grow." Pointing to the lack of sophisticated evaluative research into a major crusade or other mass evangelism event, he asserts, "If it can be shown that churches involved in the process are more effective in reaching unchurched persons for Christ and incorporating them into the church than churches engaged in everyday evangelistic activity, then mass evangelism efforts should be encouraged. If this is not the case, then evangelistic denominations should take a hard look at curtailing crusades and simultaneous revivals." Kirk Hadaway, *Church Growth Principles: Separating Fact from Fiction* (Nashville, TN: Broadman Press, 1991), 29.

14 Mathews, "Mass Evangelism: Problems and Potentials," 441. According to Mathews, "In spite of the need for answers, surprisingly little research has been done, little hard data are available on this type of mission work." Ibid., 439.

15 Arn, "Mass Evangelism: the Bottom Line," 105.

16 Henry J. Schmidt, "Crusade Decisions: Counting and Accounting for Lost Sheep," *Church Growth Journal of the North American Society for Church Growth*, 1 (1990): 33.

17 "Just As We Were," 54. The contributors in this survey include evangelical leaders such as Leith Anderson, Edith L. Blumhofer, Nigel M. de S. Cameron,

Chuck Colson, J. Samuel Escobar, John W. Kennedy, Douglas LeBlanc, Paul L. Maier, Grant McClung, David McKenna, H. W. Norton, Roger Olson, Ben Patterson, Jim Reapsome, Stephen A. Seamands, Ron Sider, Uwe Siemon-Netto, Howard A. Snyder, Agnieszka Tennant, and Elmer L. Towns.

18 To be exact, as of September 2008, a total of 1,080,079 people have made documented decisions for Jesus Christ at Luis Palau's festivals, campaigns, and rallies. LPA, "Ministry Impact Statistics," September 2008.

19 See "Bibliography" for more information on his writings.

20 Green, "Mass Evangelism for the 90s," 142.

21 Morrow, "Mass Evangelism and Church Planting," 25.

22 "Luis Palau: Evangelist to Three Worlds," *Christianity Today*, 20 May 1983, 28.

23 Luis Palau and Jerry B. Jenkins, *Luis Palau: Calling the Nations to Christ* (Old Tappan, NJ: Revell, 1978; Chicago, IL: Moody Press, 1980), 9. According to Jerry B. Jenkins, this designation was first given by a freelance journalist.

24 "Is Luis Palau the Next Billy Graham?" *ABC News*, 8 October 2005 [online]; accessed 27 September 2007; available from http://abcnews.go.com/GMA/story?id= 1195278&page=1; Internet. See also Calmetta Y. Coleman, "Luis Palau: The Next Billy Graham of Everywhere?" *Wall Street Journal*, 16 November 1995, sec. B, pp. 1, 9.

25 "The 50 Most Influential Christians in America," *The Church Report* (January 2005): 16.

26 The lack of study on Luis Palau's evangelistic ministry becomes even more apparent when one compares academic works written on Billy Graham. Substantial study has been done on Billy Graham. Besides numerous books and articles written on Billy Graham, there are thirty-two dissertations and theses published as of September 25, 2007. This statistic is based on *First Search Database* with the title search containing "Billy Graham." [online]; accessed 27 September 2007; available from http://firstsearch.oclc. org; Internet.

27 For previous research on Luis Palau, see "Bibliography."

28 According to Robert Lynn Asa, the term "evangelism" came into use in the middle of the nineteenth century. Robert Lynn Asa, "The Theology and Methodology of Charles G. Finney as a Prototype for Modern Mass Evangelism" (Ph.D. diss., Southern Baptist Theological Seminary, 1983), 10.

29 For detailed discussion on the definition of evangelism, see Miles' *Introduction to Evangelism.* In chapter 2 of this book, he presents five often-quoted and well-accepted definitions of evangelism: 1918 Anglican definition, D. T. Niles's 1951 definition, Donald A. McGavran's 1977 Church Growth definition, the 1974 Lausanne Covenant definition, and George Hunter's 1979 definition. For more discussions on the definitions of evangelism, see the following references in their chronological order: John R. Mott, compiler, "What Is Evangelism?" in *Evangelism*, vol. 3, The Tambaram Series (London: Oxford University Press, 1939), 48–62; "The Task of Evangelism" in Bryan Green, *The Practice of Evangelism* (New York: Charles Scribner's Sons, 1951), 1–15;

"Getting Our Bearings" in George E. Sweazey, *Effective Evangelism* (New York: Harper & Brothers Publishers, 1953), 19–25; "Evangelism Defined" in Robert O. Ferm, *Cooperative Evangelism* (Grand Rapids: Zondervan, 1958), 24–32; "Evangelism" in J. I. Packer, *Evangelism & the Sovereignty of God* (Downers Grove, IL: InterVarsity Press, 1961), 37–57; "Definitions of Revival and Evangelism" in Edwin B. Dozier, *Christian Evangelism: Its Principles and Techniques*, vol. 1 (Tokyo, Japan: The Jordan Press, 1963), 1–9; "The Evangel" in Michael Green, *Evangelism in the Early Church*, (Grand Rapids: Wm. B. Eerdmans Publishing Co., 1970) 48–77; "What Is Evangelism" in David Watson, *I Believe in Evangelism* (Grand Rapids: Wm. B. Eerdmans Publishing Co., 1976), 25–39; "Make the Message Plain: What Is Evangelism?" in Reid, *Introduction to Evangelism*, 3–24.

30 Miles, *Introduction to Evangelism*, 35. This originated from the Archbishops' Committee of Inquiry on the Evangelistic Work of the Church and later was adopted by the Archbishops of Canterbury and York in 1943.

31 George G. Hunter III, "Informing Apostolic Ministry: Research and Writing for Effective Evangelism," *Journal of the Academy for Evangelism in Theological Education* 15 (1999–2000): 22. According to George Hunter III, this definition is the best in traditional understanding of evangelism, even though the Anglican Church never implemented it.

32 Cf. Another competing and popular definition is the one agreed to at the International Congress on World Evangelization held in Lausanne, Switzerland, in 1974. The Lausanne Covenant defined evangelism as follows: "To evangelize is to spread the good news that Jesus Christ died for our sins and was raised from the dead according to the Scriptures, and that as the reigning Lord he now offers the forgiveness of sins and the liberating gifts of the Spirit to all who repent and believe." "The Lausanne Covenant," J. D. Douglas, ed., *Let the Earth Hear His Voice* (Minneapolis, MN: World Wide Publications, 1975), 4. This definition is a part of the article under the title "The Nature of Evangelism." As John R. W. Stott explained, only the first part is intended to be a definition and the rest describes "the context of evangelism, namely what must precede and follow it." This definition has a merit in the fact that it articulates the message of the gospel clearly. To read the rest of the article, see John R. W. Stott, *The Lausanne Covenant: An Exposition and Commentary* (Minneapolis, MN: World Wide Publications, 1975), 20.

33 Asa, "Theology and Methodology of Finney," 11. In this dissertation, Robert Asa espouses that Finney's evangelistic methods became a prototype of modern mass evangelism. According to him, Finney's new methods have transcended denominational lines and have influenced most major mass evangelists, not only in his time but also in the subsequent era.

34 Bryan Green, *The Practice of Evangelism* (New York: Charles Scribner's Sons, 1951), 121. According to Bryan Green, Georges Michonneau seems to be the first one who questioned the validity of the term "mass evangelism." With a reference to Georges Michonneau, Green stated, "To speak of mass evangelism is in the strictest sense inaccurate, for, although the term is convenient, there can be no such thing as mass evangelism. We can proclaim the Gospel to the masses, but souls can only be won for Christ individually; one by one they

must pass over into conversion." Cf. Georges Michonneau, *Revolution in a City Parish* (Oxford: Blackfriars, 1949).

35 Hollis Green, *Why Churches Die* (Minneapolis, MN: Bethany Fellowship, 1972), 176. Ford, *Christian Persuader*, 81. Ford states, "To many it smacks of mass hypnotism or crowd hysteria. But the aim is not really to win people 'en masse' to Christ. 'Mass evangelism' is a platform for personal evangelism."

36 Ford, *Christian Persuader*, 81. He states, "We should coin a new phrase, for the term 'mass evangelism' is misleading."

37 Green, *Why Churches Die*, 176.

38 The rationale of both Leighton Ford and Hollis Green comes from their perspective that reception of the gospel, which is ultimately dependent on individuals who hear the gospel, is an indispensable part of evangelism. Although decision for Christ is the ultimate goal of evangelism, the authenticity of evangelism cannot be judged on the basis of reception of people. Evangelism is sharing of the good news, whether people receive or reject it. Thus mass evangelism should be defined in terms of method and context, rather than result. Cf. Cassidy, "Limitations and Its Potentialities," 206. In the words of Michael Cassidy, "To evangelize is to sow the seed of the Word, and not necessarily to reap. All four soils of the parable (Matt. 13:1–23) were 'evangelized', though only one was really fruitful."

39 Leslie Woodson, *Evangelism for Today's Church* (Grand Rapids: Zondervan, 1973), 101–11.

40 Some have made distinction between mass evangelism and revivalism. See, for example, John Mark Terry, *Church Evangelism: Creating a Culture for Growth in Your Congregation* (Nashville, TN: Broadman & Holman Publishers, 1997), 180. Even though it is necessary to distinguish between revivalism and mass evangelism, some authors used these terms interchangeably. Thus, the word "revival(s)" may appear occasionally in this research when it is quoted in original sources.

41 For example, Robert Asa excludes media evangelism from mass evangelism, while acknowledging that there are some who connect media evangelism with mass evangelism. See Asa, "Theology and Methodology of Finney," 12. Cf. Harold J. Ockenga, "New Concepts of Evangelism," *One Race, One Gospel, One Task*, vol. 2, eds. Carl F. H. Henry and W. Stanley Mooneyham (Minneapolis, MN: World Wide Publications, 1967), 479. Cf. Reasoning that mass evangelism and city-wide evangelism are not adequately defined, Michael McGinnis developed the term "mass-cooperative evangelism," referring to "an evangelistic effort which includes the participation of two or more Christian bodies involved in the united purpose of reaching a targeted segment of society." Michael Lee McGinnis, "A Church Growth Analysis of Mass-cooperative Evangelism" (Th.D. diss., Mid-America Baptist Theological Seminary, 1985), 4.

42 Luis Palau's team named its evangelistic campaigns "festivals." Even though they are similar in nature to traditional evangelistic campaigns, their approach is more contemporary, innovative, and relevant.

43 Morrow, "Mass Evangelism and Church Planting," 20. Morrow also cites Mark Terry's statement: "These events are quite varied, and may include holiday festivals, concerts, pageants, banquet meals, dramas, sport clinics, block parties, street meetings, and felt-need seminars." Terry, *Church Evangelism*, 184–85; Alvin Reid shares the same idea of mass evangelism: "In a general sense, mass evangelism refers to any gospel message presented to a crowd, including a musical, drama, block party, or some other tool." Reid, *Introduction to Evangelism*, 266.

44 Luis Palau, "The Future of Mass Evangelism," in *Evangelism: The Next Ten Years*, ed. Sherwood Eliot Wirt (Waco, TX: Word Books, 1978), 156.

45 Luis Palau Evangelistic Association (LPEA) changed its name to Luis Palau Association (LPA) in 2005. According to Palau, this change occurred strategically to access unbelievers who shun any religious affiliations, as well as countries, such as China, that are unfriendly to the Christian faith. Luis Palau, Interview by author, Frisco, Texas, 27 June 2008.

46 See "Bibliography" for the list of books and booklets written by Luis Palau in their chronological order. To date, Luis Palau has authored forty-five books and nine booklets.

47 Some of his representative books on the Christian life include: *So You Want to Grow* (UK: Kingsway Publications, 1984; reprint, Eugene, OR: Harvest House Publishers, 1986); *Radical Renewal* (Downers Grove, IL: Inter Varsity Press, 1991; Eastbourne, England: Crossway Books, 1991); *Say Yes! How to Renew Your Spiritual Passion* (Portland, OR: Multnomah Press, 1991; Grand Rapids: Discovery House Publishers, 1994); *Healthy Habits for Spiritual Growth: 52 Principles for Personal Change* (Grand Rapids: Discovery House Publishers, 1994).

48 Palau's two books are outstanding in this area. In 1997 he coauthored *God Is Relevant* with David Sanford. The primary purpose of this book is to refute the ideas of atheism and agnosticism. He traces the historical root of both ideas and argues for the existence of God from logical and practical perspectives. Luis Palau and David Sanford, *God Is Relevant: Finding Strength and Peace in Today's World* (New York: Doubleday, 1997). More recently, he published *A Friendly Dialogue Between an Atheist and a Christian* with a renowned Chinese diplomat and atheist Zhao Qizheng. Luis Palau and Zhao Qizheng, *A Friendly Dialogue Between an Atheist and a Christian* (Grand Rapids: Zondervan, 2008).

49 Luis Palau and David Sanford, *Luis Palau: Calling America and the Nations to Christ* (Nashville, TN: Thomas Nelson, Inc., 1994; rev. 2000). Other biographies include: Jerry B. Jenkins and Luis Palau, *Luis Palau: Calling the Nations to Christ* (Old Tappan, NJ: Revell, 1978; Chicago, IL: Moody Press, 1980) and Ellen Bascuti, *Luis Palau: Evangelist to the World* (Uhrichsville, OH: Barbour Publishing, 2000).

50 Luis Palau and Mike Umlandt, *The Only Hope for America: The Transforming Power of the Gospel of Jesus Christ* (Wheaton, IL: Crossway Books, 1996).

51 Luis Palau and Timothy Robnett, *Telling the Story: Evangelism for the Next Generation* (Ventura, CA: Regal Books, 2006).

52 Luis Palau, *Our God Reigns: Scotland Messages*, ed. David L. Jones (London: Luis Palau Team [UK] Trust, 1981). This is a collection of Palau's sermons preached in 1981 during a British tour called "Our God Reigns."

53 Susan Holton and David L. Jones, *Spirit Aflame: Luis Palau's Mission to London* (Grand Rapids: Baker Book House, 1985). Susan Holton and David L. Jones were professional journalists on the Luis Palau Evangelistic Team. When this book was published, Susan was an associate editor and public relations assistant. David was director of communications. Palau's *Mission to London* is one of the best documented campaigns in his ministry.

54 Palau, *Telling the Story*, 109.

55 Roy Pointer, *Crusade Evangelism: The Fruit That Remained; A Discussion Arising from Mission to London* (Bromley, Kent [England]: MARC Europe, 1988). This was originally a thirty-five page paper written as part of Roy Pointer's doctoral program. The published book does not indicate any information about his school or doctoral program.

56 Peter Brierley, *Mission to London: Phase 1, Who Responded?* (London: MARC Europe, 1984), *Mission to London: Phase 2, Who Went Forward?* (London: MARC Europe, 1984).

57 Henry J. Schmidt, "Crusade Decisions: Counting and Accounting for Lost Sheep," *Church Growth Journal of the North American Society for Church Growth*, 1 (1990): 14–40.

58 Scott Bauer, "Crusade Evangelism" (D.Min. project, Oral Roberts University, 1995).

59 William A. Giovannetti, "A Strategy for Linking Crusade Evangelism with Church Planting" (D.Min. project, Fuller Theological Seminary, 1996). The background of this project is Luis Palau's Chicago crusade in 1996. According to Giovannetti, the purpose of this project is to make "a series of recommendations to the LPEA and to the Chicago Crusade Committee, suggesting ways to stimulate and coordinate a strategic church planting effort in connection with the Chicagoland crusade." Ibid., 3.

60 Kevin T. McBride, "Retaking the Village Green: Building Strategic Partnerships for Evangelism That Work in New England" (D.Min. project, Gordon-Conwell Theological Seminary, 2001).

61 Michael Lee McGinnis, "A Church Growth Analysis of Mass-cooperative Evangelism" (Th.D. diss., Mid-America Baptist Theological Seminary, 1985). In this work McGinnis has studied mass evangelism from the perspective of the Church Growth school of thought.

62 Ibid., 134. Moreover, the length of his discussion of Luis Palau's campaign in Rosario is only eleven pages, and its scope is limited to that one section.

CHAPTER 1

THE MAKING OF AN EVANGELIST: EARLY YEARS

Knowing Luis Palau's early life is crucial to understanding him as an evangelist, because it was during this time that he was converted, called to the ministry, and trained as an evangelist. As is the case with many other people of faith, some individuals Palau met along the way on his spiritual journey have played a crucial role in the formation of his faith and his dedication as an evangelist.

Kimberly Claassen, an associate editor for the Luis Palau Evangelistic Association (LPEA), once observed, "By most standards, Luis Palau was an unlikely candidate for international evangelist—son of a poor widow in Argentina, no connections, sole supporter of his mother and five younger sisters."[63] Despite such an unlikely background, Palau was able to become a successful evangelist because of spiritual mentors whom God brought into his life. This chapter examines Palau's life from the perspective of his formation as an evangelist, with special attention to those people who so influenced him.

Family and Religious Background

Palau was born in Ingeniero-Maschwitz, Buenos Aires, Argentina, on November 27, 1934, as the first son of the seven children of Luis Palau, Sr. and his wife, Matilde.[64] His father, a successful construction businessman, was a Spanish descendant, and his mother inherited both French and Scottish blood.[65] Palau's father attended the local Catholic church, which was the only state church in that province. Yet he was only a nominal churchgoer, simply following the religious tradition of his time. Palau's mother was more committed to the church and even played the organ in the local parish, but she still lacked a personal relationship with the Lord.

Shortly after Luis Palau, Jr. was born, both of them were converted through the witness of a British missionary tentmaker, Edward Rogers, an executive working for the Shell Oil Company.[66] It was Palau's mother who first began to attend the Plymouth Brethren Church with little Luis. After a while, Palau's father reluctantly, at the request of his wife, agreed to attend once, only to be converted dramatically during the service. While listening to the sermon, to the surprise of his wife and the other church members, he stood up and declared, "I receive Jesus Christ as my only and sufficient Savior."[67]

Following their conversion, Palau's parents became active members of the Plymouth Brethren Church and began to share the good news of Jesus Christ boldly, not only with people in their town but even in the remote countryside. Yet, as Palau recalls, the good news his father shared was "often greeted with insults, derision, stones, and worse."[68] While passing out the gospel tracts with his father to the people on the street, the young Palau was forced several times to dodge a well-aimed stone. Even in the face of such persecution, his father continued to distribute the gospel tracts.[69] It would be impossible to overemphasize the influence of Luis Palau, Sr. on his impressionable namesake. For the younger Palau, his father was the model of an evangelist:

> My father was my hero as a boy. His pride in the Gospel and boldness to share it with others marked my life. After hearing him preach so often, I began imitating his gestures, his voice, and even his words. Actually, I got quite good at it! Maybe that's why I thoroughly enjoyed playing "church" with my little sisters. They had to listen to me preach, like it or not, because I was the oldest.[70]

Faith became the highest priority in the Palau household. Sunday was sacred, with the older Palau forbidding "any other activities, except going to church, resting, reading, or participating in a Gospel street meeting."[71] When Palau became seven years old, his father decided to send him to Quilmes Preparatory School, a private British boarding school near Buenos Aires. The classes in this school were taught in both English and Spanish, thus offering a good preparation for St. Alban's College, where Palau could go next.[72] Shortly after he became ten years of age, however, Luis's life was interrupted by one of its most significant events: His father died suddenly at the age of thirty-four. After receiving a call from his grandmother, Luis hurried home by train.[73]

Despite the tremendous grief and pain of losing his father, Palau was comforted to hear what had happened right before his father's death. Despite difficulty breathing while on his deathbed, the older Palau suddenly sat up and began to sing, while clapping like a child: "Bright crowns up there, bright crowns for you and me. Then the palm of victory, the palm of victory."[74] After singing this song three times, he fell back onto his bed and announced, "I'm going to be with Jesus, which is far better."[75]

The death of his father left an indelible imprint on his young son, changing his worldview. As Palau recalls, "That molded my whole view of life, eternity, death and the future."[76] Moreover, it impacted him as an evangelist more than any other event in his life: "Without a doubt, the death of my father has had more impact on my ministry than anything else in my entire life, besides my own conversion to Jesus Christ. My wish and desire is that people get right with God, settle the big question, and die happy, knowing they will be with Jesus, 'which is better by far' (Philippians 1:23)."[77]

Along with that of his father, the impact of Palau's mother, Matilde, cannot be ignored. Like many other great men of faith, Luis Palau had a devout and godly mother. Matilde was the first in the family to accept Jesus Christ in her heart as Savior and Lord; it was she who had led her husband and children to Christ. She had raised her six children according to biblical principles, teaching them the Bible and praying for them. She also often read the stories of missionaries to her kids before they went to bed.

Palau later recalls, "My favorite was the true story of Mildred Cable and Francesca French, who carried the Gospel through Asia (particularly the Gobi desert) in spite of tremendous persecution and physical abuse."[78] These stories inspired Palau to become a bold witness for Christ later on in his life, even in the midst of opposition and persecution.[79] When Palau lost his father, his mother comforted and strengthened her disheartened son with the assurance of heaven, citing Bible verses such as John 14:1–3 and 1 Thessalonians 4:13–14.[80]

Later in his life, while working for a British bank in Argentina, Luis Palau became actively involved in outdoor evangelistic ministry. Nevertheless, he felt himself to be unready to do God's work on a full-time basis. Yet his mother, who greatly influenced his life decisions, challenged him to quit his job and pursue just such a career. At the World Evangelical Fellowship's (WEF) tenth meeting, Palau illustrated her influence:

> I was working at a British bank in Argentina, and my mother used to say, "Leave the bank. Preach the Gospel. Plant churches." I replied, "Mom, I'm waiting for the call." She exclaimed, "The call went out 2,000 years ago! The Lord's not waiting for the call; he's waiting for the answer!"[81]

Conversion and Call to Ministry

Conversion

Three months after his father's death, Luis Palau entered St. Alban's College, a boys' school that was connected to the Cambridge University Overseas Program. Because the classes were taught in both English and Spanish, he soon became a fluent bilingual student, which eventually prepared him to be a global evangelist, proclaiming the gospel not only in Latin America but also in many other parts of the world. During these school years he learned discipline, studied hard, and loved sports. Luis especially enjoyed Latin America's favorite sport, soccer, which was unfortunately forbidden on his campus in favor of British sports, such as cricket and rugby.[82]

The most important event during this period was his conversion at the age of twelve. Mr. Charles Cohen, one of the teachers at St. Alban's, invited Palau, along with other students, to a two-week summer camp in the mountains. Even though Luis made the excuse that he could not go due to his family's difficult financial situation, he ended up attending because Mr. Cohen offered to pay his expenses for the camp.

The camp was led by Mr. Cohen and several counselors from different missionary organizations. Palau recalls, "We had Bible lessons, memorizations, and singing every day, along with the usual fun and games."[83] But the most important aspect of this camping experience was the individual encounters with the message of the gospel. Every night each counselor, who was in charge of about ten boys in his tent, took one boy for a walk and gave him the opportunity to respond to the gospel.

Finally the day came for Luis Palau. When his counselor, Frank Chandler, came into the tent to counsel Palau, he pretended to be asleep, noting later, "I wanted to run and hide, I was so embarrassed I had not received Christ yet; still, I couldn't lie and say that I had. Even though I felt guilty for my sins and knew I needed to make a Christian commitment, I didn't want to face the issue with anyone."[84]

But Frank Chandler, refusing to give up, finally took Palau outside and sat down with him on a fallen tree. It was on this cold and rainy night that the future global evangelist, who would proclaim the gospel of Jesus Christ to more than 25 million people around the world, came to accept Jesus as his Savior and Lord. Palau describes his conversation with Chandler:

> It was cold and a light rain was beginning to fall. A thunderstorm was coming our way. Frank knew he had to hurry. He pulled out his flashlight and opened his New Testament. "Luis," he asked, "are you a born-again Christian or not?" I said, "I don't think so." "Well, it's not a matter of whether you think so or not. Are you or aren't you?" "No, I'm not." "If you died tonight," Frank asked me, "would you go to heaven or hell?" I sat quietly for a moment, a bit taken

> aback, and then said, "I'm going to hell." "Is that where you want to go?" "No," I replied. "Then why are you going there?" I shrugged my shoulders. "I don't know." Frank then turned in his Bible to the apostle Paul's letter to the Romans and read. … Frank looked back at me. "Luis, do you believe in your heart that God raised Jesus from the dead?" "Yes, I do," I said. "Then what do you have to do next to be saved?" I hesitated as it began to rain even harder. Frank had me read Romans 10:9 once more—"If you confess with your lips that Jesus is Lord … you will be saved." "Luis, are you ready to confess Him as your Lord right now?" "Yes." "All right, let's pray." … I opened my heart to Christ right there, out in the rain sitting on a log, in a hurry, but I made my decision. … When we finished praying, I was crying. I gave Frank a big hug and we ran back into the tent. I crawled under my blanket with my flashlight and wrote in my Bible "February 12, 1947" and "I received Jesus Christ."[85]

Luis Palau could not sleep well that night. He was rightly convinced that nothing was more important than the decision he just made, which assured him of eternal life through Jesus Christ.[86]

Call to Ministry

For Luis Palau, God's call to evangelistic ministry came in a couple of phases. After he was converted at twelve years old, Palau became an enthusiastic follower of Christ. He was a diligent student in the Bible classes at school and assisted with Crusader youth group meetings held in Mr. Cohen's home on Sunday afternoons.[87] Yet his enthusiasm did not last long. Several months later, his zeal for daily Bible reading and Crusader meetings, along with his excitement over Bible classes, were gone—along with the Bible that he carelessly left on a streetcar.[88]

Palau acknowledges that his suddenly devastated spiritual condition was in part related to a punishment he had received from Mr. Cohen. Palau, in a fit of temper directed against an art teacher, had spoken a foul word in Spanish and received a harsh punishment from Mr. Cohen.[89] Other factors also contributed to Palau's spiritual depletion during this period, not the least of which was anger against the person who had "managed" his family's business after his father's sudden death; he had swindled the Palau family and left them with nothing.

Second, the life of his non-Christian friends looked like so much fun, and Palau could not resist the temptation to join them.[90] After the incident with Mr. Cohen, his spiritual life began to slide rapidly. Turning his back on God, he joined his old friends and began to do things he believed to be sinful, such as going to school dances and reading magazines on Sundays about car racing and sports.[91] His ungodly and rebellious lifestyle continued until his graduation from St. Alban's. During this time he was dreaming of becoming "a race-car driver, a soccer player, or a big businessman."[92]

Meanwhile, after the death of Palau's father, his family suffered financially, to the point that he could not finish his last year at St. Alban's, leaving him with only the equivalent of a junior college degree in the United States. Palau's dream to study at Cambridge was shattered. It is obvious that he was deeply discouraged and angered by the circumstances around him, as expressed in the following words:

> I felt I had been the victim of a cruel joke. Eight long, double years of schooling in the British boarding schools would leave me with an intermediate degree, no money, and no future, as far as I could tell. I still feared God, but I questioned Him daily and was sometimes glad I had not served Him more.[93]

The turning point in his life took place during Carnival Week in 1952. During that week most businesses closed and people did whatever they wanted to do. According to Whalin, Palau's biographer, "Carnival was an outright mockery of everything Christian. People dressed in costumes and masks, drank, and danced around the clock."[94] Even though he had promised his friends to go to a wild dance party, Palau felt that he should not be involved in Carnival: "Somehow I knew if I went to Carnival Week, temptation would overwhelm me and I would be engulfed in sin. ... I had to get out of Carnival Week, or I would be swallowed up, finished, sunk. I'm sure the Holy Spirit was convicting me."[95]

In desperation, he began to pray to God to extricate him from this temptation. God answered his prayer in an unexpected and humorous way. When he woke up in the morning, his mouth was swollen, as though he had "a ping-pong ball in it."[96] Knowing that this was God's answer to his prayer, he refused to go to the carnival with his friends. After that, he made what he calls "the second most important decision" in his life: "to serve only Jesus Christ and to give my life to working for Him."[97] His decision was immediately followed up by action: "I went back into the house, broke my pipe in two, tore up my university club membership card, and ripped up all my soccer and car-racing magazines and many record albums."[98]

After a while Palau was hired by the Bank of London in Buenos Aires as a junior employee in training. Due to his British education and bilingual abilities, his salary was fairly high for someone his age. Although he was doing well at work and had received a couple of promotions, he felt the need to help his family in Córdoba, north of Buenos Aires four hundred miles away. To his surprise, his request to transfer to the Bank of London branch in Córdoba was accepted, even with a promotion.

Palau was not yet eighteen years old. Back in Córdoba he began to serve the Lord more zealously than ever before. Baptized by immersion, he became an active member of a local Plymouth Brethren assembly of about 130 members. The church was led by the elders and one full-time missionary, George Mereshian. Under their leadership, Palau joined the discipleship program, studied the Bible, and read many books written by famous Christian writers.[99]

Shortly after beginning to attend this church, Palau experienced a spiritual breakthrough that marked another milestone in his life. One Sunday in church, while he was singing the hymn "Am I a Soldier of the Cross?" God touched his heart. He recalls, "The lyrics by Isaac Watts burst into my mind as if God Himself was impressing an exhortation on my heart. 'You sing of being a soldier of the cross, and yet you do nothing.'"[100]

Since his prayer of dedication to God during Carnival Week, Luis's dream had been to become a lawyer or a judge to change the world, focusing specifically on the devastating conditions of poverty and injustice in Argentina.[101] While singing this song, however, God laid upon him a new burden to serve Him as His full-time servant. Palau recalls his resolution at that time:

> At this point I knew I probably wouldn't be a banker all my life. And I wouldn't be a lawyer or a judge, either. I couldn't change my nation or the world through finances or law or politics or sociology or psychology. I was going to have to become a soldier of the cross or quit singing about it.[102]

Even though he wanted to dedicate his life totally to God, Palau feared the suffering he would have to endure. He even imagined himself working with lepers in Africa as a missionary and contracting the disease himself, if not something worse. After several weeks of struggling and wrestling in prayer, he finally knelt by his bed one Saturday night and gave God full control of his life, praying, "Lord, yes, if it has to be, I'll even be a leper, for Your name's sake."[103]

Endnotes

63 Kimberly Claassen, "Reviving the Nations," *The Plain Truth* (March/April 1998): 11.

64 Ellen Bascuti, *Luis Palau: Evangelist to the World* (Uhrichsville, OH: Barbour Publishing, 2000), 8.

65 LPA, "An Overview of Luis Palau's Life and Ministry," October 2007, 1.

66 Bascuti, *Luis Palau: Evangelist to the World*, 8–9.

67 Ibid., 9.

68 Luis Palau and David Sanford, *Luis Palau: Calling America and the Nations to Christ* (Nashville, TN: Thomas Nelson, Inc., 1994; rev. 2000), 2. According to Luis Palau, the persecution against evangelical Christians in Latin America subsided in the 1960s after Pope John XXIII and Vatican II declared that those outside the Catholic church were no longer heretics, but simply "separated brethren." He continues, "Marxist-Leninist forces, however, soon proved to be a much more serious threat, infiltrating some churches and undermining the proclamation of the Gospel." Ibid.

69 Bascuti, *Luis Palau: Evangelist to the World*, 10.

70 Palau and Sanford, *Calling America and the Nations*, 3. His father was a role model of faith to the young Palau. On cold winter mornings, Palau often saw his father reading the Bible and praying in his office alone before going to work. Ibid., 4.

71 W. Terry Whalin, *Luis Palau* (Minneapolis, MN: Bethany House Publishers, 1996), 17.

72 Palau and Sanford, *Calling America and the Nations*, 5–6. Cf. Only affluent families could send their children to the British boarding school because of the high cost of the school. Palau recalls, "The majority of students were from at least middle-class families." Whalin, *Luis Palau*, 24.

73 Ibid., 7. Cf. Bascuti, *Luis Palau: Evangelist to the World*, 15. Palau later learned that his father had contracted bronchial pneumonia and had suffered for ten days. Penicillin could have saved his life, but in December 1944 the antibiotic was all sent to Europe and the Pacific for the soldiers wounded in World War II.

74 Palau and Sanford, *Calling America and the Nations*, 8.

75 Ibid. According to Palau, the story of his father's death is "such a contrast to the typical Latin American scene, where the dying person cries out in fear of going to hell."

76 Michelle Bearden, "Man with a Message," *The Tampa Tribune*, 19 November 2006.

77 Palau and Sanford, *Calling America and the Nations*, 9. The importance of his father's death to Palau is evident in the fact that he has recounted this event on many occasions throughout his sermons and writings. Mike Umlandt, "A Father's Passion," *New Man: Proclaiming Life to Men* (June 1997), reprinted from LPA.

78 Ibid., 3.

79 Bascuti, *Luis Palau: Evangelist to the World*, 31. Later, while attending St. Alban's College, Palau met these two missionary ladies, Mildred Cable and Francesca French. Hearing their testimony, Palau prayed, "God, I thought I was an outspoken Christian, but what am I doing compared to these two women? They gave up the luxuries of life to minister under terrible conditions, just because they love You and want to serve You. Lord, help me love You like that."

80 Palau and Sanford, *Calling America and the Nations*, 9–10.

81 Luis Palau, "Missions to the End of the World," in *Global Crossroads: Focusing the Strength of Local Churches*, ed. W. Harold Fuller, World Evangelical Fellowship (Mandaluyong, Philippines: OMF Literature Inc., 1998), 280.

82 Palau and Sanford, *Calling America and the Nations*, 12–14.

83 Ibid., 17.

84 Ibid., 19.

85 Ibid., 19–21. Palau later recalled, "He [Frank] probably never guessed that the Lord not only would save a big-mouthed, little fellow like me—but also would call me to be a winner of souls across the nations." Luis Palau, "That Night at Summer Camp: An Experience at Summer Camp Changed a 12-year-old Boy's Life Forever," *Decision* 36, no. 6 (June 1995): 25.

86 Whalin, *Luis Palau*, 31.

87 Palau and Sanford, *Calling America and the Nations*, 21–22.

88 Ibid., 23.

89 For detailed accounts, see *Calling America and the Nations*, 23–25. Cf. Luis Palau honestly acknowledges that he had troubles controlling his temper and tongue when he was a child. Ibid., 4–5.

90 Whalin, *Luis Palau*, 37.

91 Palau and Sanford, *Calling America and the Nations*, 25.

92 Ibid., 27.

93 Ibid., 28.

94 Whalin, *Luis Palau*, 39. Carnival Week in Latin America is the counterpart of Mardi Gras in New Orleans in the United States.

95 Palau and Sanford, *Calling America and the Nations*, 30.

96 Ibid., 31.

97 LPA, "Overview of Life and Ministry," 1.

98 Palau and Sanford, *Calling America and the Nations*, 31–32.

99 Ibid., 37–38.

100 Ibid., 39.

101 Palau later articulated that as a lawyer he wanted to defend widows and orphans free of charge. He calculated that he might be able to help about five thousand in fifty years. Yet he found that presenting Christ to them will eventually help them in a better way. Claassen, "Reviving the Nations," 11–12.

102 Palau and Sanford, *Calling America and the Nations*, 39.

103 Ibid.

CHAPTER 2

THE MAKING OF AN EVANGELIST: PREPARATION

Ministerial Training

Palau's ministerial training was achieved gradually. As part of the process of his spiritual journey and training, God brought many devout Christians into his life, who eventually became his spiritual mentors. The following discussion will examine how those mentors helped Palau by preparing him spiritually and intellectually for his role as an evangelist.

George Mereshian and Personal Discipleship

Palau's informal theological training began when he was nineteen through the Bible teaching program at the local Plymouth Brethren assembly. The missionary at the church, George Mereshian, trained Palau as though he were in seminary. For two years Mereshian discipled Palau for three hours a day, three days a week.[104] Palau was a zealous student of the Bible who devoured books on theology and church history. He comments on his learning from Mereshian during this period as follows:

> The Bible teaching program was so sound and systematic that it was like attending a seminary. I began to devour commentaries and supplementary books by great Christian preachers, teachers, and writers. Biographies of evangelists Martin Luther, John Calvin, George Whitefield, John Wesley, D. L. Moody, Charles E. Finney, George Müller, and Billy Sunday, and books by Bible teachers Oswald Chambers, C. H. Mackintosh, F. B. Meyer, J. I. Packer, S. I. Ridout, Oswald J. Smith, C. H. Spurgeon, and scores of others influenced my life and ministry.[105]

Furthermore, George Mereshian's influence on young Palau was not limited to theological education. He also profoundly shaped Palau's spirituality by offering a good example through his own life.

> On weekends we would go door to door helping the poor, older people especially, and preaching the Gospel. But I learned it on my knees. He seemed to be always on his knees. What a lesson it was to me. He taught me to love and to help, but first of all to be with the Lord.[106]

Theological training also occurred in his work place. He had become so familiar with his work at the bank that he could accomplish his duties in the foreign operations department within a few hours. At Palau's request, his supervisor allowed him to devote the rest of his working time to personal study. Spurred by his spiritual hunger and thirst, he began to study the Bible and read many theological books, to the point that his coworkers began to call him "Pastor."[107] Palau writes, "I studied whole books of the Bible, using works like Jeremiah by F. B. Meyer. I read through Bible dictionaries and commentaries such as Jamieson, Fausset, and Brown on the New Testament. I often studied several different subjects a day."[108]

During this period in his early twenties, Palau served as the Sunday School superintendent at the church. He was also actively involved on an evangelistic team that he had formed with his close friend. He recalls, "We preached all over the place, taking turns drawing the crowd, leading the singing, and then preaching.... That's really where I began to learn the basics of evangelism."[109]

Keith Bentson and Evangelistic Vision for the World Through Intercessory Prayer

Palau's first encounter with Keith Bentson occurred while he was working at the bank in Córdoba in 1959. Bentson, a representative of *Servicio Evangelizador Para America Latina* (SEPAL), the Latin American division of One Challenge International, came to the bank to open an account. Knowing that Palau was a Christian, Bentson asked him whether he knew any bilingual Christian who would translate an English magazine called *La Voz*, which means "The Voice." Coincidently, Palau was looking for a new job because of his confrontation with the bank manager over some unethical bank policies; he immediately left his job at the bank and began to work for SEPAL.[110]

After a couple of weeks at SEPAL, Palau was invited by Keith Bentson to his office to pray with him every Wednesday evening. The prayer meeting with Bentson, in fact, was an eye-opening event to Palau. Beginning with Palau's own family and the church he attended, Bentson's prayer list had enlarged each week. The two prayed together for the city of Córdoba, the towns and cities in Argentina, the Americas, and even the whole world. As Palau prayed with Bentson, his evangelistic vision began to enlarge as well; expanding his vision to the whole world as his harvest field went a long way toward preparing him to be a global evangelist.

In his speech at the Amsterdam 2000 conference, Palau shared how the intercessory prayer meetings with Keith Bentson had impacted his life:

> At that point my vision was the city of Córdoba. But the next Wednesday he came with a map of the province of Córdoba. And the following week he had a map of the whole country of Argentina. Then he had a map of the whole South American continent. Then Europe. Then Asia. Every week the prayers and the vision grew and grew, until after a

year and a half I found myself praying to be an evangelist to the whole world.[111]

Palau also comments in his autobiography, "Those prayer meetings in Keith's office revolutionized my life. My vision for those who needed Christ became international, geographical, global."[112] Speaking at WEF's tenth meeting in 1997 of the impact upon himself of prayer with Bentson, Palau also remarked, "After praying this way month after month, your vision expands. Before you know it, you become the answer to your own prayers, because the Lord lays the need on your heart."[113]

While working for SEPAL, Palau formed his own evangelistic team. He was actively involved, along with Ed Murphy, one of SEPAL's new missionaries, and others, such as Bruce Woodman and Bill Fasig, in evangelistic tent meetings and church planting.[114]

Ray Stedman and Seminary Education in the States

It was not until 1960 that Palau received formal theological education at a seminary. In 1958 Palau met Ray Stedman, a pastor at Peninsula Bible Church in Palo Alto, California, along with Dick Hillis, a former missionary to China and founder of OC International, who were visiting Argentina for a mission trip.[115] Palau had no clue that the meeting with Ray Stedman, whom he later called his spiritual father in America, would change the course of his life.

After having some conversation and spending time with Palau, Stedman invited him to come to the States for theological study at Dallas Theological Seminary. Knowing that Palau did not have enough money to live and study in the States, Stedman even contacted a businessman who was willing to support Palau financially. Due to his unwillingness to spend four more years in school and financial concern for his family, Palau declined his offer.[116] It was during that period that he quit his job at the bank and began to work for SEPAL. Stedman, however, did not give up and insisted that Palau come to the States for study at Multnomah Biblical Seminary in Portland, Oregon, which offered a one-year graduate course in theological education.[117]

In 1960 Palau finally reached the decision to leave for North America for study. After spending two months with Ray Stedman,

Palau left for Multnomah Biblical Seminary. His first semester there was tough. Within himself he was struggling spiritually, and his frustration is well expressed in his own words: "I was a sincere hypocrite. People always laugh when I say that, but I truly was, and it wasn't funny. … If I were to describe myself in those days, I would have to say I was envious, jealous, too preoccupied and self-centered, and ambitious to a wrong degree."[118]

This discouraging spiritual condition during his seminary year was overcome by two incidents. First, Palau met Patricia Marilyn Scofield, another student at Multnomah who would become his wife. Although they met early in the first semester, the couple came to know and love each other gradually. They married on August 5, 1961, a couple of months after graduation from seminary.

The other breakthrough in his spiritual condition came through one of the chapel services at Multnomah. The speaker was Major Ian Thomas, founder and general director of the Torchbearers. He preached on how God had worked through Moses and through countless Christian servants throughout history when they fully surrendered themselves to God, realizing that it was He who was at work in them. Palau summarizes Thomas's message as follows:

> The essence was that it took Moses forty years in the wilderness to realize that he was nothing. Thomas said God was trying to tell Moses, "I don't need a pretty bush or an educated bush or an eloquent bush. Any old bush will do, as long as I am in the bush. If I am going to use you, I am going to use you. It will not be you doing something for Me, but Me doing something through you."[119]

When Thomas finished his sermon by citing Galatians 2:20, Palau came to realize the source of his spiritual battle. Convicted, he ran into his room in tears and prayed to God: "Lord, now I get it. I understand. I see the light at the end of the tunnel. The whole thing is 'not I, but Christ in me.' It's not what I'm going to do for You but rather what You're going to do through me."[120] This event was so important to Palau that he called it "the intellectual turning point in my spiritual life." Going on, "Theologically, I knew better, but the experience made me feel as if I had just been converted, after trying to serve the Lord on my own for more than eight years."[121]

Billy Graham's Influence on Luis Palau

From Palau's conversion to his triumph as an evangelist, many godly individuals have served as his mentors and spiritual guides. As discussed in previous sections, people such as Palau's parents, who probably had the greatest impact on him; Charles Cohen at St. Alban's; counselor Frank Chandler; missionary George Mereshian; Keith Bentson; Dick Hillis; and Ray Stedman all played important roles in Palau's conversion and spiritual growth.

There were, however, no others who would impact Luis Palau as did the renowned evangelist Billy Graham.[122] Even though Palau is indebted to many preachers and evangelists in the history of Christian faith—men such as Luther, Calvin, Wesley, Whitefield, Finney, Spurgeon, Moody, and Sunday—their influence cannot be compared to that of Billy Graham.[123] The fact that Graham's name has been often associated with Palau's in the media is not accidental at all.[124] Hence, without understanding Graham's influence on Palau it will be impossible to properly understand Palau as an evangelist. The relationship between Graham and Palau was not static but evolved over time. In terms of their developing relationship, Graham's influence on Palau can be examined in three phases: Billy Graham as hero; Billy Graham as mentor; and, finally, Billy Graham as partner.

Billy Graham as Hero

Graham's influence on Luis Palau began long before the two met in person. From Palau's youth, Graham had been his hero and role model as an evangelist. First, through Billy Graham God gave Palau a vision to reach people via radio broadcasting. While working for the bank in Buenos Aires at the age of eighteen, Palau was listening to a shortwave radio program from HCJB in Quito, Ecuador, when he heard a preacher exhorting people in a vibrant voice to come to Jesus. After that another man began to sing a song by William T. Sleeper.

Having been touched while listening, Palau prayed, "Jesus, someday use me on the radio to bring others to You, just as this program has firmed up my resolve to completely live for You."[125] He had no clue at that time of how God would answer his prayer in the future, enabling him to reach a multitude of people through various radio stations around the world. It was only later on that he learned he had been listening to Billy Graham and George Beverly Shea.

Palau's second encounter with Billy Graham was through Graham's book *The Secret of Happiness*, which had been translated into Spanish. Before reading this book, Palau had been spiritually frustrated because he had not seen any adult converts through his preaching—only a few kids had come to accept Christ during Vacation Bible School. He expressed his discouragement as follows: "Nothing I did seemed to make any difference. I was inspired by the things I read and heard about other evangelists, but it seemed obvious I didn't have whatever they had, namely the Holy Spirit's power in my life."[126] After giving God his own deadline for seeing converts and still witnessing no fruit at all, Palau finally gave up, concluding that he did not have the gift of evangelism.

It was right after this period that Palau "happened" to read *The Secret of Happiness*, an exposition by Graham on the Beatitudes from Jesus' Sermon on the Mount in Matthew 5. Touched by Graham's exposition, especially in light of his own spiritual desperation, Palau memorized the main points of each Beatitude. That night he went to the home Bible study meeting, only to find that the designated speaker had not shown up. The elders compelled Palau to preach, even though he was not prepared at all. Reluctantly, out of allegiance to the elders, he complied.

After reading aloud the Beatitudes, Palau preached what he remembered from Graham's book. When he came to the verse "Blessed are the pure in heart, for they shall see God" (Matthew 5:8, RSV), a woman began to sob, imploring, "Somebody help me! My heart is not pure. How am I going to find God?"[127] Only after being counseled with 1 John 1:7, which says, "The blood of Jesus, his Son, purifies us from all sin," did she come to have peace in her heart, allowing her to go home with joy.

The joy in Palau's own heart was immense that night. God had answered his prayer by converting a woman through his preaching. He felt himself to have been confirmed of his gift and calling as an evangelist. Palau's excitement is well expressed in his autobiography: "I ignored the buses that night and walked all the way home, praising the Lord that He had chosen to use me."[128] It is noteworthy that it was Graham's teachings on the Beatitudes that God used to influence Palau's first adult convert in his ministry, hence confirming his gift and calling as an evangelist.[129]

Billy Graham, through the news about his own evangelistic outreach around the world, also inspired Luis Palau to have a vision as a global evangelist. Palau's friends gave him the book *Revival in Our Time*, which recorded Billy Graham's Los Angeles campaign in 1949.[130] When Palau read it, his heart was stirred and he began dreaming of becoming an evangelist. Palau also received a copy of *Moody Monthly* from Brethren missionaries and read in it an article about Graham's 1954 London campaign. Excited by the report, Palau became convicted that mass evangelism was the key to turning the multitudes to Christ.[131] Graham thus became not only Palau's hero to respect but also a role model for him to emulate. Palau records these thoughts:

> Here I had heard that the end was near and that there would be no more revival, no more great masses of people coming to Christ. … But it just wasn't true! To say that the masses weren't turning to Christ, one would have had to ignore what Billy Graham was doing. … I tore out the color picture of Billy Graham and pinned it on the wall near my bed. … I admired him, yes, but to me that picture represented what God could do through a man. And it gave a boost of hope to my growing dream to evangelize millions of Latin Americans.[132]

Motivated by Billy Graham's successful evangelistic ministry around the world, Palau prayed to God to be used as an evangelist. He states, "The more I prayed and read about mass evangelism, the more convinced I became it was where the Lord wanted me."[133]

Billy Graham as Mentor

Ever since the two met, Billy Graham has been a spiritual mentor who has challenged and encouraged Palau to live his life as a global evangelist. Palau's first face-to-face encounter with Billy Graham occurred about ten years after he had first heard him preach on radio.[134] While working for OC International as new missionaries in Fresno, California, Palau and his wife had an opportunity to work for Billy Graham's evangelistic campaign in July of 1962. Palau worked as an interpreter for the Spanish audience, while his wife served as a counselor. He was filled with enthusiasm, wanting to learn everything possible about evangelistic campaigns.

Palau remarked, "I was so sure evangelism was what I was called to that I was like a hawk in Fresno. I didn't miss a thing. I asked questions of everyone, kept a thick notebook on every detail, and learned the mechanics of mobilizing thousands of people."[135] Observing this passionate and industrious young man, Billy Graham asked him what he was planning to do for the rest of his life. To which Palau answered promptly, "I want to have crusades just like yours."[136]

When Palau met Billy Graham at a pre-crusade breakfast, Graham advised him to aim at the big cities, the major population centers, for evangelistic campaigns.[137] Through his personal conversations with Graham and other staff members, Palau learned the fundamental principles and strategies of evangelistic campaigns. In referring to the similarities of his campaigns to Billy Graham's, Palau comments, "If anyone wonders why our team's crusades resemble his in many ways, they should have seen us eagerly absorbing the basics in Fresno."[138] In his interview with the *Tampa Tribune*, Palau also frankly admitted, "I copied Mr. Graham shamelessly from the beginning. … Some of my earliest messages were his. I memorized them. I knew the Gospel, but he did it so well."[139]

Billy Graham's influence on Palau after their acquaintance became even more tangible and significant; Graham's irreproachable integrity and godly character provided a role model for Palau to emulate,[140] and Graham's passion and boldness for the gospel inspired Palau to preach the good news in any circumstances. In his interview with *Discipleship Journal*, Palau was asked, "Who has impressed you most in this [evangelism] area?" Along with Bill Bright in terms of personal evangelism,[141] Palau acknowledged Billy Graham's influence in mass evangelism.

> And then as far as witnessing openly and publicly, I have been blessed personally in my acquaintance with and in observing Billy Graham, who takes advantage of great opportunities to unashamedly confess Christ. I think many of us are willing to confess Christ under very controlled circumstances when everything is in our favor. I have observed him do it in other situations, and that has moved me to do the same—in situations where it is not the expected thing.[142]

Graham's support and mentoring have continued throughout Palau's ministry. As Palau acknowledges, Graham gave him a platform to speak on many occasions.[143] He confesses, "Billy Graham was the one who had opened doors for me as an evangelist."[144] Going on, "One day, I thanked him for getting me the opportunity to preach in some place. He said, 'Luis, I can only open the door for you, but you have to walk through it."[145] Graham's sponsorship even included financial support. After Palau's vigorous and fruitful ministries in Latin America, Billy Graham donated $100,000 in seed money to fund Palau's new evangelistic association based in Portland, Oregon, in 1978.[146] By Graham's appointment, Walter Smyth, one of the key members of Graham's team, served on the founding board of directors for LPEA. Palau recalls that Smyth's advice was particularly valuable to him.[147]

Billy Graham as Partner

Although Billy Graham has been Palau's hero and mentor, their relationship has developed beyond that; the two have worked together closely as partners in evangelism for the kingdom of God. In his early ministry, Palau often interpreted Billy Graham's preaching for Spanish audiences and also worked as an associate evangelist for Graham.[148] For his part, Graham has invited Luis Palau on many occasions to give testimony in his own evangelistic campaigns. The first of such occasions was in Phoenix, Arizona, in 1974.[149]

When a violent earthquake hit Central America in 1976, both Graham's and Palau's evangelistic associations helped Guatemala with finances, food, and other relief at the request of Guatemala's president, Laugerud Garcia.[150] Billy Graham, a senior evangelist, sometimes called Palau for advice when he felt he could benefit from Palau's particular expertise.[151]

Graham publicly and unreservedly recognized Palau's ability as an evangelist. Introducing Palau to the audience at Amsterdam '83, Graham announced the upcoming campaigns in England in 1984, which he would conduct together with Palau, commenting that "God has given Luis Palau a multiplicity of gifts. For evangelicals throughout the world, he is now in more demand than anyone, and that includes me."[152]

Their partnership in evangelism reached a climax when the two proclaimed the gospel message in England almost simultaneously in 1984.[153] While Billy Graham and his evangelistic team proclaimed the gospel in six British cities through the campaign called "Mission England," Palau and his team preached in London and its suburbs through "Mission to London."[154]

When Palau arrived in London for his engagement at Queen's Park Rangers Football Stadium (QPR), the main campaign for Mission to London, he received a letter from Graham and recorded in his diary: "It's 2:30 a.m. and I am so excited about the upcoming mission that I can't sleep. When I arrived I found a lovely letter from Dr. Billy Graham. Billy's letter was warm beyond words. He is so gracious and such a great friend. Praise the Lord for a loyal friend like Dr. Graham."[155]

During the campaigns the two evangelists invited each other to speak from their respective podiums. The results of both campaigns were spectacular. The total attendance of Mission to London was more than a half million, with about 28,000 making a public confession of faith.[156] Graham's Mission England was even more fruitful. More than 1 million attended his campaigns, and 96,982 people—9.4 percent of the audience—registered public commitments.[157]

Graham's role in the formation and growth of Palau as an evangelist cannot be overemphasized. As the primary influencer on Palau's life as an evangelist, Graham's role has evolved over time from hero to mentor and finally to partner. Even in his frail old age, Graham's support continues; although he can no longer stand beside Palau, he wants to be informed about Palau's campaigns and prays for him regularly.[158] To the question journalists frequently ask Palau, "Who is going to fill Billy's shoes once he's gone?" Palau replies without hesitation, "No one man."[159]

Conclusion

A great spiritual leader is not formed in one day. Behind every godly man and woman are people who inspire and encourage them to be bold followers of Christ. Luis Palau is not an exception. He is indebted to many godly individuals, including his parents and the other mentors who have walked alongside him on the path to his success as an evangelist.

Among such mentors Billy Graham stands out. Upon receiving an honorary doctorate of divinity degree from Talbot Theological Seminary, Palau acknowledged the tremendous impact of his spiritual mentors, "who spiritually nurtured, discipled, trained, and equipped me to serve the King of kings."[160] "If they had not come to Argentina," said Palau, "if they had not loved me, if they had not gotten close to me and prayed with me and encouraged me to get on with the Lord's work, I might still be in Argentina, still in that little chapel … doing nothing for the Lord."[161]

Endnotes

104 Jerry B. Jenkins and Luis Palau, *Luis Palau: Calling the Nations to Christ* (Old Tappan, NJ: Revell, 1978; Chicago, IL: Moody Press, 1980), 95. Cf. There is a discrepancy in the length of learning from Mereshian. Unlike Jenkins' record, Whalin says that Palau learned from Mereshian for three years. Whalin, *Luis Palau*, 52.

105 Luis Palau and David Sanford, *Luis Palau: Calling America and the Nations to Christ* (Nashville, TN: Thomas Nelson, Inc., 1994; rev. 2000), 38.

106 Luis Palau, "The Unfinished Task of Declaring His Glory," in *Declare His Glory Among the Nations*, ed. David M. Howard (Downers Grove, IL: InterVarsity Press, 1977), 226. Palau also said, "I learned as much from this humble, holy man as I did from the study itself." Jenkins and Palau, *Luis Palau: Calling the Nations*, 95–96.

107 Ellen Bascuti, *Luis Palau: Evangelist to the World* (Uhrichsville, OH: Barbour Publishing, 2000), 44.

108 Palau and Sanford, *Calling America and the Nations*, 43.

109 Jenkins and Palau, *Luis Palau: Calling the Nations*, 96. According to Palau, Palau's friend was a very gifted evangelist. He served more as an evangelist, while Palau taught Bible lessons. Every day at 5:00 a.m., Palau and his friend prayed together, and they also prayed throughout the night on Fridays.

110 Palau and Sanford, *Calling America and the Nations*, 52–53. Palau had worked for the bank for about seven years, from 1952 to 1959.

111 Luis Palau, "The Evangelist Has a Strategy for Harvest," in *The Mission of an Evangelist*, ed. J. D. Douglas (Minneapolis, MN: World Wide Publications, 2001), 232.

112 Jenkins and Palau, *Luis Palau: Calling the Nations*, 54.

113 Luis Palau, "Missions to the End of the World," in *Global Crossroads: Focusing the Strength of Local Churches*, ed. W. Harold Fuller, World Evangelical Fellowship (Mandaluyong, Philippines: OMF Literature Inc., 1998), 280.

114 See Palau and Sanford, *Calling America and the Nations*, 52–60.

115 Cf. David Sanford, "Luis Palau: Calling America and the Nations to Christ," *Life Wise* (December/January 2002): 9. Here Dick Hillis is named as one of Palau's mentors, along with Billy Graham, Ray Stedman, and Keith Bentson.

116 Palau and Sanford, *Calling America and the Nations*, 51. See also ibid., 131.

117 Ibid., 60. Ray Stedman's influence on Palau's life cannot be overemphasized. Later Palau notes, "Ray became like a father to me and even took to calling me his son when introducing me. He treated me like a son, too, mixing a lot of advice, counsel, and even reprimand, with his friendship." Ibid., 62.

118 Ibid., 64.

119 Ibid., 66.

120 Ibid., 67.

121 Ibid., 68.

122 Graham's influence on Palau cannot be overemphasized, as evidenced by the fact that his name is mentioned more often than anyone else's in Palau's autobiography. See, for example, *Calling America and the Nations*, 36–37, 42, 44–45, 46–49, 74–75, 121, and 162–63.

123 Jenkins and Palau, *Luis Palau: Calling the Nations*, 109. Cf. In his interview by the author, Palau said that his favorite subjects were church history and biographies of evangelists. In addition to the names mentioned above, he added the Chinese evangelist John Sung. They all inspired Palau to have passion for the gospel and love for souls. Luis Palau, interview by author, May 9, 2008.

124 For example, "Is Palau the Next Billy Graham?" *ABC News*, 8 October 2005 [online]; accessed 27 September 2007; available from http://abcnews.go.com/

GMA/story?id= 1195278&page=1; Internet. See also Calmetta Y. Coleman, "Luis Palau: The Next Billy Graham of Everywhere?" *Wall Street Journal,* 16 November 1995, sec. B, pp. 1, 9. To the fact that he was called "the Billy Graham of Latin America" by the media, he said, "I would never dream of drawing such a comparison to a man I have admired for so long." Jenkins and Palau, *Luis Palau: Calling the Nations*, 9.

125 Palau and Sanford, *Calling America and the Nations*, 37.

126 Ibid., 44.

127 Ibid., 45.

128 Ibid.

129 Jenkins and Palau, *Luis Palau: Calling the Nations*, 106.

130 Palau and Sanford, *Calling America and the Nations*, 46. This event was called the mid-century revival by J. Edwin Orr.

131 Ibid.

132 Jenkins and Palau, *Luis Palau: Calling the Nations*, 108. This picture shocked his mother and church elders and brought criticism to Palau, but Palau states, "Still, I talked about Billy Graham almost as if I knew him. I followed what was happening with him, because it made sense to me." Ibid., 108–9.

133 Palau and Sanford, *Calling America and the Nations*, 46.

134 Palau heard Billy Graham preach on the radio in 1952, and in 1962 he met him personally. LPA, "Overview of Life and Ministry," 1–2.

135 Palau and Sanford, *Calling America and the Nations*, 74.

136 Michelle Bearden, "Man with a Message," *The Tampa Tribune,* 19 November 2006.

137 Palau and Sanford, *Calling America and the Nations*, 74–75. According to Palau, "Paul always went to the centers of population," said Graham. "And Mr. Moody used to say that the cities were the mountains, and if you won the mountains, the valleys took care of themselves."

138 Ibid., 75.

139 Bearden, "Man with a Message."

140 Concerning Graham's integrity, Palau remarked, "He [Graham] has redeemed the term 'evangelist,' for during the first half of the twentieth century, to be called an evangelist was an insult in many countries." Luis Palau and Timothy Robnett, *Telling the Story: Evangelism for the Next Generation* (Ventura, CA: Regal Books, 2006), 29. Palau also shares an episode through which he learned humility from Graham. While visiting Graham's hotel room in Essen, Germany, they had a chance to pray for a German evangelist. When Graham's voice became muffled, Palau opened his eyes to watch Graham praying on his face, "Not on all fours, but straight-out flat, face down, on the floor!" Afterward, Graham told Palau, "You know, Luis, the Bible says, 'Humble yourselves under the mighty hand of God' (1 Peter 5:6). I believe the best thing for an evangelist is to humble himself every day, even physically. I pray a lot flat on my face. In due time, He will raise

us up!" Referring to this incident, Palau comments, "I will be indebted forever for his example." Luis Palau, *Billy Graham: A Tribute from Friends*, ed. Vernon McLellan (New York: Faithwords, 2002), 137–38.

141 Jim Mills, "An Interview with Luis Palau," *Discipleship Journal* 12 (November/December 1982): 39. Palau said the following of Bill Bright: "Of my own knowledge, I must confess that watching Bill Bright [founder of Campus Crusade for Christ] witness to cab drivers and hotel employees, as well as to generals and politicians, has always been a source of blessing.... I have been impressed by his giving attention to you as a person when you talk to him. Even though he may have only fifteen seconds if you meet him in a crowded lobby, those fifteen seconds are all yours.... I can see why God uses him in leading souls to Christ, man to man—because of his really looking at you for those moments and really giving you his full attention."

142 Ibid. Palau went on to say, "For instance, politicians do not always expect someone to lay the gospel on them—but he does it. On a television talk show he will take advantage of any little twist in the conversation and come on strong with the gospel—that is a challenge, to take advantage of opportunities like that."

143 Besides many speaking opportunities in evangelistic campaigns, Graham also invited Palau to preach at many evangelism conferences. For instance, Graham invited Palau as one of the plenary speakers for the International Conference for Itinerant Evangelists in 1983 and 1986, better known as Amsterdam '83 and '86. The first time Palau attended such conferences by Graham's invitation was the World Congress on Evangelism in Berlin, Germany, in 1966. He attended this conference as attendee while serving as a missionary in Colombia. Palau, interview by author, May 9, 2008.

144 Palau, *Telling the Story*, 133.

145 Ibid.

146 Palau, interview by the author, May 9, 2008. Palau states that $100,000 in 1978 is worth about $1 million today. See also Bearden, "Man with a Message." According to A. Larry Ross, Graham's spokesman for twenty-six years, the financial support was possible only because Palau earned Graham's endorsements. He states, "Palau's biblical knowledge, his ability to keep his message relevant with the times and his commitment to reach a generation that is outside the church 'must have made an impression on Dr. Graham.'"

147 Palau, interview by author, May 9, 2008.

148 For instance, in 1975 Palau interpreted for Billy Graham in Mexico City, and he spoke at "mini-fests" in the nine-nation European tour in preparation for Eurofest '75. Palau and Sanford, *Calling America and the Nations*, 121. In 1979 Palau also worked as an associate of Graham in Australia. Susan Holton and David L. Jones, *Spirit Aflame: Luis Palau's Mission to London* (Grand Rapids, MI: Baker Book House, 1985), 71. Cf. In his interview by the author, Palau also confirmed that his voice was heard instead of Billy Graham's for Spanish audiences on television. Palau, interview by the author, May 9, 2008.

149 Palau and Sanford, *Calling America and the Nations*, 119.

150 Billy Graham, *Just as I Am: The Autobiography of Billy Graham* (Grand Rapids: Zondervan, 1997), 437-38. According to Graham, the president of Guatemala arranged two helicopters for Graham and his companions, Cliff Barrows and Luis Palau. The president's son also accompanied them. See also Palau and Sanford, *Calling America and the Nations*, 123.

151 For example, Billy Graham called Palau before he went to the Vatican and asked Palau how the Hispanics under persecution would react if he saw the pope. Palau, *Telling the Story*, 133.

152 Holton and Jones, *Spirit Aflame*, 33. This is the transcript of Billy Graham's address at the International Conference for Itinerant Evangelists (ICIE) in Amsterdam, the Netherlands, in July 1983.

153 Cf. Palau and Sanford, *Calling America and the Nations*, 141. Similar evangelistic campaigns in conjunction with BGEA occurred in Australia during the spring of 1979. While Billy Graham preached the gospel in Sydney, Palau held a campaign in Newcastle.

154 Cf. The following statement by Palau to the media before the beginning of his campaign at Queen's Park Rangers Football Stadium well expresses his friendship and partnership with Billy Graham: "Billy Graham and I are portrayed not only as friends, but also he as my mentor. I am glad to acknowledge this. We are working together and praying together for the British Isles at this time in history." Holton and Jones, *Spirit Aflame*, 177-78.

155 Holton and Jones, *Spirit Aflame*, 177.

156 LPA, "Ministry Impact Statistics."

157 Holton and Jones, *Spirit Aflame*, 11.

158 Palau, interview by the author, May 9, 2008. They do not talk on the phone any longer because Graham is having trouble focusing and thinking clearly while talking on the phone. Rather, they communicate with each other by writing.

159 Palau and Sanford, *Calling America and the Nations*, 161.

160 Ibid., 133.

161 Ibid.

CHAPTER 3

EVANGELISTIC THEOLOGY AND PHILOSOPHY, PART 1

In his preface to *Evangelism in the Early Church*, Michael Green expresses his concern that "Most evangelists are not very interested in theology; most theologians are not very interested in evangelism."[162] The inseparable nature of evangelism and theology has also been emphasized by Lewis Drummond: "It cannot be stated too strongly that the two disciplines [evangelism and theology], when separated, part to their mutual detriment."[163]

Luis Palau is one of the well-balanced evangelists in both theology and the practice of evangelism. Since he is not a systematic theologian, he does not elaborate on every aspect of theology. Nevertheless, like the preceding great evangelists and revivalists such as Charles Finney, D. L. Moody, R. A. Torrey, and Billy Graham, his evangelistic efforts originate from his solid biblical and theological convictions. The following section does not deal with all aspects of Palau's theology but addresses his core theological and philosophical convictions concerning evangelism, which appear often in his writings and speeches.

Evangelism and the Bible

The evangelistic ministry of Luis Palau originates from his firm belief in the authority of the Bible as the inerrant Word of God.

The message of salvation he has preached is deeply grounded in the Scriptures.

Historical Review

The significance of the Bible in relation to evangelism cannot be overemphasized. As the apostle Paul states in Romans 10:17, "Consequently, faith comes from hearing the message, and the message is heard through the word of Christ."[164] It is the Word of God that contains the message of salvation. The Church in the Middle Ages, however, diminished the value of Scripture; the authority of the Bible had been replaced by human traditions, and the Church had become institutionalized, negatively affecting every aspect of the Christian life. In Palau's words, some strengths of the Christian faith "evaporated with the rapid institutionalization of Christianity."[165]

The negative impact on evangelism was serious. Since the authority of Scripture had been lost in the perception of human authority, ordinary people lost their chance to hear the message of the gospel. This miserable spiritual condition continued until the Reformation. As legitimately pointed out by Luis Palau, the primary contribution of the Reformers of the 16th century rested on their viewing "the Bible (especially the New Testament) as the religious authority, instead of human institutions."[166]

Authority of the Bible for Evangelism

Throughout his evangelistic ministry Luis Palau has often advocated the ultimate authority of the Bible for the Christian faith. In his address at the Amsterdam 2000 conference, for instance, he stressed the Scriptures as the sole authority behind the message of evangelists. Palau exhorted other evangelists: "First, evaluate the message you're preaching. My number one goal is to 'preach the Word' (2 Timothy 4:2). Everything I preach must be clearly verified by Scripture."[167]

The fierce battlefield for the authority of the Bible in Palau's ministry has been Great Britain. During his evangelistic campaigns for a six-city tour of Scotland in 1980, Palau's greatest challenge did not come "from the media, government officials, or anti-religious forces."[168] Rather, it came from within the Church. A dozen Scottish ministers met with Palau to oppose the evangelistic campaign prior to its launch, and more than half of them disavowed the authority of the Bible as the trustworthy Word of God.[169] Edwin Gunn, a Baptist minister and a committee chairman of Palau's Glasgow campaign in 1983, expressed well the deplorable conditions of evangelism in the United Kingdom due to the lack of scriptural authority:

> A number of theological students and ministers doubt that the Bible is the Word of God. Therefore, their preaching is completely weakened in authority. They preach about politics and social issues, but don't relate that to the Word with any conviction. Inevitably that weakens evangelism.[170]

During Palau's Mission to London evangelistic campaigns in 1983 and 1984, the authority of the Bible had become a focal point of debate among people in London. The scriptural authority was rejected not only by ordinary people, but also by many members of the clergy. For example, the Church of England's Canon Melinsky remarked, "One doesn't accept a thing simply because the Bible says it."[171] Donald Soper, a member of the House of Lords, also criticized the evangelistic campaigns of Billy Graham and Luis Palau saying, "To hitch the wagon of such evangelism to the so-called star 'the Bible says' ... is strictly nonsensical and therefore practically intolerable."[172]

When confronted with such attacks on the Bible, Palau upheld the inerrancy of Scripture. In his address to a British audience, he argued, "When I hear people who profess to be Christians questioning whether the Bible is God's Word, I can't help but wonder if Christians today worship too small of a God. If God is God, then couldn't He write a book that is without error?"[173] At Queen's Park Rangers Football Stadium, the main campaign for Mission to London, he also preached this message:

> London's churches are empty because people deny the authority of the Bible. They denigrate Jesus Christ. The Bible is not just another religious book. It is the Word of

> God, inspired by the Holy Spirit. It is the authority for everything we do and say as Christians. … Christians need to recover the authority of Scripture or the churches will continue to be empty. People are looking for leadership from the Church. If we have no authority, all we have is "I think, I think, I think."[174]

Palau always affirms scriptural authority before he reads a Bible passage for his sermon. His message at QPR stadium offers a typical example:

> I want to read a Bible passage so relevant that it could be in tomorrow morning's newspaper. As I read it, remember that the Bible is the Word of God, inspired by the Holy Spirit. The Bible is without error. You can trust it 100 percent. Everything it affirms is the truth of God. Although it was written 2,000 years ago, it is relevant tonight here in London and all over the world.[175]

In his recent conversation with a Chinese government official and atheistic scientist, Zhao Qizheng, Palau confirmed his belief in biblical inerrancy once again: "The Bible is inspired by God. Even though the authors wrote freely, God overruled—if you can use that word—so that the end result was what God wanted us to know about him."[176] It is this conviction that has driven Palau to become a bold witness of the Word of God to multitudes of people.

Palau's conviction in the authority of the Bible and defense of the truth against those who deny biblical authority are commendable. Without conviction in the truth revealed in the Bible, evangelism loses its footing. The Bible firmly declares, "Then you will know the truth, and the truth will set you free" (John 8:32). When there is no conviction of the truth, there can be no knowledge of that truth and consequently no freedom. The Bible is the inerrant Word of God, containing the perfect message for the salvation of human beings.

Evangelism and the Sovereignty of God

There has been a theological controversy as well about whether evangelism is solely the work of God, a human responsibility, or a matter of collaboration between God and people.[177] In Palau's view it is the sovereign God who brings about salvation of human beings from beginning to the end. Still, he emphasizes that God normally works through human agency, the faithful witness of the gospel message.

God's Sovereignty in Evangelism

Evangelism in essence is the sovereign work of God. Although the involvement of a messenger and the response of the recipient of the gospel are both necessary, it is God alone who brings sinners to salvation. In his interview with *Discipleship Journal*, Luis Palau clearly states that "Conviction, conversion, and regeneration—these are all the work of God."[178]

The awareness of God's sovereignty in evangelism causes evangelists not to trust in themselves but to rely totally upon the Holy Spirit. In his Amsterdam '86 speech, Palau emphasized this point: "Any ministry that is not anointed by God's Spirit is not really ministry, but manipulation. The power of persuasion never must [*sic*] be confused with or substituted for the power of the Holy Spirit Himself."[179] Along with sound doctrine and the integrity of the evangelist, the power of the Holy Spirit is an indispensable element for genuine evangelistic fruit:

> For the evangelist, a truly Spirit-empowered ministry manifests itself in the hearts of the audience. The fire of the conviction of sin is the work of the Holy Spirit. He alone can convict the world of sin and righteousness and judgment. No one can experience regeneration apart from His intervention.[180]

Palau's firm belief in the sovereignty of God and the work of the Holy Spirit has led him to utilize several reliable methods to promote the message of the gospel. Commenting on the words of the apostle Paul in 1 Corinthians 2:3–5,[181] Palau asserts the following:

> God does the work of evangelism through us, no matter what method we use. It is through the power of the Holy Spirit and by God's grace—not our impressive techniques—that people are saved. Polished evangelism presentations are weak and ineffective without His anointing.[182]

Even though evangelists proclaim the message of the gospel using any available means, it is God who speaks to the hearts of people, brings conviction of sin, and leads them to the decision to believe in Jesus. Thus, Palau decisively concludes, "Only a very uninstructed evangelist would think that he himself actually does the conversion."[183]

The Role of the Evangelist in Evangelism

If evangelism is solely the work of God, what is the role of the evangelist in bringing sinners to Him? Although Palau asserts that God sets in motion the salvation of human beings, he does not negate the active role and involvement of evangelists. The role of evangelists cannot be ignored, since God uses human beings as His instruments. As Palau puts it, "Evangelism is really the activity of God, and the human instrument is to be *available* to God and *obedient* to God" [emphasis in original].[184] To Palau, the obedient participation of evangelists is crucial for any successful evangelistic endeavor. Thus, while emphasizing the sovereignty of God in evangelism, Palau stresses the role of evangelists, as seen in the following statement:

> We are so much the instruments of God that James actually says in his epistle, "Anyone who converts a soul from sin has covered a multitude of sins." There is a point at which we are so much the instrument of God that in some sense, if it is properly understood, it can be said that the evangelist, as the working instrument, actually converted the person.[185]

This statement may sound radical, but it should be understood in light of his firm conviction that God is at work in the whole process of salvation.

Palau's belief in the vital role of the human agency somewhat resembles that of Charles Finney, who advocated that revival is the work of both God and people. Like Finney, Palau has developed and utilized innovative methods to spread the gospel.[186] Nevertheless, recognizing the truth that God works through human agency should not incite self-pride in any evangelist; rather, it should drive the preacher to pursue the work of evangelism under the direction of the Holy Spirit with more passion and urgency, as exemplified in the life of Luis Palau.

Evangelism and Its Urgency

The urgency in evangelism has been the driving force and motivation for Palau's passionate evangelistic endeavors. Paul negates the popular idea that evangelism just happens when Christians live a godly life.

> I know great worshipping people who just don't share their faith, and godly men and women for whom evangelism never happens. If evangelism happened naturally, the Lord wouldn't have repeatedly commanded it. Evangelism must stay a priority for us to continue the work of Christ.[187]

Palau laments that most churches in North America "devote very little time to evangelism of *any* kind."[188] He believes that the urgency of evangelism ought to drive every Christian to make it their first priority in life. With this urgency and priority, every believer should make an intentional effort to share the gospel.

Biblical Mandate

The urgent need for evangelism stems from several sources, foremost of which is biblical mandate. For Palau, "In its essence, evangelism is a chosen act of obedience to God's revealed will."[189] Throughout the Scriptures God's will is clear:

> It is the highest, most important act of obedience for a Christian, because there is nothing more important to God, "who wants all men to be saved" (1 Timothy 2:4). "The Lord … is patient with you, not wanting anyone to perish, but everyone to come to repentance" (2 Peter 3:9). Jesus made His mission very plain: "For the Son of Man came to seek and to save what was lost" (Luke 19:10). We know His final command to "go and make disciples of all nations" (Matthew 28:19) as the Great Commission, not the great suggestion.[190]

While serving as the president of Overseas Crusades (now OC International), Palau challenged missionaries to proclaim the gospel with urgency. With a special emphasis on the present tense in the Bible verse, "The harvest *is* plentiful," from Matthew 9:37–38, Palau stressed, "It's ready now! Therefore, we must go get it <u>now</u>. Many times the tendency is to point out the mistakes that are made, forgetting that the harvest is sitting out there—ready. While we sit around discussing problems, mistakes, and concepts, some humble guy who can't even read or write is winning souls!" [emphasis in original].[191]

Human Destiny and Limited Time

The urgency for evangelism also stems from the undeniable fact that humankind is lost without Christ. Unfortunately, many believers today do not share this conviction. As Palau points out, "In today's church there's no urgency to evangelize partly because we don't deeply believe the lost are really lost."[192] He goes on to say, "We don't out and out deny it because that would sound heretical; but we don't embrace it, because if we did, we'd be much more *desperate* [emphasis in original] to persuade lost and dying people to turn to Christ."[193]

Furthermore, humanity's time on Earth is limited and running out. According to Timothy Robnett, director of Next Generation Alliance (NGA), 165,000 people die every day in the world, and many of them face eternity without Christ.[194] Palau also argues that the fact that there are more than 3 billion people alive who do not know Christ may serve as an excuse for some Christians not to share the gospel.

However, he urges, "We must not forget the actual people—including those we know and love—behind that number who live 'without hope and without God in the world' (Ephesians 2:12)."[195]

Moreover, Palau solemnly admonishes that the time for believers who have the message of eternal life is also running out. During the inauguration rally for Mission to London at Trafalgar Square in 1983, Palau challenged eight thousand Christians with these words: "As far as you and I are concerned, today is the only time we have. None of us knows when the Lord will call us home. We must therefore take Britain for Christ with authority, in the name of Jesus Christ, before it's too late."[196]

Changing Situations and Opportunity

Finally, the pressing imperative for evangelism comes from the changing situations in the world, which entail great opportunity and the possibility of world evangelization with the present generation. Palau insists that God is opening the doors to the gospel in many countries around the world: "The overwhelming sense I have as I travel is that we live in a time of great opportunity."[197]

Many countries in the Third World that had very limited access to the gospel now witness a tremendous harvest of souls. With the collapse of Marxism, people in the former Soviet Union and Eastern Europe are embracing Christian faith. A similar process is taking place, in Palau's judgment, in the People's Republic of China, opening the doors to the gospel to this once closed country. God's supernatural intervention is also taking place in many countries in the Middle East where evangelization seemed impossible before. Many Christians who were converted from a non-Christian background testify that they met Jesus in a dream or vision, in which He spoke directly to them that He is the Savior of the world. Hence, Palau asserts, "I look forward to the day when I will preach in Riyadh, Saudi Arabia, or Tehran, Iran."[198]

Other factors also contribute to new opportunities for global evangelization. Technological advances in mass media help proclaim the gospel more effectively. Inevitably, as Palau observes, "Mass communication has made it possible to reach even closed nations with the message of life."[199] Palau notes further that the "world is in flux. Large populations and ethnic groups are moving from country to country, region to region, city to city."[200] Quoting Donald McGavran, he continues, "Such times of transition provide the best moments to lead people to God through Jesus Christ."[201]

Sharing his confidence in the evangelization of the world in his own generation, Palau challenges people, "We need the conviction that it must be done in our society and it must be done urgently. … It is urgent that we move now."[202] Palau also warns that Christians must seize the opportunities while they last:

> For they [opportunities] will pass, as history teaches us. In some now-open areas, persecution is rising, and already evangelism is becoming much more difficult. … Now is the moment—perhaps a unique moment in history that may not return for several hundred years. Let us press on.[203]

All of the factors mentioned above—the biblical mandate, the eternal destiny of humanity without Christ, the limited time for both unbelievers and believers, and changing situations and opportunities—compel Palau to proclaim the message of eternal life with urgency. Speaking of the joy of winning a soul, he exhorts, "There's no greater thrill. Give evangelism all you've got. This life is your only chance."[204]

Endnotes

162 Michael Green, *Evangelism in the Early Church* (Grand Rapids, MI: Wm. B. Eerdmans Publishing Company, 1970), 7. Cf. Thomas Paul Johnston, "The Work of an Evangelist: The Evangelistic Theology and Methodology of Billy Graham" (Ph.D. diss., Southern Baptist Theological Seminary, 2001), 53. While acknowledging the lack of works in the area of theology of evangelism, as compared to the number of books written on systematic theology, Johnston still argues that there are some exceptional works on the theology of evangelism. For example, he provides the following list of books in their chronological order: Henry Cook, *The Theology of Evangelism: The Gospel in the World of To-Day* (Carey Kingsgate Press, London: 1951); T. A. Kantonen, *The Theology of Evangelism* (Philadelphia, PA: Muhlenberg, 1954); Julian N. Hartt, *Toward a Theology of Evangelism* (New York: Abingdon, 1955); C. E. Autrey, *The Theology of Evangelism* (Nashville, TN: Broadman, 1966); Ernest D. Pickering,

The Theology of Evangelism (Clarks Summit, PA: Baptist Bible College Press, 1974); and Lewis A. Drummond, *The Word of the Cross: A Contemporary Theology of Evangelism* (Nashville, TN: Broadman, 1992).

163 Lewis A. Drummond, *Leading Your Church in Evangelism* (Nashville, TN: Broadman Press, 1975), 35. Drummond presents several reasons for uniting theology and evangelism: "The first and by far the most important reason is that they are never divorced in the Scriptures. … A second reason for the wedding of theology and mission is that without sound theological content, evangelism soon degenerates into sentimentalism, emotionalism, and gimmicks. … The third reason for fusing theology and evangelism is the pragmatic fact that God has honored most profoundly the ministry of those who do. ... Other reasons could be given for the necessity of a strong theology for effective evangelism. For example, a knowledge of theology makes the presentation of the gospel message plain; it makes the evangelist more sure of his message; a genuine understanding of the rich content of the Bible will fill one with zeal; theology is an important agent in conserving evangelistic results." Ibid., 35–37.

164 Scripture quotations, unless otherwise indicated, are from NIV.

165 Luis Palau and David Sanford, *God Is Relevant: Finding Strength and Peace in Today's World* (New York: Doubleday, 1997), 18.

166 David L. Jones and Luis Palau, *Scottish Fires of Revival* (Cupertino, CA: D.I.M.E. Publishers, 1980), 17.

167 Luis Palau, "The Evangelist Has a Strategy for Harvest" in *The Mission of an Evangelist*, ed. J. D. Douglas (Minneapolis, MN: World Wide Publications, 2001), 234.

168 Luis Palau and David Sanford, *Luis Palau: Calling America and the Nations to Christ* (Nashville, TN: Thomas Nelson, Inc., 1994; rev. 2000), 146.

169 Ibid.

170 LPEA, *Let the Whole World Hear the Voice of God* (Portland, OR: LPEA, 1983), 16.

171 "Storm over Marriage Guide," *Today*, March 1984; quoted in Susan Holton and David L. Jones, *Spirit Aflame: Luis Palau's Mission to London* (Grand Rapids: Baker Book House, 1985), 52.

172 Donald Soper, "Why I'm Bothered about These Campaigns," *Methodist Recorder*, March 1, 1984, p. 1; quoted in Holton and Jones, *Spirit Aflame*, 52. "The Bible says" is the phrase that Billy Graham and Luis Palau often use in their preaching. During Mission to London, Soper and Palau debated the authority of the Bible on LBC's radio program called *Nightline*. Holton and Jones, *Spirit Aflame*, 52. Cf. Another controversy on the Bible arose during Palau's Mission to London. Rev. David Jenkins, a former professor of religion at Leeds University, expressed his doubts on some of the fundamental doctrines of the Bible, such as the virgin birth of Jesus and His physical resurrection. A survey showed that a third of the Church of England's bishops agreed with Jenkins' statements, and he was elected as Bishop of Durham on July 6, 1984, at York Minister, Britain's largest medieval cathedral. Ibid., 53–57.

173 Holton and Jones, *Spirit Aflame*, 52.

174 Ibid., 52-53.

175 Ibid., 214.

176 Luis Palau and Zhao Qizheng, *A Friendly Dialogue Between an Atheist and a Christian* (Grand Rapids: Zondervan, 2008), 14. Cf. LPA's statement of beliefs accurately represents its view on the Bible: "We believe that the Bible is the verbally inspired Word of God, without error in the original writing, and the supreme and final authority in doctrine and practice." LPA, "Beliefs" (Portland, OR: LPA).

177 For example, see J. I. Packer, *Evangelism & the Sovereignty of God* (Downers Grove, IL: InterVarsity Press, 1961), 18–36. Packer acknowledges both divine sovereignty and human responsibility in evangelism. He calls the coexistence of these elements "antinomy." According to him, "An antinomy exists when a pair of principles stand side by side, seemingly irreconcilable, yet both undeniable." Ibid., 18.

178 Jim Mills, "An Interview with Luis Palau," *Discipleship Journal* 12 (November/December 1982): 40. Cf. Sterling Huston also made an insightful observation on this aspect: "Effective Crusades are not built on persuasion, personality, or promotion. They are built by depending on the Holy Spirit to do a lasting work. … If we could organize or persuade people into the Kingdom, we could also organize and persuade them out again. This kind of evangelism would merely be human manipulation." Sterling W. Huston, *Crusade Evangelism*, rev. ed. (Minneapolis, MN: World Wide Publications, 1996), 45.

179 Luis Palau, "The Evangelist and the Ministry of the Holy Spirit," in *The Calling of an Evangelist*, ed. J. D. Douglas (Minneapolis, MN: World Wide Publications, 1987), 141. Cf. Palau often emphasized the work of the Holy Spirit in today's churches. "If there's anything the Church needs today, it's fire—not the short-lived fire of human effort or the flesh, but the mighty fire of the Holy Spirit." Palau and Sanford, *Calling America and the Nations*, 190.

180 Palau, "Evangelist and Ministry of the Holy Spirit," 141. Palau also states, "If the evangelist's message is anointed by the Spirit, it will be delivered with authority. All the physical and mental energy in the world, combined with all the witty, persuasive speech imaginable, cannot manufacture the Spirit's power. Too many evangelists miss the obvious: Only the Holy Spirit can produce Holy Spirit authority. He must speak for Himself. He must have the last word if people are to repent and give their lives to Christ."

181 "I came to you in weakness and fear, and with much trembling. My message and my preaching were not with wise and persuasive words, but with a demonstration of the Spirit's power, so that your faith might not rest on men's wisdom, but on God's power" (1 Cor. 2:3–5).

182 Luis Palau and Mike Umlandt, *The Only Hope for America: The Transforming Power of the Gospel of Jesus Christ* (Wheaton, IL: Crossway Books, 1996), 77.

183 Mills, "Interview with Luis Palau," 40.

184 Ibid.

185 Ibid. Palau gives an example of a Bible verse in this respect: "For instance, Scripture says in 2 Corinthians 5:11 that we persuade men—'Knowing the fear of the Lord, we persuade men.' And there are other passages in which the evangelist is talked about almost as though *he* [emphasis in original] is doing the work." Ibid. Cf. One may also ponder what the apostle Paul said in 1 Corinthians 3:9, "We are God's fellow workers," which shows clearly the responsibility and significance of human agency.

186 From his confidence in human agency, Finney employed and developed certain methods to promote revivals that were called "New Measures." He contended that measures are not fixed but flexible. For Finney, the purpose of a measure was to "make known the Gospel in the most efficient way, to make the truth stand out strikingly, so as to obtain the attention and secure the obedience of the greatest number possible." Charles Grandison Finney, *Lectures on Revivals of Religion* (New York/Chicago/Toronto/London/Edinburgh: Fleming H. Revell Company, 1868), 211. According to Robert L. Asa, Finney's new methods had transcended denominational lines and influenced most major mass evangelists, not only in his time but also in the subsequent era, becoming a prototype of modern mass evangelism. Robert Lynn Asa, "The Theology and Methodology of Charles G. Finney as a Prototype for Modern Mass Evangelism" (Ph.D. diss., Southern Baptist Theological Seminary, 1983), 6-9. Palau's innovative methods will be discussed in the section "Evangelism Rooted in Cultural Relevancy and Creativity."

187 Luis Palau and Timothy Robnett, *Telling the Story: Evangelism for the Next Generation* (Ventura, CA: Regal Books, 2006), 107.

188 Palau, *The Only Hope for America*, 17.

189 Palau and Sanford, *Calling America and the Nations*, 195.

190 Ibid.

191 Luis Palau, "Evangelism in the Future," in *Evangelical Missions Tomorrow*, ed. Wade T. Coggins and E. L. Frizen (South Pasadena, CA: William Carey Library, 1977), 181.

192 Palau, *The Only Hope for America*, 22.

193 Ibid. Palau quotes Billy Sunday, who said, "God keeps no halfway house. It's either heaven or hell for you and me." He also cites John Wesley's words: "The moment a soul drops the body and stands naked before God, it cannot but know what its portion will be to all eternity. It will have full in its view, either everlasting joy, or everlasting torment." Cf. Palau expressed the same concern in his interview with *Christianity Today*: "If we believed that people were irrevocably lost without Christ, we would take advantage of every chance to preach the gospel." Luis Palau, "Whatever Happened to Evangelism? Luis Palau Wants to Rekindle Our Passion for the Lost," *Christianity Today*, 8 April 1996, 39.

194 Robnett, *Telling the Story*, 151.

195 Palau, *Telling the Story*, 153.

196 Holton and Jones, *Spirit Aflame*, 136.

197 Luis Palau, "Which Part of the Great Commission Don't You Understand?" *Christianity Today*, 16 November 1998, 76.

198 Ibid.

199 Palau, *Telling the Story*, 154.

200 Palau, "Which Part Don't You Understand?" 76.

201 Ibid.

202 Luis Palau, "Working Together," in *Believing and Obeying Jesus Christ: The Urbana '79 Compendium,* ed. John W. Alexander (Downers Grove, IL: InterVarsity Press, 1980), 112.

203 Palau, "Which Part Don't You Understand?" 76.

204 Palau, *The Only Hope for America*, 24.

CHAPTER 4

EVANGELISTIC THEOLOGY AND PHILOSOPHY, PART 2

Evangelism and the Evangelist

The Great Commission is given to every believer who confesses Jesus as Savior and Lord. However, the Scriptures acknowledge some Christians who are especially gifted for the task of evangelism, calling them "evangelists."[205] From the biblical era down through Christian history, the message of the gospel has been carried out effectively and extensively by these evangelists.[206] Although there has been a tendency among Christians to ignore the gift of the evangelist, the church must regain the biblical teaching and, as Robnett puts it, "identify, train and position these gifted ones from God for the purposes He has given them."[207]

The most important element for any successful mass evangelism is the evangelist himself. Unfortunately, some popular mass evangelists such as Jim Bakker and Jimmy Swaggart disappeared from the public scene due to outrageous scandals. As pointed out by Michael Cassidy, the lack of qualified evangelists is one of the primary limitations of mass evangelism.[208] Luis Palau acknowledges this point.

To the question why only a few evangelists among many are called great, Palau replies, "I've examined that question and found that the answer has little to do with method or technique."[209] Rather, the answer lies in certain characteristics these individuals share in common. As a renowned evangelist himself, Palau has had many opportunities to speak to fellow evangelists and has often discussed the essential characteristics of evangelists. These qualities are based on biblical teaching, and Palau has implemented them in his own life. And now he and his organization are making an investment into the lives of hundreds of evangelists in much the same way Graham encouraged Palau. The following section will review some of the core characteristics for evangelists, as espoused by Luis Palau and which he is teaching to younger men and women.[210]

Vision

Fulfilling the Great Commission requires a clear vision. In his exposition on John 14:12–15, Palau asserts that Christians must dream great dreams. As Jesus promised, believers can do what Jesus did and even more. The reason so few Christians accomplish great things for Christ is, in Palau's words, that "Christians too often lose the ability to dream great dreams."[211] For Palau, a large vision gives a person "perspective and stability."[212] He compares such a vision to flying in a jumbo jet with big wings:

> When you have a big vision, the wings move a little, but the airplane doesn't rock very much. If your vision is small, however, your little airplane may feel like it's falling apart. Vision helps you to go through the clouds and the storms without being shaken up and tempted to give up.[213]

The vision of evangelists must entail geographic dimensions, just as Jesus "went about all the cities and villages."[214] Since Jesus commanded His followers to preach the gospel to the ends of the world, the vision of evangelists should not be limited by any geographical boundaries, as long as God continues to use them.[215] As a global evangelist, Palau himself has been a man of vision, a vision that God has gradually expanded in conjunction with his ministry around the world. Testifying of how his vision had grown over time from the city of Córdoba in Argentina to Latin America, Palau remarks, "But God wasn't through with me yet. Today, in faith, our evangelistic association wants to let the whole world hear the voice of God."[216]

Compassion

Compassion for souls without Christ is another essential attribute for evangelists. Compassion was the driving force of Jesus' ministry on Earth. When Jesus saw the multitudes of people, whom he perceived to be like sheep without a shepherd, He felt compassion and directed His disciples to ask God to send more workers for the harvest (Matthew 9:36–38).[217] Palau confesses that evangelists are often tempted to fall into mannerisms; many thus end up preaching the gospel without sincere love for people who are without Christ.[218] While acknowledging this tendency, Palau shares his firm resolution:

> One thing I am asking the Lord, in my planning and charting is that I will not lose my compassion and warmth for the lost. It's easy to forget. It's easy to get in front of a TV camera to preach and "get plastic." To begin to think of numbers and statistics. To forget the suffering of people. The Lord Jesus had compassion on them. … I feel that evangelism in the future demands we keep compassion for souls on fire.[219]

As an evangelist, Palau makes a deliberate effort to be a man of compassion. His compassion is well revealed in his preaching at Urbana '76:

> Do you know how I get compassion? I remember that in Latin America every two months an average of 500,000 people die. Every two months! And my heart breaks when I think of it. I have a book with pictures of Latin America—the Indians and city people, rich people and poor people. When I begin to feel that my heart is getting hard, I go through this book and look at the old people and poor people and the blind, and I begin to cry almost every time. We must not be embarrassed to cry a little bit for those who are lost.[220]

While the role of most evangelists is limited to preaching the gospel, Palau has shown genuine interest in the real life and suffering of people. Through extensive counseling he has heard firsthand reports of people's suffering and given biblical advice in love.[221]

Holiness

Evangelists are often faced with temptations and traps that can lead to their downfall; among these are as sex, fame, money, competing spirit, pride, and ungodly lifestyle.[222] Billy Graham once observed that most evangelists last less than ten years. In Palau's judgment, they "don't last because they dishonor the name of the Lord due to a lack of holiness in the areas of money, sex and pride."[223]

Holiness has been the characteristic of Christian leaders most emphasized by Luis Palau. Scripture abounds with exhortations for holiness, as Palau points out:

> God must be honored! The Holy Spirit, if grieved, cannot do His work as He pleases among men. Scripture says, "*Do not grieve the Holy Spirit*" (Eph. 4:30); "*Do not quench the Holy Spirit*" (1 Thess. 5:19); and finally it says "*be filled with the Spirit*" (Eph. 5:18) [emphasis in original].[224]

As a teenager Palau did not quite understand the indwelling of the Holy Spirit, thinking of this as a figure of speech. It was during his time of study in the States that he came to realize that the indwelling of the Holy Spirit is real.[225] In his view, "Holiness means that we walk close to the Lord. Holiness means that we walk in the light. Holiness means that we stay close to Jesus Christ and to His Word. And when you stay close to the Lord in holiness, the Lord can use you."[226]

Holiness is also possible because of the indwelling of the Holy Spirit. Hence, holiness is the condition for an evangelist to be used by God. An evangelist must, in and through the power of the Holy Spirit, have a clean and pure heart, after repenting of his own sin and thus restoring his relationship with God, the evangelist is able to stand before God and be used by Him as His spokesperson.[227] Palau adds, "There is authority in holiness. A holy person may not be brilliant, not be extremely eloquent, but there is a power evident in a holy person."[228] Palau endorses what Robert Murray M'Cheyne (1813–1842), one of the greatest Scottish evangelists, wrote in his letter to Jonathan Edwards: "According to your holiness, so shall be your success. … Mr. Edwards, a holy man is an awesome weapon in the hand of God."[229]

Boldness

Boldness, which originates from absolute trust in the power of God,[230] is another important quality for the evangelist. Without boldness, one cannot advance the kingdom of God on Earth, which is full of hostility against the gospel. Proclaiming the gospel requires boldness, since there will often be criticism and opposition. Citing examples of great men of faith from the past, such as John Calvin, Martin Luther, Nicolaus Ludwig Zinzendorf, and George Whitefield, Palau states, "These evangelists had *holy audacity* [emphasis mine]. Like them, we must learn to launch out in the name of the Lord, take risks and even face death with courage."[231]

Palau himself has been such a bold witness of Christ that he was once dubbed by a columnist "God's good gaucho."[232] In fact, he has faced the threat of being harmed for holding evangelistic campaigns. For instance, during his campaign in Lima, Peru, in 1984, a Maoist terrorist group called *Sendero Luminoso* (Shining Path) threatened to kill him if he did not leave the country within twenty-four hours. Palau decided to stay and continued his campaign as planned. Even though there was some disturbance by the terrorist group, God protected Palau and the campaign was successful, with 250,000 in attendance over the eight days.[233]

In his speech at Lausanne II in Manila in 1989, Palau predicted that some of the participants of the Lausanne II meeting might be killed for the sake of the gospel by the year 2000. Yet he affirmed his conviction in God's protection:

> George Whitefield said, "I am immortal till my day is done." None of us will be killed one hour before the Lord says, "OK boy, you've done your duty. Come on home." … The

Lord says, "Never will I leave you; never will I forsake you." So we say with confidence, "The Lord is my helper; I will not be afraid. What can man do to me?" (Hebrews 13:5–6).[234]

Evangelism and the Evangelistic Campaign

Campaign evangelism has been criticized by many in the past and is still being disparaged today. Such criticisms come from various quarters. Generally speaking, some criticize evangelists, others disapprove of the theology of campaign evangelism, and still others find fault with the methods of evangelistic campaigns.[235] Luis Palau himself acknowledges the weaknesses of mass evangelistic campaigns. However, he believes that "despite all the weaknesses that are properly pointed out, it [campaign evangelism] *is* [emphasis mine] still a valid method to proclaim the gospel."[236] In the following section, Palau's views on evangelistic campaigns will be examined from the biblical, historical, practical, and future perspectives.

Biblical and Historical Precedents

Evangelistic campaigns have contributed significantly toward the carrying out of the Great Commission. According to Michael Green, preaching to a crowd in the open air was not uncommon among the Jews in Jesus' time.[237] Palau also observes that Jesus is reported to have spoken to "the multitudes" nearly 150 times and that He "often addressed himself to cities as a whole in his declarations ('Oh Jerusalem, Jerusalem!'), ('Woe unto you, Bethsaida!') (Matt. 9:35–38; Luke 4:14–22; Matt. 5:1)."[238] After Jesus' death and resurrection, His apostles and disciples continued to practice this evangelistic method. The best example can be found in the ministry of the apostle Paul, who used the marketplace, where people were gathered, to preach the message of the gospel.[239]

Throughout Christian history, this method has continued to be employed, becoming one of the most effective ways to reach unbelievers "en masse" with the gospel of Jesus Christ. Godly individuals such as "John Wesley, George Whitefield, Jonathan Edwards, Charles G. Finney, Dwight L. Moody, Elias Schrenk,

R. A. Torrey, Billy Sunday, John Sung, [and] Billy Graham" have conducted citywide evangelistic campaigns and brought multitudes into the kingdom of God.[240] Moreover, since their evangelistic campaigns have often transformed the lives of believers, they have also been referred to as revivals.[241]

Strategic Role of Evangelistic Campaigns

Like all other methods of evangelism, campaign evangelism has its strengths and weaknesses. Luis Palau shares his convictions on its positive aspects. Some of these characteristics, those that are more pertinent and unique to this form of evangelism, are discussed in this section.[242]

First, campaign evangelism proclaims the gospel to multitudes of people by all available means, giving unbelievers opportunities to hear the truth, believe in Jesus, and confess Him publicly.[243] The scale and scope of evangelistic campaigns cannot be compared to those of any other form of evangelism. While affirming the importance and effectiveness of personal evangelism, Palau still contends the following:

> History has shown that a nation of millions cannot be converted by one-on-one evangelism, because eventually the chain breaks down and the multiplication peters out. You can prepare the groundwork, but eventually it's necessary to move the masses, sway public opinion, influence the thought patterns of the nation and the media.[244]

Second, through evangelistic campaigns, citywide or even nationwide "God-consciousness" is created: "An awareness of the Gospel sweeps across whole nations. … Conversations in restaurants, hotels and private homes often revolve around God, Jesus Christ and the Bible."[245] Third, "God-consciousness" can be expedited by utilizing all available mass media, including newspapers and radio and television broadcasts. This in turn grabs the attention of national leaders, people in the upper class, and professionals who might not otherwise be interested in the Christian faith.[246]

Fourth, believers are trained in this way for personal witness and often have their first opportunity to lead someone to Christ. New converts from campaigns also make local churches grow when they are properly assimilated into existing churches or formed into new congregations.[247]

Fifth, the unity and cooperation expressed through campaigns enhance the self-image of Christians and often lead them to spiritual awakening.[248] Sixth, in the society as a whole, the prophetic voice of God is proclaimed, expelling the powers of darkness that dominate the regions. Through campaigns, "the climate for calls to justice and honesty at all levels in a nation" cause "a transformation in the family and business life of a nation."[249]

Future of Campaign Evangelism

There have been many skeptical voices concerning the future of campaign evangelism. As a matter of fact, Palau already sees the passion and fervor for evangelistic campaigns growing weak in the West, although he encounters more opportunities and responses in many other regions of the world.[250] His confidence in the future of mass evangelism is reflected in the following statement:

> Does mass evangelism have a future? My answer is a resounding "Yes!" I believe that mass evangelism, practiced in the power of the Holy Spirit and proclaiming the true Gospel of Jesus Christ, will move both those who practice it and those who observe it to exclaim in the words of St. Paul, "To the King of ages, immortal, invisible, the only God, be honor and glory for ever and ever. Amen" (1 Tim. 1:17).[251]

Luis Palau, who has preached the gospel throughout his lifetime, is convinced that campaign evangelism is effective and viable in spite of some pessimistic prospects. His conviction is justified on the basis of biblical, historical, and practical grounds. Furthermore, in Palau's judgment, the future of campaign evangelism is even brighter because more opportunities for campaigns are opening, especially in Third-World countries, brought by political and social changes. With this conviction Palau has carried out evangelistic campaigns, pursuing unity and cooperation that are indispensable for their success.

Evangelism Founded on Christian Unity and Cooperation

Biblical Basis for Christian Unity and Cooperation

The principle of Christian unity and cooperation is firmly rooted in the Scriptures. The Bible abounds with exhortations for Christians to be united in Jesus Christ for the well-being of the kingdom of God.[252] One of the best examples is found in John 17, in which Jesus prayed for the unity of His disciples before His death on the cross. In his exposition on John 17, Luis Palau writes, "Evangelism that does not flow from unity and that does not lead to unity of the Body of Christ cannot fulfill the will of Jesus. Evangelists can be those unifying persons who call the Church to partnership, cooperation and supportive ministry."[253]

Palau advocated Christian unity and cooperation in his speech at Urbana '79.[254] He preached on the principles of cooperation for Christian workers from Romans 12:6–8:

> In Christ we complete, not compete (vv. 6–8). In the power of the resurrected Christ we can conquer nations for God. Foreigners and nationals can work together arm in arm, not competing for results but complementing each other's work. Theologians and evangelists, local pastors and traveling preachers can work together for the common good and the glory of our living God. . . . Therefore, work together for Christ. Begin to discover what your gifts from Christ may be now. Let him be the great synchronizer of the church worldwide.[255]

Christian unity and cooperation for the kingdom of God are impossible without an attitude of mutual respect, accompanied by genuine love (Romans 12:10).[256] They are also impossible without a servant's heart and humility (Romans 12:11). Just as Jesus washed the feet of His disciples, so Christian workers must serve one another. To wash the feet of others, Christian workers must be on their knees, bowing before their brothers and sisters.[257]

Implementation of Unity and Cooperation for Evangelism

Campaign evangelism is the venue in which Christian unity and cooperation are required and demonstrated more powerfully than in any other evangelistic endeavors. One can share the gospel on a personal level, in a small-group setting, or even in the united effort of a local church, but apart from evangelistic campaigns it is hard to see the unity and cooperation of Christians within a whole city or region, encompassing various denominations.[258] Campaign evangelism thus requires harmony among the evangelist and his team, the various committees for a campaign, local church leaders, and congregations. Without accord and collaboration among these entities, success cannot be achieved. Accordingly, the scope and degree of unity in an evangelistic campaign surpass those of any other evangelistic efforts.

Palau's ministry has been marked by unity and cooperation. He has worked with people of diverse denominational, cultural, and ethnic backgrounds. The spirit of oneness and mutual support is well expressed in one of LPA's Statements of Core Values: "We are committed to accomplishing our mission by partnering with churches, evangelists, and other ministries."[259] In compliance with this value, Palau and his team have worked well with various Christian organizations.[260]

According to Palau, the primary task of evangelistic campaigns "is not touching the nonconverted [*sic*]. It is bringing the churches together to touch the unconverted."[261] From this perspective, Palau attempts to embrace as many Christians as possible with his campaigns. As a result, unity and cooperation among different groups of people have been demonstrated in many of them. During Mission to London, for instance, more than 1,700 churches participated and worked together.[262] A glimpse of the composition of the entire body of volunteers during this campaign well displays the spirit of unity and diversity that is typical in Palau's campaigns:

> Vocations represented included mechanics, executives, housewives, ministers, students, missionaries, teachers, policemen, and the unemployed.
>
> No one was too young or too old to help with the mission. Ten-year-old children and 90-year-old great-grandmothers

> donated their time and money to the mission. Race was not a factor either, as black, white, yellow, and brown all worked together in one Body during *Mission to London*. Nor was denomination a factor. Anglicans, Baptists, Methodists, Pentecostals, and many others united to proclaim the Gospel to their city.[263]

Working together in a unified spirit for evangelism reaps many benefits. In Palau's words,

> Unity brings focus in purpose and work. … When the Church works together in cooperative evangelistic efforts, relationships among Christians are strengthened, new ministries are often formed, people are brought into the Kingdom, churches are planted, and a God consciousness often comes over the city.[264]

"To a watching world," notes Palau, mass evangelism presents "a strong and united front as the Body of Christ." He goes on say, "We tell the world that we have a common core of Biblical faith that binds us to Jesus Christ and to one another despite real differences on secondary matters."[265]

Despite its manifold benefits, unity cannot be achieved without overcoming some obstacles. Observing Palau's Mission Maine in 1999, for instance, McBride comments, "In an area where many evangelical churches are struggling for survival, the possibility of losing more members to another church is frightening."[266] There are also conflicts that originate from different faith backgrounds and practices. These may be related to certain theological beliefs, manner of prayer, style of music, dress code, and so on. For a successful evangelistic campaign, all participating church leaders and congregations must overcome peripheral and trivial issues, while refusing to compromise biblical truth. McBride rightfully points out that participants in the campaign must conquer any spirit of jealousy, competition, and mistrust—issues that arise frequently during campaigns.[267]

Evangelism Rooted in Cultural Relevancy and Creativity

The world is changing constantly and rapidly. Although churches must be ready to meet changes in societies, it is true that most established churches are slower to adapt to rapidly changing culture. Mass evangelism is in the same dilemma; it must respond to the changing culture in a relevant way. If not, it will be ineffective and obsolete, as many already claim.

Relevancy and Creativity: Two Principles of Method

About a half century ago, the renowned church-growth scholar Donald McGavran remarked that "the methods of achieving church growth must change to fit the different characteristics of this new age."[268] Speaking of adopting new methodology for evangelism, he gave this solemn warning:

> If we stubbornly cleave to the *status quo*, [emphasis in original] God's redemptive purpose will be frustrated for hundreds of thousands of souls each year. ... If there are more effective ways in which the Church may be planted, or more efficient methods for inducting those now ready to accept their Saviour into the Church, they should be set forth and adopted.[269]

Like McGavran, Luis Palau has advocated the need for new methods to reach new generations. It is his conviction that the method should be time-sensitive even though the message is timeless. Palau states, "The idea that God advocates one form of evangelism over another is a serious theological error. Evangelism methods aren't sacred. They are simply vehicles for proclaiming the Gospel of Jesus Christ to the unsaved."[270] He also remarks: "God's principles are rock solid and never change. But methods are to be adapted in every generation. An evangelist's ministry is never predictable. Approach your goals with a teachable spirit, open to new ideas. Let God's Holy Spirit creatively work through you."[271] To attempt new approaches in evangelism, insists Palau, evangelists need "holy audacity":

> Holy audacity also prompts us to try new approaches. Some of you may be prepared to use an approach that older folks will question. But you should try it anyway in the name of the Lord. Try it with humility. Try it with counsel. You don't have to do everything the way it has always been done. As far as I'm concerned, any method is valid as long as it is ethical and moral. There are no biblical restraints on methodology (as long as it is done in love), only on the message. The message is sacred, and it never changes. Yet the methods should vary depending on whom we're trying to reach with the gospel.[272]

Palau's principles in adopting and utilizing new methodology might be summarized in two words that are closely related to each other: relevancy and creativity. As a matter of fact, relevancy and creativity in evangelistic outreach are not at all new. These principles can be found in the Bible, as well as in the later history of the Christian faith. For example, the apostle Paul's ministry is marked by relevancy: "I have become all things to all men so that by all possible means I might save some" (1 Corinthians 9:22).

Evangelists in the past also have used relevant and creative ways to reach the lost in their own generations. Their methods might not have been totally new, but as Robnett states, "Effective evangelism requires that old methods be retooled with new approaches."[273] Perhaps the best example of relevancy and creativity in modern mass evangelism can be traced back to Charles Finney, who was called the "founder of professional evangelism"[274] and the "father of modern revivalism."[275]

Using an innovative method called "new measures,"[276] Finney proclaimed the gospel relevantly and creatively in his generation. Finney's new measures stirred a major controversy among pastors and evangelists, and he has been censured for his theology and methods, both by his contemporaries and by modern critics.[277] According to Timothy L. Smith, however, by the 1840s revivalists throughout American Protestantism were using new measures.[278]

Dwight L. Moody also provides a good example in this respect. In the words of William McLoughlin, "Charles Finney made revivalism a profession, but Dwight L. Moody made it a big business."[279] To proclaim the gospel effectively, Moody employed secular tactics and business methods. Winthrop S. Hudson states, "By utilizing every technique of efficient business promotion—'planning, organization, publicity, vast sums of money, a host of workers, skilful executive direction'—Moody ... became the first and foremost representative of a new breed of professional evangelists."[280] Quoting Robert Huber, William Evans referred to Moody as "God's salesman of salvation."[281] By employing cutting edge methods in their time, both Finney and Moody evangelized their generations effectively.

Implementation of Relevancy and Creativity

Following in the footsteps of preceding evangelists like Finney and Moody, Luis Palau has preached the gospel in relevant and creative ways for more than four decades. He has adopted and utilized every possible means to communicate the good news of Jesus Christ effectively.[282] Cultural relevancy can be determined by two criteria among others: geographical and generational differences.

First, as a global evangelist, Palau has preached the gospel around the world. In his interview with *Christianity Today*, Palau was asked whether he saw a difference in terms of methodology between evangelism in Latin America and in North America. While conceding that his message is basically the same, except for some changes in the illustrations, he answered: "Methodologically, we try to adapt to the local culture. … In comparison to Latin America, we'll stage more in-the-vicinity-of-the-city campaigns before we come to the big united effort."[283]

Before they launch a campaign, the staff at LPA conduct in-depth research on the region they are planning to target. Palau himself also studies the history and recent political and social issues of the area, in order to reach people in the most relevant possible way.[284] Speaking of the preparation for his first Asian campaign in Singapore in 1986, for example, Palau recounts, "I attended Chinese conferences, interviewed Chinese Christian leaders, and then thoroughly studied the books they had recommended."[285]

Generational difference is another decisive factor in determining methods of evangelism. Even within the same society, there are diverse generations living together. Although they share much in common, each generation is also unique, since people are going through different passages of life. Through evangelistic campaigns called "festivals," Palau's team adopted a multi-generational approach, aiming and effectively reaching each generation.[286] To connect with a younger generation, his team adopted loud contemporary Christian music. Palau confesses, "To be honest, I don't love the loud music, but I love the kids who love this kind of music. And we're seeing thousands of them commit their lives to Jesus Christ."[287] As Kevin Palau, son of Luis Palau and president of LPA, puts it, "The more an event is culturally sensitive, one that people will want to bring their friends to, the better."[288]

Another characteristic of Palau's evangelistic ministry is creativity and knowing when to reinvent his organization's evangelistic methods. According to David L. Jones, vice president of corporate affairs for LPA, after 2000 90 percent of LPA's ministry had changed to accommodate changes in the world. Among many, he specified, the biggest changes employed were the "festival model, Next Generation Alliance, and Livin It."[289] Livin It, as an example, was created to reach out to youth across America. This extreme-sports ministry includes skateboarders and BMX riders who will draw the attention of young people. In his interview with Palau, John Freeman Gill, the *New York Times* reporter, stated that "Mr. Palau is so convinced of skateboarding's effectiveness in youth ministry that he said he suspected that Jesus himself would be a skater if he walked the earth today. 'Yeah, I mean, he was young; I think he'd get on a skateboard and go for it,' Mr. Palau said. 'I know St. Paul would.'"[290]

Palau's statement may sound too pragmatic. Nevertheless, it cannot be disputed that the methods of evangelism must continuously be adapted to a rapidly changing world. In the words of researcher George Barna, "Not only is change inevitable, occurring at a blistering pace and invading every dimension of our lives, but also the pace of change is accelerating at what seems to be a geometric rate."[291]

Changing cultures demand new approaches to evangelism. Therefore, engaging cultures in relevant and creative ways in evangelism is not optional but inevitable. Furthermore, Palau's relevancy and creativity in evangelistic methods are not new. As discussed previously, evangelists such as Finney and Moody were sensitive to their changing cultures and employed innovative strategies to reach their contemporaries with the gospel.

The times in which Finney and Moody lived were different from our own day, but the principle remains the same. Finney's "new measures" are now "old measures." Thus it is the duty of contemporary evangelists to find new "new" measures. In this respect, Palau's effort to reach people in relevant and creative ways provides a good example to current and future evangelists. Jones, who has been with Palau since 1978, says that while Palau's message has not changed during the four decades they have worked together, methods must change to remain culturally relevant.

Endnotes

205 Charles V. Bryant, *Rediscovering the Charismata: Building the Body of Christ Through Spiritual Gifts* (Waco, TX: Word Books, 1986), 80–81. The word *evangelist* comes from the Greek transliterated *euangelion*, which means "to declare, announce, proclaim, or herald good news." According to Bryant, it is used only three times with reference to persons in the New Testament (Acts 21:8; Eph. 4:11; and 2 Tim. 4:5). For example, in Ephesians 4:11 Paul states, "The gifts he gave were that some would be apostles, some prophets, some evangelists, some pastors and teachers." For more biblical and theological discussion on the term "evangelist," see Billy Graham, *A Biblical Standard for Evangelists* (Minneapolis, MN: World Wide Publications, 1984), 6–8; Leonard Sanderson, "The Role of the Vocational Evangelist," in *Evangelism Today and Tomorrow*, ed. Charles L. Chaney and Granville Watson (Nashville, TN: Broadman Press, 1993), 146. Cf. There seems to be no consensus in defining the role of evangelists. According to Billy Graham, for example, "An evangelist is a person with a special gift from the Holy Spirit to announce the good news of the Gospel." Graham, *A Biblical Standard for Evangelists*, 6; Sterling W. Huston defines the gift of an evangelist as follows: "The gift of an evangelist is that special ability God gives to some members of the Body of Christ which enables them to share clearly the Gospel with unbelievers so that they will commit their lives to Christ." Sterling W. Huston, Crusade Evangelism, rev. ed. (Minneapolis, MN: World Wide Publications, 1996), 168.

206 The best example of an evangelist in the Bible is Philip, one of the most important pioneers of the early Christian mission. He was the first one who proclaimed the gospel in one of the cities of Samaria, which had unfriendly relations with the Jews (Acts 8). F. F. Bruce, *The Spreading Flame: The Rise and Progress of Christianity*, vol. 1, *The Dawn of Christianity: The Story of the Infant Church to the Fall of Jerusalem, A.D. 70* (Grand Rapids: William B. Eerdmans, 1956), 111–12.

207 Luis Palau and Timothy Robnett, Telling the *Story: Evangelism for the Next Generation* (Ventura, CA: Regal Books, 2006), 16.

208 Michael Cassidy, "Limitations of Mass Evangelism and Its Potentialities," *International Review of Mission* 65 (April 1976): 204. Cf. Quoting George Barna, Rusty Wright insists that "credibility" and "relevance" are two most needed qualities for evangelists in North America. According to Wright, evangelists in North America have a bad reputation among people. In a recent survey, to the question of what people think of when they hear the word "evangelist," most responded with negative terms such as "fanatic," "pontificating," and "fascist." Rusty Wright, "'Credibility' Gap Worries Evangelists," *Christianity Today*, 15 August 1994, 53.

209 Palau, *Telling the Story*, 22.

210 His convictions on the life of an evangelist are scattered in his writings and speeches, but one can find recurring and consistent themes that are discussed in this section.

211 Palau, *Telling the Story*, 48.

212 Ibid., 25–26.

213 Ibid., 26.

214 Matthew 9:35.

215 Luis Palau, "Evangelism in the Future," in *Evangelical Missions Tomorrow*, ed. Wade T. Coggins and E. L. Frizen (South Pasadena, CA: William Carey Library, 1977), 174. This is his preaching in Urbana '76 at the University of Illinois. Palau also quotes John Wesley, who said, "The world is my parish." Palau, *Telling the Story*, 26.

216 Palau, *Telling the Story*, 53. Cf. For Palau, it was Keith Bentson who helped him broaden his vision for world evangelization through a weekly prayer meeting. Jerry B. Jenkins and Luis Palau, *Luis Palau: Calling the Nations to Christ* (Old Tappan, NJ: Revell, 1978; Chicago, IL: Moody Press, 1980), 54.

217 Palau, "Evangelism in the Future," 179.

218 Palau, *Telling the Story*, 23.

219 Palau, "Evangelism in the Future," 179.

220 Luis Palau, "The Unfinished Task of Declaring His Glory," in *Declare His Glory Among the Nations*, ed. David M. Howard (Downers Grove, IL: InterVarsity Press, 1977), 226.

221 For example, Palau's book *Where Is God When Bad Things Happen?* is full of real-life stories that Palau himself encountered. Luis Palau and Steve Halliday, *Where Is God When Bad Things Happen? Finding Solace in Times of Trouble* (New York: Doubleday, 1999; Thorndike, ME: G.K. Hall, 1999; Cambridge: Lutterworth Press, 1999).

222 Palau, *Telling the Story*, 131–32. According to Robnett, these temptations aggravate all the more since evangelists on many occasions have to travel apart from their families. Ibid., 121.

223 Ibid., 25.

224 David L. Jones and Luis Palau, *Scottish Fires of Revival* (Cupertino, CA: D.I.M.E. Publishers, 1980), 66.

225 Palau, interview by the author, May 9, 2008.

226 Luis Palau, "Missions to the End of the World," in *Global Crossroads: Focusing the Strength of Local Churches,* ed. W. Harold Fuller, World Evangelical Fellowship (Mandaluyong, Philippines: OMF Literature Inc., 1998), 285–86. On another occasion he describes holiness as follows: "It's a life walked in the light, being transparent before God and others." Palau, *Telling the Story*, 25.

227 Luis Palau, "The Evangelist and the Ministry of the Holy Spirit," in *The Calling of an Evangelist,* ed. J. D. Douglas (Minneapolis, MN: World Wide Publications, 1987), 136. Cf. See Jeremiah 15:19. This is part of his preaching at the second International Conference for Itinerant Evangelists, better known as Amsterdam 1986. According to *Christianity Today,* Palau switched his topic at the last minute, making some people upset. In his interview, Palau commented, "I sensed things were out of control here in the States. There was an unhealthy emphasis, for example, on numbers, people getting saved over the phone, or stories of experiences that didn't sound real. And then there were the astonishing displays of luxury." "Evangelism: The Best Form of Social Action," *Christianity Today,* 17 February 1989, 51.

228 Palau, "Evangelism in the Future," 183.

229 Jones and Palau, *Scottish Fires*, 65. Palau asks his readers to pray for evangelists for holiness in their lives. "Will you join us in prayer that God would do that in our hearts and lives as a Team? Would you ask God that our Board of Directors, our staff and traveling Team members will all be filled with the Spirit day after day according to the commandment of Scripture? That is the greatest prayer intercession ministry that you can have on our behalf as a Team of evangelists. We need your prayers!" Ibid., 66.

230 Lewis A. Drummond, *The Evangelist* (Nashville, TN: Word Publishing, 2001), 121. Drummond follows Joseph Thayer's definition of boldness, which states, "freedom in speaking, unreservedness in speech; openly, frankly without concealment." Ibid., 120.

231 Palau, *Telling the Story*, 27.

232 James D. Douglas, "God's Good Gaucho and Roundup Time in Glasgow," *Christianity Today*, 17 July 1981, 90.

233 John Maust, "Terrorist Death Threat Fails to Force Palau Out of Peru," *Christianity Today*, 18 January 1985, 51. On the first day of the campaign in Lima, the terrorist group blasted seven high-tension towers, cutting off the electricity for the evening. See also Luis Palau and David Sanford, *Luis Palau: Calling America and the Nations to Christ* (Nashville, TN: Thomas Nelson, Inc., 1994; rev. 2000), 166–67. Shining Path had killed more than forty pastors and four hundred other believers. Cf. For a similar life-threatening situation in Bogotá, Colombia, in 1989, see ibid., 182–83.

234 Luis Palau, "Fear Not," in *Proclaim Christ Until He Comes: Calling the Whole Church to Take the Whole Gospel to the Whole World*, ed. J. D. Douglas (Minneapolis, MN: World Wide Publications, 1990), 369.

235 Some issues concerning the value of campaign evangelism are persistent. Leighton Ford, for example, mentioned "financial policies, emotionalism, sensationalism, follow-up procedures, public invitations, and other techniques" as the recurring debate. Leighton Ford, "The Strategic Role of Mass Evangelism," *Christianity Today*, 24 November 1961, 31. For criticism and debate of validity on evangelistic campaigns, see introduction and chapters 3–5.

236 Jim Mills, "An Interview with Luis Palau," *Discipleship Journal* 12 (November/December 1982): 40. Palau is confident that mass evangelism has been the most effective method to reach people, especially in Latin America. See Luis Palau, "The Future of Mass Evangelism," in *Evangelism: The Next Ten Years*, ed. Sherwood Eliot Wirt (Waco, TX: Word Books, 1978), 155.

237 Michael Green, *Evangelism in the Early Church* (Grand Rapids: Wm. B. Eerdmans Publishing Company, 1970), 196. History of open air preaching goes even further back than Jesus' time. According to Michael Green, the Jewish practice of open-air preaching was not their invention. He states, "It had long been carried on both in Palestine and elsewhere, in courtyards, open fields, river banks and market places."

238 Luis Palau, "Citywide Crusade Evangelization," in *Let the Earth Hear His Voice: International Conference on World Evangelism*, ed. J. D. Douglas (Minneapolis, MN: World Wide Publications, 1975), 602. This article was reproduced in other books, with some variations of title and content. See Palau, "Why Mass Evangelism," in Susan Holton and David L. Jones, *Spirit Aflame: Luis Palau's Mission to London* (Grand Rapids: Baker Book House, 1985), 36-42; Luis Palau and Mike Umlandt, *The Only Hope for America: The Transforming Power of the Gospel of Jesus Christ* (Wheaton, IL: Crossway Books, 1996), 99-113; Palau, "The Future of Mass Evangelism," 154–65.

239 Palau, "Citywide Crusade Evangelization," 602–3. For example, see Acts 19 and 28.

240 Ibid., 601. Referring to the names mentioned above, Palau goes on to say, "What a sense of vibrating excitement grips the imagination at the very reading of the names of such great men! They are more than individuals; they symbolize potent movements of God. God used them to write history—nation-changing history."

241 Palau, "Why Mass Evangelism," 40.

242 Palau presents twenty-seven reasons for the use of evangelistic campaigns. For the full account, see Palau, "Why Mass Evangelism," 36–42.

243 Palau, "Why Mass Evangelism," 37, 41. See "Reason numbers 1 and 24."

244 Jerry B. Jenkins and Luis Palau, *Luis Palau: Calling the Nations to Christ* (Old Tappan, NJ: Revell, 1978; Chicago, IL: Moody Press, 1980), 110. He goes on to say that "A nation will not be changed with timid methods. The nation must be confronted, challenged, answered, hit with the truth."

245 Palau, "Why Mass Evangelism," 37. See "Reason number 2."

246 Ibid., 37, 39, 40. See "Reason numbers 3, 11, and 20."

247 Ibid., 40-41. See "Reason numbers 19 and 21."

248 Ibid., 38-42. See "Reason numbers 10, 14, 16, and 26."

249 Ibid., 39, 41. See "Reason numbers 12, 13, and 25."

250 Palau, interview by the author, May 9, 2008. See also Luis Palau, "Which Part of the Great Commission Don't You Understand?" *Christianity Today*, 16 November 1998, 74–76. A recent survey by *Christianity Today* also confirms his point. To the question, "Are city-wide crusades a thing of the past?" 62 percent of participants of the survey answered no. One of the reasons was the growing demand and response of people to mass evangelism in the two-thirds world. "Just As We Were," *Christianity Today*, 5 July 2007, 54.

251 Palau, "Why Mass Evangelism," 42.

252 For instance, referring to planting the seed of the gospel in the church of Corinth, the apostle Paul said, "I planted the seed, Apollos watered it, but God made it grow. So neither he who plants nor he who waters is anything, but only God, who makes things grow. The man who plants and the man who waters have one purpose" (1 Corinthians 3:6–8). Thus, the unity and cooperation of believers for evangelism under the overarching sovereignty of God is essential. Cf. For a detailed biblical discussion on the unity of Christians, see chapter 2, "Biblical and Historical Basis of a United Church." Kevin T. McBride, "Retaking the Village Green: Building Strategic Partnerships for Evangelism that Work in New England" (D.Min. project, Gordon-Conwell Theological Seminary, 2001), 51–82.

253 Palau, *Telling the Story*, 146.

254 Urbana '79 was held at the University of Illinois in Urbana for the twelfth national missions convention sponsored by Inter-Varsity Christian Fellowship. Preaching from Romans 12:1–13, Palau observed three major emphases: "the foundation for working together (vv. 1–2), the functional basis for working together (vv. 3–8) and the fuel to keep us working together (vv. 9–13)." Luis Palau, "Working Together," in *Believing and Obeying Jesus Christ: The Urbana '79 Compendium*, ed. John W. Alexander (Downers Grove, IL: InterVarsity Press, 1980), 113.

255 Ibid., 125. Palau also presented seven points as benefits of Christian unity and cooperation for evangelism. "1. Working together with Jesus Christ as the master strategist, you and I are more productive servants. 2. Working together brings balance into your life—it purifies sectarianism and cultism out of your heart and gives you Scriptural understanding instead. 3. Working together develops responsibility because you use the gifts of the Holy Spirit in your life and you begin to understand and care for the weaker brother. 4. Working together under the master strategist broadens your perspective. You begin to understand the traditions of other Christians, and you get historical equilibrium that keeps you from extremism. 5. Working together puts you in your place. There is a healthy ego-deflation that takes place, not in the sense of discouraging you, but

of looking at yourself properly. As Romans 12:3 says, 'I bid every one among you not to think of himself more highly than he ought to think, but to think with sober judgment.' 6. Working together brings in the harvest. John 4:34-38 is one of the most thrilling passages in relation to our subject today: 'one sows and another reaps.' 7. Working together builds the house of God in accordance with 1 Corinthians 3:9–11." Ibid., 126.

256 Ibid., 127–30. Romans 12:10: "Love one another with brotherly affection; outdo one another in showing honor" (ESV).

257 Ibid., 131–32.

258 Palau states, "The sense of God's presence and blessing among His people in a united effort can seldom be experienced under any other circumstance." Luis Palau, "Why Mass Evangelism," in *Spirit Aflame: Luis Palau's Mission to London*, eds. Susan Holton and David L. Jones (Grand Rapids: Baker, 1985), 39.

259 LPA, "Core Values" (Portland, OR: LPA).

260 Besides local churches, for example, he has worked with organizations such as Wycliffe Bible Translators, World Vision, Habitat for Humanity, and others.

261 Luis Palau, "Whatever Happened to Evangelism? Luis Palau Wants to Rekindle Our Passion for the Lost," *Christianity Today*, 8 April 1996, 39.

262 The *Baptist Times* listed "the 'impressive' level of cooperation among the churches" as one of the reasons for the success of Mission to London, along with "the 'unexpectedly high' responses at the meetings, the 'thorough' and 'effective' follow-up by local churches." "We'll feel the effects for years," *Baptist Times*, June 21, 1984, p. 1; quoted in Holton and Jones, *Spirit Aflame*, 85–86.

263 Gordon Thornton, the Blackheath mission administrator, also expressed his impression of the unity during Mission to London as follows: "For the first time in my experience, Christians of all denominations have worked together, sat on committees together, prayed together, and worshiped together. It's been fantastic. The unity displayed has been a tremendous inspiration." Holton and Jones, *Spirit Aflame*, 139.

264 Palau, *Telling the Story*, 146–47.

265 Palau, "The Future of Mass Evangelism," 159–60.

266 McBride, "Retaking the Village Green," 96.

267 Ibid., 96. Listing some examples of conflicts during Mission Maine, McBride tells how they overcame these obstacles. Ibid., 96–111.

268 Donald A. McGavran, "New Methods for a New Age in Missions," *International Review of Missions* 44 (1955): 394.

269 Ibid., 403.

270 Palau, *The Only Hope for America*, 77.

271 Luis Palau, "The Evangelist Has a Strategy for Harvest," in *The Mission of an Evangelist*, ed. J. D. Douglas (Minneapolis, MN: World Wide Publications, 2001), 233.

272 Palau, *Telling the Story*, 27. Referring to great evangelists in the past, Palau states, "Those we call great were highly recognized because they took advantage of unique new methods, sanctified them, and used them to evangelize the masses." Ibid., 28. Palau also espoused intentional efforts to promote new methods. He argues, "There must also be the determination to *plan* [emphasis in original] to do it, under God, and the determination to rejoice over any methodology that the creative Holy Spirit of God may lay on anyone's heart to accomplish the job." Palau, "Working Together," 113.

273 Robnett, *Telling the Story*, 68.

274 William G. McLoughlin, *Modern Revivalism: Charles Grandison Finney to Billy Graham* (New York: Ronald Press, 1959), 11.

275 Lewis A. Drummond, *The Life and Ministry of Charles G. Finney* (Minneapolis, MN: Bethany House, 1983), 9.

276 Charles Grandison Finney, *Lectures on Revivals of Religion* (New York/Chicago/Toronto/London/Edinburgh: Fleming H. Revell Company, 1868), 211. From his conviction that human agency is important in evangelism, Finney employed and developed certain methods to promote revivals. For Finney, the purpose of measure was to "make known the Gospel in the most efficient way, to make the truth stand out strikingly, so as to obtain the attention and secure the obedience of the greatest number possible."

277 James E. Johnson, "Charles Grandison Finney: Father of American Revivalism," *Christian History* 20:7. According to Johnson, "Particularly offensive were his allowing women to pray in mixed public meetings; the use of an anxious bench at the front of the church; the adoption of protracted meetings; informal, instead of reverential, language, especially in prayer; and the hasty admission of new converts to church membership."

278 Timothy L. Smith, *Revivalism and Social Reform: American Protestantism on the Eve of the Civil War* (Gloucester, MA: Peter Smith, 1976), 45–62. According to Asa, Finney's evangelistic techniques became a prototype of modern mass evangelism and were adapted by subsequent evangelists even to the present day. Robert Lynn Asa, "The Theology and Methodology of Charles G. Finney as a Prototype for Modern Mass Evangelism" (Ph.D. diss., Southern Baptist Theological Seminary, 1983), 6–9.

279 McLoughlin, *Modern Revivalism*, 166.

280 Winthrop S. Hudson, *Religion in America: An Historical Account of the Development of American Religious Life*, 2nd ed. (New York: Charles Scribner's Sons, 1973), 228–29.

281 William Glyn Evans, *Profiles of Revival Leaders* (Nashville, TN: Broadman Press, 1976), 72.

282 For specific examples, see chapter 4.

283 "Luis Palau: Evangelist to Three Worlds," *Christianity Today*, 20 May 1983, 33.

284 Palau, interview by the author, May 9, 2008.

285 Palau and Sanford, *Calling America and the Nations*, 170.

286 For more information, see "New Forms of Evangelistic Campaigns" in Chapter 8.

287 David Sanford, "Luis Palau: Calling America and the Nations to Christ," *Life Wise* (December/January 2002): 11.

288 Kevin Palau, "Cooperative Evangelism," in *The Mission of an Evangelist,* ed. J. D. Douglas (Minneapolis, MN: World Wide Publications, 2001), 319.

289 Robnett, *Telling the Story*, 95.

290 John Freeman Gill, "Jesus on the Half-Pipe," *New York Times*, 18 March 2005 [online]; accessed 27 May 2008; available from http://travel.nytimes.com/2005/03/18/travel/escapes/18skate.html?scp=2&sq=Luis+Palau&st=nyt; Internet.

291 George Barna and Mark Hatch, *Boiling Point: It Only Takes One Degree* (Ventura, CA: Regal, 2001), 18-19. Barna also presents some examples of changed values in America from two generations ago. Ibid., 87.

CHAPTER 5

EVANGELISTIC THEOLOGY AND PHILOSOPHY, PART 3

Evangelism and Social Reform

As a young man and a Christian in Argentina, Luis Palau faced the need for solutions to social problems. Because most countries in Latin America had endured severe social and political revolutions, it was imperative that Christians offer biblical answers to such situations and respond accurately. Conservative evangelicals traditionally shunned social action because of their historical opposition to the social gospel espoused by Walter Rauschenbusch and others. The liberals in Latin America, on the other hand, were actively engaged in social reform.[292] Amid these social upheavals and controversial reactions, Palau, as one of the leading evangelists representing evangelical voices in Latin America, presumably had to address such questions such as "Are Christians responsible for the transformation of the society?" "How much should they be involved?" and "What is the role of an evangelist in terms of social reform?"

Priority of Evangelism over Social Reform

Christians must be concerned about the social problems of the world, just as Jesus cared for suffering people. Experiencing poverty in his youth in Córdoba, Argentina, Luis Palau dreamed of becoming a lawyer in order to help change the miserable social conditions of his country.[293] Even though he realized later in his life that social reform was not the answer to human depravity and suffering, Palau still believes that Christians are responsible for caring for people in need. He expresses his deep concern for and commitment to people who are enduring suffering as follows:

> I now feel I better understand and more deeply care about the poor because I've been there. As a result, my family and evangelistic team make it a priority to do what we can—individually and working with others—to help widows, orphans, and others in need here in the States and around the world.[294]

Palau also observes that the "world is weighed down by famines, poverty, injustice, oppression, and environmental disasters," noting that in the midst of these massive problems Christians are called "to serve as Jesus served, feeding the hungry, caring for the sick, breaking the chains of injustice—and leading people to receive the gift of life in Jesus Christ."[295]

Although Palau is committed to social improvement, he strongly argues that evangelism must neither be confused with nor replaced by social reform:

> Although we participate in social action parallel with evangelism—and that's why we love the Lausanne Covenant—nevertheless let's never forget that social action itself is not evangelism. Evangelism is preaching Christ crucified, resurrected with power to change people's lives. … Evangelism is the presentation of Christ in the power of the Spirit so that lives are changed.[296]

In Palau's view, "No greater blessing and no more effective social action for the good of nations exists than to proclaim the Lord Jesus—the Jesus who died on the Cross, rose from the dead, and ascended into Heaven."[297]

At the World Evangelical Fellowship's (WEF) Tenth General Assembly held in Abbotsford, British Columbia, in May of 1997, Palau preached on the three distinct ministries of Jesus on Earth, as recorded in Matthew 9:35—10:1: teaching, preaching the gospel, and healing disease and sickness. While interpreting "preaching the Gospel" as evangelism and "healing" as social action, Palau cautioned that Christians must not lose that balance in stressing the priority of evangelism over social work: "When you get involved in only [*sic*] social action, you can lose your evangelistic perspective, because the physical needs of the world are so overwhelming. But we must not forget that their souls last for eternity."[298] In Palau's view evangelism must not be divorced from social concern, as some have done in the past,[299] but he also stresses that evangelism definitely takes priority over social reform.

Historical Precedents of Social Reform Through Evangelism

Critics of mass evangelism often claim that this approach neglects social concerns. Yet history confirms the impact of the gospel on society as a whole. Refuting critics' charges, Leighton Ford states, "The scholarly works of men like Timothy Smith, J. Edwin Orr, Kenneth Scott Latourette, John Wesley White, and others have amply documented the impact of this kind of evangelism on social reform."[300] Mark Terry also acknowledges the contributions of evangelists to society: "The evangelists lifted moral standards. Billy Sunday influenced the approval of prohibition, and Billy Graham contributed to improved race relations by insisting that his crusades be integrated."[301]

Palau underscores that great evangelists in the past have been passionately involved in social justice. Drawing attention to the fact that many people do not realize what the gospel has accomplished in the past, he insists, "Stop and think about it: We enjoy freedom of speech, justice under the law, respect for individual rights, and we need not live in fear of [the] secret police. The Gospel generates transforming power."[302] Moreover, Palau points out the peaceful nature of changes that came about as the result of gospel proclamation: "Most societies change by coercion. The few that change by internal compulsion, without machine guns, are those that have had spiritual revivals."[303]

One of the best examples of social reform through the transforming power of the gospel can be found in the ministry of John Wesley (1703–1791). Endorsing the view of many scholars that John Wesley saved Great Britain from a bloody revolution by the working class—an outcome that did in fact occur in France and other European countries—Palau observes, "In fact, it can be argued that, as an indirect result of Wesley's ministry, gin traffic was stopped, slavery was eventually abolished, the development of medicine was furthered, Sunday Schools became popular, and prison reform was initiated."[304]

More recently, in Palau's judgment, Billy Graham provides a good example of involvement in social reform. Graham's campaign in South Africa, for example, brought blacks and whites together for the first time in the history of that nation, resulting in racial harmony and reconciliation.[305] Such examples provide convincing proofs that evangelism does bring about social reform.

Evangelism as the Best Form of Social Transformation

Although Palau is convinced that evangelism must take priority over social reform, he also believes that "Evangelism always has social implications, because it takes place in a social context."[306] Furthermore, evangelism is the best form of social reform because "evangelism deals with the root of the problem, not with the symptoms," and "The root is man's alienation and sinfulness."[307] Humanity's heart is at the root of all the problems in the world, since "The heart is deceitful above all things, and desperately wicked" (Jeremiah 17:9, KJV). Hence, claiming that "Political campaigns, family counseling, and education do nothing about the condition of human depravity," Palau decisively declares, "Unless there's a change of heart, nothing's happened to change a person."[308] Individual lives transformed through Christ will ultimately bring about the transformation of society.[309]

Citing the example of Zacchaeus, who experienced changes in his life after he had met Christ, Palau elaborates:

> Imagine a city where a million people become new creations, like Zacchaeus. The Gospel can change society

> because it changes individuals, who then begin to change their families, which then change neighborhoods. And as those individuals live out their faith at home, in schools, in the military, in business, and in government, a quiet revolution occurs.[310]

With this conviction, Palau has preached the gospel throughout his life, while refusing to ignore victims of social problems.

Christians show differing attitudes toward the injustice and sufferings in the world. Some emphasize the gospel while ignoring social actions, while others are committed to changing the world while marginalizing the gospel. The truth is that one must be careful not to stress one above the other at the sacrifice of its counterpart. Christians must share God's love both in words and in actions. The key lies in balance and priority, as revealed in Jesus' words, "Man does not live on bread alone, but on every word that comes from the mouth of God" (Matthew 4:4).

Along with the priority of evangelism, believers must strive to feed the hungry, heal the sick, rectify human rights violations, and change the social structures to reflect the biblical ideal. As Palau believes, changing the world through the gospel may be slow, but it is the surest way to achieve success. Disciples of Christ, who experience transformation in their own lives, will ultimately change the world. And while Palau's organization strives to proclaim the love of Christ in both word and deed, the evangelist asserts that "evangelism is the greatest form of social action."

Evangelism and Discipleship

Biblical Perspectives on Discipleship

The Great Commission given by Jesus in Matthew 28:19–20 involves not only preaching the gospel but also teaching new converts to obey Jesus' teachings. Therefore, the ultimate goal of evangelism is to make disciples of Jesus Christ, as commanded by Jesus Himself. In this sense, evangelism is the initial stage in the process of disciple-making. In the words of Arthur C. Archibald, "The Great Commission is a command for both evangelism and conservation." And the latter requires "more patience, skill, preparation, and persistence of effort."[311] The significance of discipleship is obvious when one considers the great number of occurrences of the term "disciple(s)" in the New Testament. Richard N. Longenecker observed that, in the Gospels and Acts, the most common designation for one committed to Jesus is "disciple."[312]

While acknowledging the importance of human endeavor for follow-up and discipleship, Luis Palau stresses the essential and indispensable role of the Holy Spirit in this process. Palau addressed Paul's words in Philippians 1:6, "He who began a good work in you will complete it until the day of Jesus Christ":

> The Holy Spirit is working on His people. Follow-up and discipleship on our part are vitally important, but we must remember God's part too. Those whom the Lord calls, He justifies. And those He justifies, He also sanctifies and ultimately glorifies. Nobody follows up better than the Holy Spirit Himself.[313]

Discipleship is in essence the forming of character according to the teachings of Jesus Christ. One of the most important but often ignored aspects of discipleship is the issue of discipline within the Body of Christ. How does the Church respond to and help Christians with problems like alcohol and drug addiction, incessant gossiping, and sexual immorality? Palau provides helpful and practical guidelines to these issues, based on 1 Corinthians 5; Matthew 18:15–20; and other passages. In addressing people's tendency to avoid the subject of discipline, he remarks, "But we cannot lead victorious Christian lives until we understand Christian discipline. The more we learn about what God teaches on this subject, the better equipped we will be to handle crises in our personal lives, our families, and our churches."[314]

Palau's Commitment to Discipleship

Throughout his ministry Luis Palau has been committed to discipleship, as well as to evangelism. The evangelist's role and influence on discipleship is limited by the nature of his ministry. Palau, however, has devoted much of his time and energy to discipleship and has personally discipled many individuals. In his interview with this author, he affirmed that he cares for the new converts and disciples by calling, writing, and meeting with them periodically. "Most of them," he noted, "are leaders of society in the realm of politics, business, law, and so on."[315]

Another convincing proof of Palau's dedication to discipleship is found in his own writings. He has, in fact, authored more books on discipleship than on evangelism. The specific topics include holiness, spiritual renewal and growth, and prayer. If discipleship means the formation of Christian character after Jesus' teachings, Palau's books on other aspects of the Christian life should be included in this category as well.[316] Thus, in spite of the limitations imposed by the nature of his ministry, Palau has devoted himself to nurturing new converts so that they can grow in the knowledge of truth. Although the primary role of evangelists is proclaiming the gospel, they must not ignore helping new converts grow spiritually, so that they can be true followers of Jesus Christ.

Implementation of Discipleship in Evangelistic Campaigns

Waldron Scott aptly points out that "The dynamic interdependence between discipleship and evangelism … is one of the least noted but most important relationships affecting the Christian enterprise worldwide."[317] The comparison between the evangelistic ministries of John Wesley and George Whitefield verifies the importance of linking evangelism with discipleship. While Wesley formed "class meetings" for new converts, in which they could grow as disciples of Christ, Whitefield did not utilize such a follow-up system. As a result, according to Ford's judgment, "Although George Whitefield was in some ways a greater evangelist than Wesley, Wesley's ministry had the most enduring results."[318]

Palau's commitment to discipleship in his campaigns is appreciated by Waldron Scott. Discussing the close connection between evangelism and discipleship, Scott expresses his deep concern over the low rate of assimilation of new converts into the local churches through campaigns.[319] However, he presents Luis Palau as an example of one evangelist who is committed to the follow-up of new converts, acknowledging that "There may never be a wholly satisfactory solution. Yet current efforts by Latin American evangelist Luis Palau, an ardent admirer of Graham, to forge stronger links between his 'converts' and the churches may yet prove to be a breakthrough."[320]

Two phases of discipleship take place in conjunction with campaign evangelism—before and after campaigns. First, before campaigns begin, Palau and his team invest much of their time and energy in training volunteering Christians in personal witness and counseling of new converts. In this process these volunteers are equipped to lead the lost to Christ and nurture them in the basic elements of Christian life. This process of training is a discipleship course for the participating believers.

The Rosario Plan (Argentina in 1976) represents a great example of discipleship for participating Christians. Describing the Rosario Plan as "a combination of intensive mass evangelism ... and biblical discipleship,"[321] the main architect, Edgardo Silvoso, argues that "Discipleship and mass evangelism need not to be divorced, neither opposed to each other. When properly combined they produce solid, visible results."[322] In Rosario, discipleship for volunteering Christians began two years prior to the campaign, and many of these trainees ultimately became the leaders of new churches after the campaign.[323] Although the Rosario Plan represents the best example of discipleship, some form of training of Christians takes place in all of Palau's campaigns.

The second stage of discipleship takes place after campaigns. The trainees are new Christians who need nourishment and guidance. They must be cared for so they may grow and become mature Christians. Unfortunately, evangelists have been blamed for the lack of discipleship of new converts, and they must pay attention to this criticism.

Still, the assumption that evangelists must do the work of discipleship of new converts is presumptuous. As pointed out by Roy Pointer and Scott Bauer, the primary responsibility for discipleship rests with the local churches, not with the evangelist or his or her team.[324]

The latter must strive to connect new converts to the local churches. Following the referral stage, however, the local churches must provide necessary nurture and discipleship to the new converts.[325]

Criticisms of Theology and Philosophy of Evangelism

Luis Palau, like other evangelists in the past and present, has been criticized throughout his ministry. Some of these critiques deserve consideration,[326] while others originate from intolerant and biased attitudes.[327] Many are found to be groundless, arising from sheer speculation and misunderstanding. For instance, Bryan Gilling, a lecturer in history and religious studies at the University of Waikato, New Zealand, analyzed from a third-party perspective the theological accusations of four Anglican bishops against Luis Palau during the Mission to Auckland in 1987. Gilling found that many of the criticisms were only speculative.[328]

Ironically, criticisms leveled against Palau sometimes show extremely polarized attitudes on issues in which the charges seem to contradict each other. For example, some claimed that Palau, in an effort to draw more people to accept Christ, has compromised the message of the gospel by preaching the love of God without mentioning God's wrath.[329] By contrast, others have alleged that he was too preoccupied with "Satan, judgment, and hell" and that the threat of hell appears "to be the motivator of mission, rather than the love of Christ."[330] Such obvious contradiction of criticisms seems to originate from the lack of serious research into Palau's theology.

Two lingering and recurring charges against Luis Palau will be scrutinized in this discussion. On the one hand, Palau has been criticized by liberal Protestants for his association with right-wing politicians in Latin America. On the other side, fundamentalists have blamed Palau for the ecumenical nature of his campaigns. Do such charges against him have a solid foundation? And what are Palau's responses to such criticisms? These questions need to be clarified and answered in order to properly understand Palau's theology.

Political Alliance with Right-wing Regimes

During his evangelistic campaigns in Latin America, Luis Palau was often condemned by liberal Protestants, who claimed that Palau had a suspicious alliance with right-wing political leaders in Latin America, as well as with U.S. foreign policy that upheld such regimes. In Mexico, Palau and his team were even labeled as "Yankee Imperialists" and accused by the press of being CIA agents.[331] This allegation spread to Palau's campaigns in other parts of the world. For example, during Mission to Auckland in 1987, four Anglican bishops in Auckland, New Zealand, viewed Palau with suspicion, accusing him of being an American tool in Latin America and charging that Palau "failed to challenge the oppressive social structures," and thus was distorting the message of the gospel by ignoring the social concern.[332]

One of the most critical events occurred in 1982, when Palau was invited to preach at the centennial celebration of Protestantism in Guatemala. Palau stood by the president, Efraín Ríos Montt, an army general who had taken power only eight months before this evangelistic event. Ríos Montt, Latin America's first evangelical dictator, was alleged to have killed thousands of Mayan Indians in the process of suppressing a communist insurgency.[333] Yet according to David Stoll, evangelicals in the United States denied such massacres and even "heaped him with praise, and offered to send large amounts of aid."[334] While referring to such incidents, Stoll criticizes these actions:

> In contrast to liberal Protestants and much of the Catholic Church, prominent figures [from evangelicals] such as Luis Palau advised Latin Americans to concentrate on improving themselves rather than working for structural change. Such leaders claimed to be apolitical, but they customarily supported any regime in power.[335]

Such a claim cannot simply be ignored when one considers the deteriorating political and social circumstances in which Palau has preached the gospel. Palau's relationship with unethical dictators such as Ríos Montt raises serious ethical issues since Palau represents the evangelical circles of Latin America. What was the motive behind Palau's actions? Did he support the political ideas of such dictators or want to gain access to the people in power to acquire fame? Neither seems to be the case. The truth, as pointed out by Palau's critic David Stoll is that Palau has been *apolitical* throughout his career. Palau himself stresses the nonpolitical nature of his actions. Although he openly acknowledges his relationship with dictators in Latin America,[336] he denies the notion that he supports their political ideas or actions, as some claim.

> For instance, the fact that I am a friend of several strong Chinese government leaders does not mean that I am a Marxist-Leninist. I respect them and I disagree with them. We talk for hours. I present the Gospel and they talk about atheism and Marxism. But that doesn't make me support Marxism-Leninism, atheism, and communism in the People's Republic of China.[337]

Furthermore, Palau has met not only with right-wing dictators of Latin America but also with many left-wing dictators in the old Soviet Union countries. But Palau contends that he has "*never* [emphasis in original] been criticized for meeting with 'left-wing' dictators in Eastern Europe."[338] Palau also defends his actions as merely strategic for evangelism, without any political intention. In fact, he will work with anyone for the cause of the gospel, regardless of their political viewpoints. While emphasizing that he is neither Republican nor Democrat, Palau declares, "I'm for evangelizing both!"[339] He also asserts, "No matter who [*sic*] I am talking to, whether it is a president of a country, whether it is a dictator of left-wing or right-wing, I always give them the pure Gospel of Jesus Christ."[340]

Palau's arguments are persuasive and consistent with his theological conviction. He believes that political reform is not the answer to the problems of the world. The change must begin with the human heart, which can be transformed only by the message of the gospel.[341] His evangelistic motive is evident even in his address at Guatemala's centennial ceremony, as summarized by Stoll: "The

Gospel could liberate Guatemalans from the chains of sin, Palau went on, and it could liberate them from the chains of poverty, misery, and oppression. Through the Gospel of Jesus Christ, the evangelist promised, the new man could build a new Guatemala."[342]

Judging from Palau's arguments and ministries, his association with right-wing political leaders may be justified simply as evangelistic endeavor. In fact, his relationship with them has provided him special opportunities and contributed significantly to the advance of the gospel.[343] Palau's apolitical position and noncritical attitude toward dictators, however, could still lead people to assume that he supports the political ideas of those dictators he has visited. In addition, he has to consider the possibility that befriending dictators could be exploited for political propaganda, no matter where his motives lie.

Consequently, Palau's actions could do more harm than good for the cause of the gospel in the long run. Perhaps Jesus' admonition to His disciples in His commission is appropriate at this point: "I am sending you out like sheep among wolves. Therefore be as shrewd as snakes and as innocent as doves" (Matthew 10:16). Though he may be innocent, Palau could in some cases have been shrewder in his strategy.

Palau's longtime mentor, Billy Graham, may provide a good case in point. Throughout his ministry Graham has been the target of a similar criticism. Being a spiritual advisor to eleven presidents, from Harry Truman to George W. Bush, Graham has always stood by presidents, regardless of their political positions. He was looking for neither wealth nor fame, but the friendships with presidents provided him unique opportunities to proclaim the gospel around the world.

After their investigation into Graham's relationships with the various presidents, Nancy Gibbs and Michael Duffy conclude, "There were places he could not go without the power of the presidency behind him to open doors. That was the practical benefit of these friendships, and its impact was felt literally all around the world."[344]

As Graham acknowledged, however, he sometimes crossed the line and acted as political advisor rather than as spiritual counselor. Graham's friendship with Richard Nixon brought particular criticism in this regard. Gibbs and Duffy concur:

> It was one thing to serve as Eisenhower's or Johnson's private pastor. But it was quite another to act as Nixon's political partner, carrying private messages to foreign heads of state, advising on campaign strategy and assembling evangelical leaders for private White House briefings.[345]

Learning from his mistakes the hard way, in 1981 Graham acknowledged his fault and declared that "Evangelicals can't be closely identified with any particular party or person. We have to stand in the middle, to preach to all people, right and left. I haven't been faithful to my own advice in the past. I will in the future."[346] Despite such a resolution, observe Gibbs and Duffy, "To his critics, the pastoral was political. The left deplored his spending the night with Bush on the day the Gulf War began; the right objected to his praying at Clinton's Inaugural."[347]

To avoid unnecessary misunderstandings and conflicts, evangelists and religious leaders must be careful in terms of their activities in political realms. However, the cynical attitudes of critics might end up being the same no matter what positions they take. Neither Graham nor Palau is without fault, but as long as their motives are pure and evangelical, their approach is to be justified as biblical. What Robert Ferm said of Billy Graham in that evangelist's defense may be applied as well to Palau: "As Jesus did, so Billy Graham [Luis Palau] has many times sat to eat with twentieth-century publicans and sinners. As Paul did, so Billy Graham [Luis Palau] has endeavored to become all things to all men that he might win some."[348]

Ecumenical Nature of Evangelistic Campaigns

While Palau has been criticized by liberal Protestants because of his actions toward and relationships with those in politics, he has been a target of vehement criticism by fundamentalists for the ecumenical nature of his ministry, and especially for inviting Roman Catholics to attend his campaigns.[349] In fact, whether or not an evangelist will work with certain faith groups is a delicate matter and thus requires sound discernment and judgment. Based on the biblical teachings on separation and fellowship, Ferm aptly warns against both extremes:

> Separation can be carried to such an extreme that we fail to make an impact on the world in need of evangelizing. Likewise, the inclusive attitude may be carried to an unwarranted extreme, leading to a relationship of compromise with either individuals or groups who are hostile to a revealed faith.[350]

Palau's sympathy toward Catholics began from his childhood experiences. The churches Palau attended in his youth did not welcome Catholics; rather, they insulted them, particularly on such issues as the veneration of the Virgin Mary, saints, and purgatory. As a result, the churches never grew, Palau recalls:

> There was nobody converted because when you would invite someone to your church it was only to insult them and their views. Of course, their theological views needed to be explained biblically. But it's one thing to explain things gently, humbly, and biblically; it is another to insult and offend them, turning them away.[351]

Palau also acknowledged that his view on working with Christians from other backgrounds has changed over time:

> When I started out I was afraid of working with people who did not verbalize their faith exactly as I liked. And I was confrontational; I would go to war on doctrinal issues. When John Stott spoke at Lausanne of being more tolerant, I thought he was getting soft. Now I see he was making sense. I would never compromise the gospel. But those who are secure in their faith have no reason to fear mingling with other people.[352]

Palau recognizes the differences among denominations, but he insists that unless one tolerates differing views on negotiable issues there will be no unity among Christians.[353] This does not mean compromising the absolute biblical truths revealed in the Bible. It is also imperative that Christian unity and cooperation be based on the inerrant Scriptures. Apart from the Scriptures, "any other unity is sheer illusion."[354] From this conviction, Palau differentiates "the true unity of the Body of Christ" from "phony ecumenism," which denies the basic truths of Christianity.[355] In his speech at Urbana '79, Palau expounded on this:

> Biblical, godly, Christ-exalting oneness already exists in the body of Christ. We are one body. This is not ecumenism. Ecumenism speaks of false union, and this is not at all what we are talking about. There is no compromising of basic truth in the union that our Lord Jesus prayed about. No playing "footsie" under the table with those who are traitors to the message of the cross, the blood of Christ and the resurrection of our Lord. That would be intolerable.[356]

From this principle and conviction Palau has espoused and practiced working with believers from different faith backgrounds, embracing as many denominations as possible without compromising the integrity of the gospel. When asked about his relationship with Catholic bishops and priests, Palau maintains that he has been faithful and humble with them. Yet he makes clear his theological position and explains what he believes to them.

> I always emphasize the authority of Scripture, the forgiveness of sin with Romans 8, the temple of the Holy Spirit which is often missing in the Catholic Church, eternal life by faith in the Lord, how to receive Jesus Christ not by baptism but by faith, the priesthood of all believers, and so on.[357]

Working with Christians from different denominational backgrounds can be both dangerous and confusing. In order to avoid unnecessary conflicts and misunderstandings, evangelists and their teams must elucidate the fundamental beliefs that in their view cannot be compromised and that will serve as biblical criteria for participating churches. Setting forth the biblical criteria for people from different doctrinal backgrounds, however, can be complicated and controversial.

While acknowledging this difficulty, Palau suggests using 1 Corinthians 3:1–8 as the guideline "as to how to be non-sectarian and yet firmly planted on basic biblical doctrines." He comments, "This is a delicate balance, indeed, but one that can be achieved and one that the Lord looks for in you and me."[358]

According to Ferm, Christian history provides ample examples that support nonsectarian attitudes and cooperation. For instance, like Palau, evangelist Billy Graham has been criticized for his practice of working outside evangelical circles with liberals, Charismatics, and Catholics.[359] In his defense of Graham's inclusive policy, Ferm reviews the history of the inclusive and cooperative natures of the evangelistic ministries of major evangelists of the past, including Jonathan Edwards, George Whitefield, John Wesley, Charles G. Finney, Dwight L. Moody, and Billy Sunday.[360]

While negating the concept that these evangelists were exclusive to other faith traditions, Ferm firmly states, "The great evangelists were separated unto God and separated from sin, but they were certainly not separated from the people who needed their message."[361] Perhaps this statement best describes Palau's motive for working with people of all denominations. In addition, one must remember that a vast majority of the population in Latin America is Catholic. If Palau were to ignore this segment of the population, he would never get a chance to share the love of Christ with most of Latin America.

Palau's Attitudes Toward Criticism

Palau has often acknowledged criticisms and accusations from other Christians.[362] Criticism seems to come even from other Christians who might be expected to help his evangelistic endeavors. His disappointment is expressed in the following statement:

> Will there be agonies? Yes. In our evangelistic crusades in Latin America and Europe, we run into an enormous amount of cynicism from people we expect support from. We hear sarcasm from the intelligentsia when we expected

> them to at least thank God that we were giving them a helping hand. And often both cynicism and sarcasm come from people who otherwise claim that they would love to see the body of believers united worldwide.[363]

Despite such disapproval, Palau is not discouraged; rather, he states that "It's a sign that you're doing something right when certain people begin to get upset because of what you represent and preach."[364] He also argues as follows:

> Sure, others will criticize. "You're too much of a dreamer," they'll say; or, "Do you really expect to see lasting results from all of your evangelistic efforts?" Answering honest questions is important. But we cannot afford to waste precious time on critics who have no desire or concern to see the world won to Christ.[365]

Palau is determined in his endeavors, refusing to let go of his passion for souls amid vehement criticisms.

Conclusion

Over more than four decades Luis Palau has proclaimed the gospel throughout the world, proving the viability and effectiveness of mass evangelism in today's rapidly changing milieu. Palau's ministry flows from his firm theological beliefs—beliefs that are biblically sound and historically proven. First, his fundamental convictions for evangelism are rooted in the inerrant Word of God. In this respect, Palau passes the timeless test of the evangelist. For Palau, the Bible is the perfect Book, wherein is contained the message of salvation. The Word is also the source of his evangelistic theology and philosophy, which have been discussed in these three chapters.

Second, Palau's theological views in many aspects resemble those of his predecessors, men such as Charles Finney, D. L. Moody, and Billy Graham, among others. Perhaps Palau's most significant theological contribution to evangelism is his confidence in campaign evangelism. Within an atmosphere of mistrust in evangelists and gloomy predictions for the future of campaign evangelism, Palau still believes in the strategic role of evangelistic campaigns for world evangelization, when accomplished in the power of the Holy Spirit.

Like evangelists in the past, Palau has been criticized in some areas. Although he is not without fault, he still provides reasonable and well-grounded defense of his theology. Palau's theological convictions have led him to pursue evangelism vigorously and with specific strategy. Two principles stand out in his evangelistic methodology: cultural relevancy and creativity. Within these principles, he has employed every possible means to share the message of God's love. The following chapters will examine Palau's specific strategies of mass evangelism.

Endnotes

292 Peter Wagner, "Evangelism and Social Action in Latin America," *Christianity Today*, 7 January 1966, 10. Wagner mentions a recent book, *The Christian's Social Responsibility*, written by a left-wing liberal group of Latin America, the River Plate theologians. The controversial point of this book is: "*The changing of the structures of society, and not the proclamation of a message geared to win converts, should be the true evangelistic burden of today's Church*" [emphasis in original]. Ibid.

293 Luis Palau and David Sanford, *Luis Palau: Calling America and the Nations to Christ* (Nashville, TN: Thomas Nelson, Inc., 1994; rev. 2000), 33. Some questions were persistent in his youth: "How could people play and party and carry on when others were going broke and being cheated and living in poverty? How could they ignore the lower class, when widows and orphans were begging for help?"

294 Ibid., 43. For information on Palau's outreach to the poor through social work, see "Reaching the Underprivileged Through Servant Evangelism" under "Reaching Affinity Groups Through Specialized Programs" in chapter 8.

295 Luis Palau, "Evangelist Luis Palau: Changing the World from the Inside Out," *World Vision* (April/May 1990), 4–5.

296 Luis Palau, "Fear Not," in *Proclaim Christ Until He Comes: Calling the Whole Church to Take the Whole Gospel to the Whole World,* ed. J. D. Douglas (Minneapolis, MN: World Wide Publications, 1990), 369. Cf. Peter Wagner espoused the same idea: "It is a good thing that evangelicals in Latin America and elsewhere are becoming more and more concerned for social action, but it is important that we never allow social action to replace evangelism." Wagner, "Evangelism and Social Action in Latin America," 12.

297 Luis Palau, "You Can Change the World," *Discipleship Journal* 33 (May/June 1986): 38.

298 Luis Palau, "Missions to the End of the World," in *Global Crossroads: Focusing the Strength of Local Churches,* ed. W. Harold Fuller, World Evangelical Fellowship (Mandaluyong, Philippines: OMF Literature Inc., 1998), 281. Cf. Palau is worried because some Christian circles are trying to replace "evangelism with *only* [emphasis in original] social actions." Luis Palau, "Whatever Happened to Evangelism? Luis Palau Wants to Rekindle Our Passion for the Lost," *Christianity Today,* 8 April 1996, 38.

299 For the historical sketch of the divorce between evangelism and social reform, see David O. Moberg, *The Great Reversal* (Philadelphia, PA: J. B. Lippencott, 1977).

300 Leighton Ford, *The Christian Persuader* (New York: Harper and Row Publishers, 1966), 82. Ford continues, "Those who say that mass evangelism has not been involved with nor concerned about social problems should read their history again." To prove his point, he gives examples of Charles Finney, Lyman Beecher, Stephen Grollet, Elihu Burritt, William Booth, John Hambleton, Keir Hardie, and D. L. Moody. Ibid., 82–83.

301 John Mark Terry, *Evangelism: A Concise History* (Nashville, TN: Broadman & Holman Publishers, 1994), 171.

302 Palau, "You Can Change the World," 37.

303 Palau, "Changing the World," 8.

304 David L. Jones and Luis Palau, *Scottish Fires of Revival* (Cupertino, CA. D.I.M.E. Publishers, 1980), 42. Palau also observed that Wesleyan revival "roused concern for public health, prison reform, and public education." Palau, "Changing the World," 8

305 Palau, "Changing the World," 8. See also William Warren Sweet, *Revivalism in America* (Nashville, TN: Abingdon Press, 1944), 171.

306 Palau, "Changing the World," 8.

307 Palau, "Fear Not," 369. In his interview with *Christianity Today*, Palau also confirmed his position: "I'm concerned about justice and poverty. But I am persuaded that evangelism is the best and deepest social action because it changes people, and that's what's needed to change society." Luis Palau, "Evangelism: The Best Form of Social Action." *Christianity Today,* 17 February 1989, 52.

308 Luis Palau, "The Only Hope for America," LPA [online]; accessed 14 March 2008; available from http://www.palau.org/articles/index.php; Internet.

309 Palau and Sanford, *Calling America and the Nations*, 97. Here Palau affirms, "The people of this world create the problems of this world. If we can lead them to Christ, we will create a climate for other positive, practical changes to take place."

310 Palau, "Changing the World," 8.

311 Arthur C. Archibald, *Establishing the Converts* (Philadelphia, PA: The Judson Press, 1952), 24.

312 Richard N. Longenecker, "Introduction," in *Patterns of Discipleship in the New Testament*, ed., Richard N. Longenecker (Grand Rapids,: Wm. B. Eerdmans Publishing Co. 1996), 4. According to Longenecker's research, the frequency

of the word "disciples" referring to followers of Jesus is as follows: sixty-seven or sixty-eight times in Matthew, forty-four times in Mark, thirty-four times in Luke, and seventy-three times in John. In Acts "disciple" appears in the masculine gender some twenty-eight times, and one time in Acts 9:36 in feminine form. Longenecker also shows the data regarding references to the "disciples" of John the Baptist in the Gospels (Matt. 9:14; 11:2; 14:12; Mark 2:18; Luke 5:33; 7:18–19; 11:1; John 1:35, 37; 3:25; 4:1), to "disciples" of the Pharisees (Matt. 22:16; Mark 2:18), to "disciples" of Moses (John 9:28), and to relationships between disciples and teachers generally (Matt. 10:24–25; Luke 6:40).

313 Luis Palau, "The Evangelist and the Ministry of the Holy Spirit," in *The Calling of an Evangelist,* ed. J. D. Douglas (Minneapolis, MN: World Wide Publications, 1987), 141.

314 Luis Palau, "Discipline in the Church," *Discipleship Journal* 16 (July/August 1983): 18.

315 Palau, interview by author, May 9, 2008. He did not reveal the specific names of individuals.

316 For the list of Palau's representative books on discipleship and Christian life, see footnote 47 in the introduction. In these books Palau dealt with family issues, such as dating, marriage, sex, divorce, and education of children, as well as with some psychological and social problems, including grief, loneliness, suicide, and alcoholism. Discussing Palau's writings on discipleship in detail is beyond the scope of this study. It will be limited to the issues related to evangelism.

317 Waldron Scott, "Discipleship Evangelism," in *Evangelism: The Next Ten Years*, ed. Sherwood Eliot Wirt (Waco, TX: Word Books, 1978), 103.

318 Leighton Ford, "The Strategic Role of Mass Evangelism," *Christianity Today,* 24 November 1961 32. Ford records Whitefield's own statement: "My brother Wesley acted more wisely than I. The souls that were awakened under his ministry he joined together in class and so preserved the fruit of his labors. I failed to do this, and as a result my people are a rope of sand." See also Ford, *Christian Persuader*, 89–90.

319 Scott, "Discipleship Evangelism," 107. Scott mentions a report by the Institute of American Church Growth indicating that only 15 percent of new converts of Graham's campaigns in 1976 still remained as active members of the local churches after a year.

320 Ibid. Scott goes on to say, "Palau, following the lead given by Dr. Vergil Gerber, prefers to call his approach 'follow through' rather than 'follow up.'"

321 Edgardo Silvoso, "In Rosario It Was Different—Crusade Converts Are in the Churches," *Evangelical Missions Quarterly* 14, no. 2 (April 1978): 84.

322 Ibid., 87.

323 The Rosario Plan will be discussed in more detail in "Planting New Churches Through Evangelistic Campaigns" chapter 8.

324 Roy Pointer, *Crusade Evangelism: The Fruit That Remained; A Discussion Arising From Mission to London* (Bromley, Kent [England]: MARC Europe, 1988), 23. Scott Bauer, "Crusade Evangelism" (D.Min. project, Oral Roberts University, 1995), 93. Here Bauer states, "It is unfair to saddle the evangelist with the responsibility to disciple or follow-up on converts. The operation of the evangelist in the Church brings people to faith in Christ by the work of the Holy Spirit. The operation of the pastor/teacher in the Church brings converts to discipleship. These two processes are radically different, but they are related and must interface with each other." Cf. Research by Glenn Firebaugh after Billy Graham's Seattle campaign in 1976 reveals the same conclusion. Firebaugh states, "An overwhelming majority (90 percent) of the local church leaders feel that the local church, not BGEA or the crusade committee, has primary responsibility for follow-up." Glenn Firebaugh, "How Effective Are City-wide Crusades?" *Christianity Today*, 27 March 1981, 28.

325 For specific process of follow-up in Palau's campaigns, see "Bridging New Converts to Local Churches" in chapter 7.

326 For instance, at a press conference in Beijing, China, in 2005, Palau urged house churches of China to register their churches officially to the government so that they can obtain religious freedom. To such a claim, house church leaders of China and other Christian leaders who are familiar with religious situations in China criticized Palau for his lack of accurate knowledge and judgment. Sheryl Henderson Blunt, "Palau Pulls Back," *Christianity Today*, 6 February 2006, 22.

327 In 2005, for example, the Cardiff City Council cancelled a civic reception for Palau because of his "extreme evangelical beliefs." Palau was called "a right-wing reactionary individual" by his critics in Wales. He was criticized for his evangelical beliefs on ethical issues such as homosexuality and on his perceived negative views on other religions. See Rob James, "Extreme Orthodoxy," *Christianity Today*, 1 January 2005, 22.

328 Bryan Gilling, "Mass Evangelistic Theology and Methodology and the 1987 Luis Palau Mission to Auckland," *Transformation* 8 (January–March 1991): 9. For details of the charges, read the article. David Jones, a spokesman for LPEA at that time, also refuted the claims of the four bishops as groundless: "Many of the bishops' undocumented accusations were quickly demonstrated to be false and other criticisms were answered either before or during Mission to Auckland." David Jones, "A Response from the Luis Palau Evangelistic Association by David L. Jones," *Transformation* 8 (January–March 1991): 14. Another example is to be found during Madison '82. Palau was charged by the local press, the *Capital Times*, with the headline, "Fundamentalist Crusade Splits Campus Groups." In reality, however, the event was the most cooperative one in the history of the University of Wisconsin at Madison. Mike Moore, a student chairman of this event, stated, "Madison '82 drew together 36 of the 45 Christian ministries on the campus. Previously, the most cooperating at any one time was five. In addition, 40 area churches endorsed the mission." Rodney Clapp, "Luis Palau Invades the University of Wisconsin: Is the Time Ripe for More Campus Evangelism?" *Christianity Today*, 19 March 1982, 38-40.

329 Matt Sedensky, "Luis Who? Man Could Be Nation's Next Top Evangelist," *The Associated Press*, 29 April 2007 [online]; accessed 27 September 2007; available from http://www.ocala.com/apps/pbcs.dll/article?AID=/20070429/NEWS/204290362/1368/googlesitemapnews; Internet.

330 Gilling, "Mass Evangelistic Theology and Methodology," 10. This charge was brought to Luis Palau by four Anglican bishops in Palau's evangelistic campaign in Auckland in 1987.

331 Palau and Sanford, *Calling America and the Nations*, 175. This happened during Palau's campaign in Mexico in 1988.

332 Gilling, "Mass Evangelistic Theology and Methodology," 9. In their criticism of Palau's message, they also said, "The focus is so 'next-world' oriented, that Gospel-centered social action in order to change *this* [emphasis in original] world is by-passed." Ibid. Another protest against Palau occurred during the campaign in London in 1984. A group of protesters that called itself "the Campaign for Real Life" handed out leaflets condemning Palau's alleged association with right-wing rulers in Central America and even staged a brief demonstration at the opening meeting for the campaign. John Capon, "Billy Graham and Luis Palau: Fanning Revival Fires in England—Events and Strategies Behind a Remarkable Summer of Evangelism," *Christianity Today*, 13 July 1984, 53.

333 For instance, *Time* reported that "Despite government denials, Ríos Montt's antiguerrilla campaign has cost the lives of thousands of innocent noncombatants. Perhaps as many as 1 million Guatemalans have been made homeless by the fighting. Guatemalans who refuse to join the civil defense patrols are sometimes shot summarily as guerrilla sympathizers." George Russell and James Willwerth, "Surprise in the Sermon," *Time*, 23 May 1983 [online]; accessed 1 December 2008; available from http://www.time.com/time/magazine/article/0,9171,953896-2,00.html; Internet. Ríos Montt was also indicted for his genocide against indigenous Mayans by some human rights groups. For more detailed information, see "Ríos Montt: Record of Human Rights Abuses in Guatemala" [online]; accessed on 1 December 2008; available from http://www.lawg.org/countries/guatemala/Rios-montt.htm; Internet. This website offers a collection of various reports, testimonies, and statistic graphs concerning the violence and abuse under Ríos Montt's regime.

334 David Stoll, *Is Latin America Turning Protestant? The Politics of Evangelical Growth* (Berkeley and Los Angeles, CA: University of California Press, 1990), 20. For information on Palau's visit to Guatemala in 1982, see ibid., 1–3.

335 Ibid., 19. Stoll also asserts, "When much of the Catholic clergy turned against military regimes in the 1970s, evangelical leaders usually did not. Some energetically preached submission to dictatorships and defended the status quo as if it were God's handiwork. ... At a time when other Christians were challenging structures of oppression, they seemed to be propping the same structures up." Ibid.

336 Palau and Sanford, *Calling America and the Nations*, 159. Palau states, "Other critics have severely criticized Billy Graham and myself for meeting with presidents, prime ministers, and other top government officials, as if they didn't

need Christ, too! Even to this day, I'm still criticized, especially whenever I go to Western Europe, for meeting with Guatemala's President Jose Efraín Ríos Montt in 1982, with Paraguay's President Alfredo Stroessner six years earlier, and with other so-called 'right-wing dictators' at Presidential Prayer Breakfasts and private meetings."

337 Palau, interview by the author, May 9, 2008.

338 Palau and Sanford, *Calling America and the Nations*, 159.

339 Ibid. This is Palau's response to journalists during his meeting with President Ronald Reagan at the National Religious Broadcasters (NRB) convention in Washington, D.C.

340 Palau, interview by the author, May 9, 2008.

341 For instance, Palau stated, "I believe the only way to change a nation is to change it from the inside out by changing the hearts of the nation's people. Only Jesus Christ can change hearts and transform lives." Susan Holton and David L. Jones, *Spirit Aflame: Luis Palau's Mission to London* (Grand Rapids: Baker Book House, 1985), 64.

342 Stoll, *Is Latin America Turning Protestant?* 2.

343 For more discussion on this point, see "Reaching Affinity Groups Through Specialized Programs," in chapter 8.

344 Nancy Gibbs and Michael Duffy, *The Preacher and the Presidents: Billy Graham in the White House* (New York: Center Street, 2007), 344.

345 Nancy Gibbs and Michael Duffy, "Billy Graham, Pastor in Chief," *Time*, 9 August 2007 [online]; accessed 2 July 2008; available from http://www.time.com/time/magazine/article/0,9171,1651625,00.html; Internet.

346 Ibid.

347 Ibid.

348 Robert Oscar Ferm, *Cooperative Evangelism* (Grand Rapids: Zondervan Publishing House, 1958), 87.

349 Some of Palau's campaigns with Catholic involvement are as follows: Managua, Nicaragua, in 1975; New Zealand in 1987; Kingston, Jamaica, in 1993; West Michigan in 1994; Londonderry, Ireland, in 1995; Chicago in 1996; Olympia, Washington, in 1998; and Omaha, Nebraska, in 2007. "Luis Palau and Rome," *Way of Life Literature* [online]; accessed 12 May 2008; available from http://www.wayoflife.org/fbns/luis-palau-and-rome.html; Internet. For criticisms on the involvement of Catholics in Palau's campaigns, see also http://obadiah1317.wordpress.com/2007/02/13/luis-palau-began-well-but-along-the-way-compromised-the-gospel/; http://www.irishcalvinist.com/?p=810; http://www.defendusinbattle.org/2007/07/luis-palau-and-sin-of-ecumenism.html.

350 Ferm, *Cooperative Evangelism*, 33.

351 Palau, interview by the author, May 9, 2008.

352 Palau, "Evangelism: The Best Form of Social Action," 52.

353 Palau, *Telling the Story*, 30-31. Palau also states, "Secondary issues *are* [emphasis in original] important. We don't pretend they don't matter to us anymore. ... I don't have to pretend that everyone agrees with me or that I agree with everyone else." Ibid., 31.

354 Luis Palau, "Working Together," in *Believing and Obeying Jesus Christ: The Urbana 79 Compendium*, ed. John W. Alexander (Downers Grove, IL: InterVarsity Press, 1980), 117.

355 Palau, *Telling the Story*, 30. Cf. Palau avoids the term "ecumenical" due to people's misunderstanding immediately connected with the term even though the term itself, meaning "worldwide," is not wrong. Palau, interview by the author, May 9, 2008.

356 Palau, "Working Together," 117. Palau preached from John 17:20–23, in which Jesus prayed for the oneness of His disciples. Palau also said, "In other words, we must focus on the positive, fundamental teachings of Scripture and in the process decide who we can work with in the preaching of Jesus Christ and his call to eternal life by repentance and faith. Don't compromise Christ's teachings by entertaining traitors to the cross." Ibid., 118.

357 Palau, interview by the author, May 9, 2008.

358 Palau, "Working Together," 127. An example of providing common biblical criteria for participating churches was set during Mission Maine. According to McBride, some churches hesitated to join the campaign at first because of Catholic involvement. However, they all agreed that LPA's statement of faith should serve as the criteria, so that anyone who agrees would join. Kevin T. McBride, "Retaking the Village Green: Building Strategic Partnerships for Evangelism that Work in New England" (D.Min. project, Gordon-Conwell Theological Seminary, 2001) 96, 103–107. See appendix 1 for "LPA Statement of Faith."

359 Cf. Throughout his career, Billy Graham has changed his stance on many issues, such as racial relations, communism, and the Roman Catholic and Jewish communities. According to Richard V. Pierard, Graham moved from evangelical exclusivism to ecumenical openness. To see how Graham's view has been changed, see Richard V. Pierard, "From Evangelical Exclusivism to Ecumenical Openness: Billy Graham and Sociopolitical Issues," *Journal of Ecumenical Studies* 20, no. 3 (Summer, 1983): 425–46.

360 Ferm, *Cooperative Evangelism*, 48–86.

361 Ibid., 48.

362 For instance, Palau states, "The funny thing is that you get a lot of praise, but you also get a lot of criticism." Jim Mills, "An Interview with Luis Palau," *Discipleship Journal* 12 (November/December 1982): 40.

363 Palau, "Working Together," 115–16.

364 Palau, *Telling the Story*, 28.

365 Palau, "Evangelist and Ministry of the Holy Spirit," 137–38.

CHAPTER 6

EVANGELISTIC STRATEGY: PREACHING

In his discussion of mass evangelism, William Brad Morrow correctly observes that "Each new generation of evangelists has built upon the methods of the previous generation. These changes have always coincided with changes in context. Mass evangelism has not been a static methodology but a fluid approach that has transformed over time."[366] This statement best describes Luis Palau's strategy of evangelism.

As Morrow acknowledges, Palau has learned from Billy Graham, who in turn also learned from previous evangelists. Nevertheless, Palau has been sensitive to changing circumstances and has utilized every possible means to proclaim the good news of Jesus Christ in a relevant and creative way. Chapters 6–10 examine Palau's strategies of evangelism in four areas: preaching, evangelistic campaigns, mass media, and mentoring and working with young evangelists.

Evangelistic Preaching of Luis Palau

Preaching is the most important and integral part of ministry for evangelists. In essence, evangelism is the communication of the gospel, and as Palau properly remarks, "You're only being an evangelist when you clearly communicate the content of the gospel."[367] While mentioning some of the renowned evangelists in Christian history, Palau asks, "What made them great evangelists?" Going on, "The answer has little to do with method or technique. … No, it wasn't their method, but their message."[368] In light of the centrality of preaching for the evangelist, this section discusses the characteristics, content, and style of Palau's preaching.[369]

Characteristics of the Message

There are some distinct characteristics in Palau's message that should be noted. First, Palau stresses the importance of preaching from the Bible, and his own preaching has been based solely on the truth revealed in the Bible. At Amsterdam 2000, Palau exhorted other evangelists: "First, evaluate the message you're preaching. My number one goal is to 'preach the Word' (2 Timothy 4:2, NIV). Everything I preach must be clearly verified by Scripture."[370] Palau is convinced that the Bible is relevant to human life and provides the answer to human dilemmas. But he has this advice for believers, even before they go to the Scriptures: "Listen to the Word of God. This is not just some book on psychology, this is the best psychology book there is. This is not simply another book on marriage counseling, this is the best book on marriage counseling."[371]

A comment by the renowned theologian John Stott on Palau's preaching during Mission to London is noteworthy: "I think Luis is wonderfully faithful. He doesn't pull his punches, but preaches straight from the Bible. Many people today know nothing about the Bible, and he's wise to know about this ignorance. He teaches, teaches, teaches from the Bible."[372] According to Palau, about 80 percent of his preaching comes directly from the Bible, while "The other 20 percent is cultural, historic and psychological."[373]

Second, the content of Palau's preaching has been the same throughout his ministry, except for some changes in his introduction and illustrations. Evangelists may face the temptation to change the message of their preaching after repeating the same one for many years. In reference to Billy Graham's preaching, David Barnes of Paris once remarked that preaching "the same message must be a very humiliating thing for a man who is well read and intelligent. One of the greatest evidences of Billy Graham's commitment to Christ and his humility is that he sticks to that to which he has been called."[374] Luis Palau honestly confesses that he is also tempted to preach something other than the gospel; yet the message of the evangelist cannot be altered, because "The Gospel hasn't changed in nearly two thousand years!"[375] His conviction of the unchangeable nature of the message for evangelists is well articulated in the following statement:

> I am convinced, when twenty years of evangelism have gone by, that the temptation is to want to speak various enriching messages. But the gospel is the same all the time. You have to repeat yourself. It is a great temptation, I think, to an evangelist, when he reaches a certain age, to want to let people know, "Hey, I am not really a dumb evangelist. I do read theology. I am up with what is going on in the world. I do grow in the Lord. I could do Bible teaching." But because I am an evangelist I must repeat the gospel—over and over and over again, because the gospel does not change. Some of the dressing may change, but even that has its limits.[376]

At Amsterdam 2000 Palau also encouraged the audience, "Brothers and sisters, we are acting as the very mouth of God Himself (see Jeremiah 15:19–21). *Never* take that responsibility lightly. *Always* preach the same old message—the simple, biblical Gospel of Jesus Christ" [emphasis in original].[377]

Third, Palau's preaching has been characterized by its positive message; he preaches God's love, not His wrath. Palau provides his own rationale for taking this approach. First, God is a loving God, not an angry God.[378] Second, the nature of the gospel itself is the good news evangelists are called to preach.[379] Third, people are tired of hearing bad news and often are already convicted of sin.[380] Fourth, an evangelist's calling and role are different from those of pastor and prophet. Unlike the latter, who must point to and denounce people's sins, evangelists must preach God's love, demonstrated on the cross.[381]

Palau's approach is not without precedent. The best example is found in the preaching of D. L. Moody, who was called "an apostle of the love of God."[382] According to William Evans, "Moody was perhaps the first major evangelist in America who preached the love of God as the main ingredient in God's attitude towards men."[383]

Preaching the positive message, however, has stirred controversy, and some have accused Palau of preaching a "watered-down gospel."[384] In fact, preaching God's love and salvation without mentioning the seriousness of sin and judgment can jeopardize the integrity of the gospel. People may not fully understand the significance of the good news without knowing the bad news that humanity faces without Jesus. Along with God's love and eternal life through Christ, evangelists must preach the eternal consequences for unbelievers. The fact that Jesus often preached on judgment and eternal punishment of sinners stands as a solemn reminder to every evangelist.[385]

Fourth, like other strategies of his evangelistic ministry, Palau's message has been marked by relevancy to the life of his audience. Palau's relevant approach to the particular audience can best be observed in his selection of topics and illustrations.[386] In his teaching on evangelistic preaching, Palau argues, "The chosen topic should interest the listeners and relate to their situation. As we speak, our teaching should go from what the listeners know to what they don't know, from what they're looking for to what they're not looking for but need."[387] The relevancy in Palau's preaching was well observed during Mission to London by Dave Pope, a well-known British singer and evangelist:

> In a nutshell, he scratches where people itch. He preaches in such a way that Joe Public can understand what he is all about. He's not preaching platitudes, theological nuances, and niceties. It's down-to-earth preaching, relating the God of creation to the man in the street.[388]

Preaching the gospel in a relevant way for a particular audience is not only practical but biblical. Jesus' preaching, and especially His use of parables, was characterized by relevancy to His audience, and as pointed out by Michael Green, the apostle Paul's preaching was "intensely relevant, alike to circumstances, concerns and consciences of the hearers."[389] Nevertheless, the evangelist must be careful not to compromise the truth while being relevant to the culture of his audience. John Stott provides insightful commentary in this regard:

> We should be praying that God will raise up a new generation of Christian communicators who are determined to bridge the chasm; who struggle to relate God's unchanging Word to our ever-changing world; who refuse to sacrifice truth to relevance or relevance to truth; but who resolve instead in equal measure to be faithful to Scripture and pertinent to today.[390]

The evangelist must strive to keep this balance in his preaching when he contextualizes the Word of God for his audience.

Fifth, in developing his evangelistic sermon, Palau has adopted a problem-solution approach.[391] He ordinarily delineates many problems in the world, related to family, economics, politics, and so on, and presents Jesus Christ as the only solution to these problems.[392] For example, in his evangelistic event called Madison '82 at the University of Wisconsin at Madison, Palau addressed topics relevant to university students such as "sexuality, loneliness, and the fear of failure."[393] According to Rodney Clapp, who reported on this event, Palau's sermon always culminated in this declaration: "Whatever else you do, student, you must face the claim of Jesus Christ on your life."[394]

Palau's problem-solution approach resembles that of Billy Graham.[395] One of the clear indications that Graham has greatly influenced Luis Palau can, in fact, be observed in this approach. Billy Graham's biographer, William Martin, describes a typical tactic of Graham's sermons: "As in virtually all his sermons, he recited a laundry list of problems: poverty, drugs, broken hearts, emptiness, guilt, loneliness, spiritual blindness, and fear."[396] Martin goes on, "To no one's surprise, Graham proclaimed, with monumental conviction and certainty, that the sole and sufficient answer to these problems is Jesus Christ."[397]

The problem-solution approach seems appropriate for evangelistic preaching. Without convincing people of the problems they face without Christ, the preaching of the gospel, which is the solution to problems, will have a very limited appeal. Therefore, before he presents the message of the gospel, the evangelist must persuade the audience to recognize and acknowledge their dilemmas.

Major Themes

Like other evangelists in the past, Palau's message has been Christ-centered. Palau contends, "The core of any evangelistic sermon has to be Jesus Christ's work on the cross. Otherwise, the message ignores the gospel and is not evangelistic."[398] Evangelists may preach different titles, topics, introductions, and illustrations, "but eventually about halfway through each message, we [evangelists] speak about the Cross, the resurrection, repentance, faith and commitment. Otherwise, we haven't preached the gospel."[399]

As observed, Palau's basic pattern in presenting the gospel has been a problem-solution approach. He presents humanity's problems without Christ, following with God's solution through Christ. Another essential part of his preaching is the invitation to repent and accept Christ into one's heart.

Humanity's Problem: Hopeless Situations Without Christ

After his introductory stories or remarks, Palau typically begins the body of his sermon with the hopeless and desperate situations people face without Christ in their lives. This approach is reasonable since, as Green has pointed out, "Faith is born out of man's despair of himself."[400] Sin separates human beings from God and results in many desperate situations, affecting social, intellectual, psychological, relational, and theological aspects of human life.[401] Palau declares, "Without God, the heart has no peace, life has no meaning, education has no purpose, economics has no direction. The human soul clamors for God."[402] During his Scotland campaign, Palau spoke of the rich young ruler in Mark 10:

> You need God in your life. ... We were not created to live alone, without God. Emptiness and loneliness were never God's intention for us. ... Unless Jesus Christ is at the centre of our lives, my dear friends, no matter how attractive, good, prosperous, handsome, moral, or even how "religious" you may be, unless Christ is in your life, you are as lost as lost can be.[403]

On another occasion, during Mission to London, Palau stated, "People are lonely today. They want to run away and escape, but they don't know how to do it. Some escape with drink, some with drugs. Some run from man to man or woman to woman, searching, searching."[404] Concerning the psychological worries of people, he said, "Today the whole world is afraid. Here in the West we have a feeling of gloom. We fear diseases, missiles, invasion, and atomic warfare. ... Many people even in the so-called free societies are slaves to all kinds of fears—fear of death, betrayal, and bankruptcy."[405] In dealing with family problems, he also observed, "Throughout Britain, North America and Latin America—all over the world—families are hurting and falling apart. People hurt each other and step on each other. Some of you may have ugly memories of a home where Jesus Christ was never King."[406] Duncan Whyte, a member of the council for the Mission to London, remarked that "Luis's preaching is related to people's personal problems. He's talking about family problems, husbands and wives not getting along, children in rebellion, drug problems—and he's showing the Christian answer to the daily problems of Londoners."[407]

God's Solution: Hope of Salvation Through Christ

The solution to human dilemmas can be found only in God's initiation of salvation in Christ. God takes the initiative in restoring the broken relationship with human beings to bring happiness to them. Before he presents the gospel, Palau usually mentions a couple of points.[408] First, he reminds people of God's creation and love. Human beings are created by God, who loves them no matter what they have done apart from Him. To an audience in Seattle Palau preached, "He

[God] says I know your name. It's written on the palm of My hand. You are not a surprise to God. You are not lost all over the place. You are not little stars floating in the universe. God knows you and He is for you!"[409] Second, Palau emphasizes that each person consists of three parts: body, soul, and spirit. He urges people to give priority to the spirit and the soul over the physical and material.[410]

When it comes to the gospel, Palau preaches it simply and plainly. The message of the gospel is in essence God's love, as shown through Jesus Christ as found in John 3:16, and the content of the gospel is Jesus' death, burial, and resurrection, as summarized by the apostle Paul in 1 Corinthians 15:1–6.[411] At a Promise Keepers' rally, Palau preached the gospel from Bible verses such as Romans 1:16; John 3:16; and 1 Corinthians 15:3–6, stating, "It's simple enough for a child to understand, profound enough to amaze the most brilliant theologians."[412] Palau speaks of the facts of sin, guilt, and repentance. But rather than using these terms, he describes them in plain language.[413]

In proclaiming the gospel Palau often tells people what it means to be a Christian. He describes the Christian life from the perspectives of past, present, and future.[414] First, Christians are those whose sins are forgiven. The Bible says, "God will remember no more" our sins and iniquities (Hebrews 8:12). Second, as the apostle Paul confessed on behalf of all Christians, "It is no longer I who live, but Christ lives in me" (Galatians 2:20). Furthermore, when an individual accepts Christ into their heart, he or she becomes God's temple, where the Holy Spirit dwells (1 Corinthians 3:16; 6:19). Thus, Christians must acknowledge Christ's lordship and live holy and pure lives on Earth in the present. Third, from the future perspective, to be a Christian is to have eternal life (John 3:16; 1 John 5:13). As God has promised, this eternal life cannot be forsaken, since no one can snatch God's children out of God's hand (John 10:28).

Invitation: Response of Repentance and Faith

Evangelistic preaching typically ends with an invitation to respond to the message of the gospel. According to Roy Fish, the invitation was an integral part of apostolic preaching in the New Testament and has been employed by many evangelists throughout

Christian history.[415] Palau has been faithful to this principle.[416] After preaching the hopeless situation of humanity without Christ and the hope offered by God through Christ, he invites people to respond to God's message of love. To Palau, evangelistic preaching without an invitation is unthinkable, since "The Gospel is an invitation."[417]

He exclaims, "Without a call to commitment, an evangelistic sermon is dysfunctional. … Without an invitation, you are not preaching the full good news of Jesus Christ."[418] Thus he challenges other evangelists to "*Always* pull the net. *Always* give listeners an opportunity to receive Jesus Christ as Lord and Savior" [emphasis in original].[419] On another occasion he pleads, "Give an invitation to receive Christ every time you preach the Gospel. Remember, it might be somebody's last chance to receive the Lord."[420]

Behind Palau's invitation lies his belief in the instantaneous conversions of souls.[421] He laments that the United States and Western Europe do not see many conversions compared to many countries in Asia and Latin America because they are not sure "if Christ has the power to convert people on the spot."[422] In response to criticisms against urging people to accept Jesus as their Savior and Lord, Palau comments, "We worry about hurrying a person in his decision; but, I tell you, when the person is ready, just get to the point and help him or her settle the issue. When you sense the Holy Spirit at work, time and technique can be irrelevant."[423]

Palau's invitation has been characterized by a lack of emotion. During his Glasgow campaign in 1981, one national magazine reported that "There is no play on the emotions. … They [inquirers] walk off as matter-of-factly as if he had asked for volunteers to help with the washing-up."[424] Holton and Jones also mention the lack of emotionalism in Palau's preaching observed by many journalists during Mission to London. For instance, one wrote that "There was no hysteria, and certainly he [Palau] did not play upon our emotions … no whipping up of enthusiasm."[425] Another Christian reporter wrote, "I looked for, but could not find emotionalism that evening; nor emotional blackmail being applied; nor pressure exerted on people to make decisions to follow Christ for motives other than wanting to get right with God."[426]

Palau's favorite verse in giving his invitation is Revelation 3:20. The following, with some variations, is typical of his invitation:

> All of us must decide. God brought you here tonight. He wants you to make a decision. The Lord is speaking to your heart. The Bible says that Jesus says, "I stand at the door and knock. If anyone hears My voice and opens the door, I will come in to him, and eat with him, and he with Me."[427]

Although God has honored this simple but sincere plea and brought forth multitudes to profess Jesus as their Savior and Lord, the use of Revelation 3:20 as an invitation for unbelievers to accept Christ requires careful scrutiny. This verse was also used as an invitation to accept Christ in the *Four Spiritual Laws*, the Gospel tract written by Bill Bright. Scholars such as David Aune and Robert Mounce, however, do not endorse such interpretation.[428] A solid exegesis of the passage to which this verse belongs reveals that these words were addressed to the believers in the local church, not to unbelievers.

Style and Delivery

The focus of evangelistic preaching is to present the gospel in such a manner that hearers understand and accept Jesus Christ as Savior and submit their lives to Him as Lord. To make this possible, as pointed out by Lloyd M. Perry and John R. Strubhar, those present must be convinced in their minds, moved in their hearts, and persuaded in their wills.[429] This cannot be achieved without a clear presentation of the message of the gospel, accompanied by effective communication.

Simple and Plain Language

Choice of language for evangelistic preaching is crucial for effective communication. Certainly, one of the most noticeable differences between preaching to believers and to nonbelievers is the choice of language. Hence, Palau advocates choosing simple and understandable terms, avoiding any theological jargon that may not be understandable to nonbelievers. He points out, "Biblical terms like 'regeneration,' 'redemption' and 'justification' need contemporary equivalents, without diminishing their depth of meaning."[430] Instead of the term "gospel," Palau uses "good news gospel" since most nonbelievers do not know the meaning of the word. Otherwise he paraphrases the meaning of the gospel in a simple way, such as, "I've got a free ticket to heaven. Do you want to hear about it?"[431]

Palau's approach is not much different from that of evangelists in the past. In their analysis of Palau's preaching during Mission to London, Holton and Jones found similarity between Palau's presentation and Moody's in the fact that "Both evangelists preached straight from the Bible, relating God's Word to their audiences in direct, simple language."[432] William McLoughlin also observed that Billy Sunday used "slangy humor and florid rhetoric" to reach the people by using familiar language.[433] Due to the simplicity of the language he chooses, Palau has effectively communicated the message of the gospel to ordinary people without religious backgrounds.

Forceful Gestures and Tones

Palau is an energetic and enthusiastic preacher who uses forceful gestures and motions. In reporting on Palau's campaign at Colorado Springs in 1984, newspaper reporter Sura Rubenstein keenly described Palau's spontaneous gestures and motions:

> Dubbed "the hot gospeler" and "a missionary superstar" by the European press, the 50-year-old Palau is in constant motion on the podium, moving his hands and arms like a symphony conductor as he underscores his message that biblical faith is the answer to life's questions, no matter how trivial or how important.[434]

She also vividly portrayed Palau's motions and changing tones as he preaches on heaven and hell, pleading with people to make decisions to accept Jesus in their hearts:

> His voice is now mellow with the Latin accents of his youth, now urgent with the immediacy of his message as he pleads for his listeners to let the Lord into their lives. "I stand at your door and knock," Palau says, his voice as deep and entreating as the lines on his forehead, his hands—never still—now open wide in pleading, now knocking for emphasis on the wooden lectern. ... Standing with his arms up, beseeching, like a humble servant presenting his master's case, he pleads: "If you open the door"—he opens the left side of his jacket as if rending his own heart—"let Jesus into your heart." He makes his case as if this moment is the crucial one that could change the world.[435]

Palau is not as dynamic and energetic as Billy Sunday, who "jumped off the stage, slammed his hand on the pulpit, stood on tables, [and] contorted his body into a variety of stances."[436] But he uses more motions and gestures than his mentor, Billy Graham.[437]

Down-to-earth Illustrations

After some introductory remarks and the reading of Scripture, Palau normally begins his sermon with illustrations chosen for their relevancy to the particular audience. Without being contemporary and applicable to the life of the audience, illustrations cannot draw people's attention. The best way to achieve this is by using stories from everyday life.[438]

The sources of Palau's illustrations are diverse. He uses current information from newspapers, personal stories, the testimonies of others, real-life stories of his audiences, and so on.[439] Palau's search for relevant illustrations begins long before the launch of a campaign. He not only studies various issues related to earlier audiences but also searches for illustrations from the moment he lands at the airport of that city. He poses questions to taxi drivers, hotel desk clerks, restaurant waiters, and others to diagnose the spiritual condition of people and find suitable illustrations based on real life.[440]

The relevancy in Palau's use of illustrations is obvious. During his campaign in Scotland in 1981, for example, Palau quoted American pop-singer Bob Dylan's song, "Gotta Serve Somebody," which was familiar to his audience. After quoting the lyrics from the song, Palau stated, "Do you know, that is the message of the Bible. You and I must serve somebody. It may be the devil or it may be the Lord, but you and I must serve somebody. Who do you serve tonight? Do you serve the Lord or do you serve the devil? There are no other options."[441]

Conclusion

The most important role of the evangelist is to preach the gospel. With this conviction, Luis Palau has preached again and again the same messages of salvation, all of which are centered around Jesus' vicarious death and resurrection. His message has been positive, with an emphasis on God's love rather than His wrath, leaving the conviction of sin to the Holy Spirit. This approach has inevitably resulted in criticism, something Palau may be unable to escape unless he preaches a more balanced message.

The most significant characteristic of Palau's preaching is relevancy. This is evident in his choice of language, topics, and illustrations. In many respects Palau has been influenced by Billy Graham, although he uses more vigorous gestures and more humor. The resemblances between the two evangelists include their Christ-centered messages, choices of topics and illustrations, problem-solution approaches, and even Palau's adoption of Graham's frequent phrase "the Bible says." Palau has preached the gospel with both passion and compassion. His evangelistic preaching has been the most essential part of his campaigns.

Endnotes

366 William Brad Morrow, "Mass Evangelism and Its Effect on Church Planting: A Filipino Case Study" (Ph.D. diss., Southern Baptist Theological Seminary, 2003), 26.

367 Luis Palau and Timothy Robnett, *Telling the Story: Evangelism for the Next Generation* (Ventura, CA: Regal Books, 2006), 77.

368 Luis Palau and Mike Umlandt, *The Only Hope for America: The Transforming Power of the Gospel of Jesus Christ* (Wheaton, IL: Crossway Books, 1996), 76.

369 For general references on evangelistic preaching, see C. H. Dodd, *The Apostolic Preaching and Its Development* (London, England: Hodder and

Stoughton, 1936); Martyn Lloyd-Jones, *Preaching and Preachers* (Grand Rapids: Zondervan, 1972); Lloyd M. Perry and John R. Strubhar, *Evangelistic Preaching* (Chicago, IL: Moody Press, 1979); Craig A. Loscalzo, *Evangelistic Preaching That Connects* (Downers Grove, IL: InterVarsity, 1995).

370 Luis Palau, "The Evangelist Has a Strategy for Harvest," in *The Mission of an Evangelist,* ed. J. D. Douglas (Minneapolis, MN: World Wide Publications, 2001), 234.

371 Palau, "God's Blueprint for the Scottish Home," in Luis Palau, *Our God Reigns: Scotland Messages,* ed. David L. Jones (London: Luis Palau Team [UK] Trust, 1981), 31.

372 Susan Holton and David L. Jones, *Spirit Aflame: Luis Palau's Mission to London* (Grand Rapids: Baker Book House, 1985), 97. During Mission to London Rev. Michael Cole, minister of All Saints Church, Woodford Wells, made a similar statement: "The first thing that a minister recognizes in Luis Palau is his faithfulness to the teaching of Scripture. Luis has been doing straight Bible exposition each night. I'm amazed that up to 15,000 people will show up in London today to hear a man simply expounding the Scriptures." Ibid., 185.

373 Janet Chismar, "Luis Palau Heats Up New England," *Religion Today*, 6 June 2001 [online]; accessed 12 July 2008; available from http://www.crosswalk.com/news/religiontoday/525940/; Internet.

374 John Pollock, *Billy Graham: Evangelist to the World* (San Francisco, CA: Harper and Row, Publishers, 1979), 118–19. To this comment, Graham later responded that it is not humiliating but exhilarating to preach the same gospel.

375 Palau, *The Only Hope for America*, 76.

376 Jim Mills, "An Interview with Luis Palau," *Discipleship Journal* 12 (November/December 1982): 42.

377 Palau, "The Evangelist Has a Strategy," 234.

378 Palau, *Telling the Story*, 82. Palau also states, "We may be angry, but we should never impose our personal feelings on the way we present God."

379 Ibid., 80. Here Palau quotes Luke 2:10: "I bring you good news of great joy that will be for all the people."

380 Ibid., 83–84. Lisa McGinley of the *New London Day* records her interview with Palau: "People already feel unworthy, he said, his mission is to make them feel happy." William K. Piotrowski, "Evangelism in a Chilly Climate," *Religion in the News* 4, no. 2 (Summer 2001): 29.

381 Palau, *Telling the Story*, 82, 84. To the plausible criticism against preaching the good news without the bad news, Palau replies, "Leave that [bad news] to the Holy Spirit. John 16:8 says that 'He will convict the world of guilt in regard to sin and righteousness and judgment.' We have been sent out to proclaim the good news. We have not been sent out to convict the world of sin, righteousness and judgment. That is the work of the Holy Spirit, and the third person of the blessed trinity is constantly at His convicting work." Ibid., 83-84.

382 Palau, *The Only Hope for America*, 79. Palau notes that Moody preached from John 3:16 night after night. Cf. Palau also observes, "Because Moody was totally consecrated to God, and because his message was simple, nondenominational, and based on God's love and not His wrath, he was used to help unite the church and lead thousands to Christ." David L. Jones and Luis Palau, *Scottish Fires of Revival* (Cupertino, CA: D.I.M.E. Publishers, 1980), 81.

383 William Glyn Evans, *Profiles of Revival Leaders* (Nashville, TN: Broadman Press, 1976), 64. Evans notes, "Other doctrines appeared in his messages—atonement, the Bible, the sovereignty of God, Christian service, rewards—but God's love was the cornerstone of everything he uttered."

384 According to Biblical Discernment Ministries, "So not to offend with the Gospel, Palau is, in effect, saying that he preaches a watered-down gospel that is no gospel at all." Chismar, "Luis Palau Heats Up New England."

385 For instance, Jesus often preached on hell. See, for examples, Matthew 5:22; 5:29–30; 11:20–24; 23:33. For the full list of references on Jesus' utterances on hell, see *Dictionary of Jesus and the Gospels*, ed. Joel B. Green, Scot McKnight, and Howard Marshall (Downers Grove, IL: InterVarsity Press, 1992), s.v. "Hell in the Gospels," by J. Lunde.

386 See "Style and Delivery of Preaching" for relevancy of illustrations in Palau's preaching.

387 Palau, *Telling the Story*, 85. The best example of this relevancy, according to Palau, can be found in the preaching of the apostle Paul. As recorded in 1 Corinthians 9:19–22, Paul approached his audience with different topics relevant to their life: "When he wanted to lead a Jew to Christ, he talked about topics of relevance to the Jewish way of thinking. When he talked to the Gentiles, he became like a Gentile." Based on Acts 17, Palau also observes, "Remarkably, Paul could adapt his message to reach any and every audience. In one week, he could preach in the Jewish synagogue (see Acts 17:17a), in the marketplace (see Acts 17:17b), and then to the intelligentsia of Athens (see Acts 17:18–31). His sermon to the Areopagus demonstrates our need to target our presentation of the same gospel message to the specific groups before us." Ibid., 86.

388 Holton and Jones, *Spirit Aflame*, 100.

389 Michael Green, *Evangelism in the Early Church* (Grand Rapids: Wm. B. Eerdmans Publishing Company, 1970), 195–96.

390 John R. W. Stott, *Between Two Worlds* (Grand Rapids: Eerdmans, 1982), 144.

391 Palau's preaching had been expository sermons in the past when campaigns lasted longer than now. This can be best observed in *Our God Reigns*, which is the collection of Palau's messages during his British tour in 1981. But with transition to a shorter period of campaigns, his preaching has been more topical than expository. Palau himself acknowledged this change in his interview by the author. He still preaches an expository style of sermon in the settings other than evangelistic campaigns but normally preaches topical sermons with a need-based approach in evangelistic campaigns. Palau, interview by author, Frisco, Texas, June 27, 2008.

392 For the best example of a sermon based on this approach, see Luis Palau, "A Message from Luis Palau: Jesus Christ Is for Today," in Holton and Jones, *Spirit Aflame*, 214–26. Relevancy of Christ to every area of human life and society has been an often-repeated theme in Palau's preaching.

393 Rodney Clapp, "Luis Palau Invades the University of Wisconsin: Is the Time Ripe for More Campus Evangelism?" *Christianity Today*, 19 March 1982, 38. This event was organized by students at the University of Wisconsin, and Palau was invited to speak.

394 Ibid.

395 James Kilgore observed the same approach in Graham's evangelistic preaching: "Whether a sermon has two, three, or four points, there are two elemental steps in Graham's preaching. First, he shows the need of relationship to Christ, and second, he declares the biblical 'plan' for establishing that relationship. ... Usually the first part of a sermon is aimed at arousing a sense of guilt, fear, or estrangement from God. The second part calls for a decision that will free from fear, remove guilt, and restore relationship with God." James E. Kilgore, *Billy Graham the Preacher* (New York: Exposition Press, 1968), 27–28.

396 William Martin, *A Prophet with Honor: The Billy Graham Story* (New York: William Morrow and Company, Inc., 1991), 28. From Graham's San Francisco sermon on April 27, 1958, Kilgore also observed: "He [Billy Graham]... begins to speak of national and international problems—fear, the arms race, the uncertain peace, economics, technological, racial, and youth problems, tensions, revolt. ... The point is that things are worse than they were before. In a sense it is a note of doom." Kilgore, *Billy Graham the Preacher*, 27.

397 Martin, *Prophet with Honor*, 29.

398 Palau, *Telling the Story*, 86.

399 Ibid., 32.

400 Bryan Green, *The Practice of Evangelism* (New York: Charles Scribner's Sons, 1951), 106.

401 Palau presented humanity's problems in these areas in his sermon "A Message from Luis Palau: Jesus Christ Is for Today." Holton and Jones, *Spirit Aflame*, 214–26.

402 Luis Palau, "Is God Relevant?" *The Plain Truth* (March/April 1998): 60.

403 Palau, "Rich, Moral and Yet Lost," in *Our God Reigns*, 9–10.

404 Palau, "A Message from Luis Palau: Jesus Christ Is for Today," 218.

405 Ibid., 220–21.

406 Ibid., 221–22.

407 Holton and Jones, *Spirit Aflame*, 97.

408 Palau, interview by the author, May 9, 2008.

409 Luis Palau, "First Love: The Original Plan," sermon delivered October 2003 at Key Arena in Seattle (Portland, OR: LPA, 2003), DVD.

410 Luis Palau, "What Is a Real Christian?" sermon delivered at Bellingham, Washington (Portland, OR: LPA, n.d.), compact disk.

411 Palau, *Telling the Story*, 24, 76.

412 Luis Palau, "The Great Commission," in *Seven Promises of a Promise Keeper*, rev. exp. ed. Bill McCartney, Greg Laurie, and Jack Hayford (Nashville, TN: Thomas Nelson, 1999), 196.

413 Palau, interview by the author, May 9, 2008.

414 Ibid.

415 Roy J. Fish, *Giving a Good Invitation* (Nashville, TN: Broadman, 1974), 9–19. Fish argues that invitations are sound biblically, historically, and psychologically. According to Fish, "The resurrection of the public invitation occurred in the mid-eighteenth century" by Separate Baptists and early Methodists, and it was adopted by many evangelists in a number of different forms thereafter. Ibid., 15–16. For examples of invitations recorded in the New Testament, see Palau, *The Only Hope for America*, 131–32. For more detailed discussion on invitation, see William Oscar Thompson Jr., "The Public Invitation as a Method of Evangelism: Its Origin and Development" (Ph.D. diss., Southwestern Baptist Theological Seminary, 1979); R. Alan Streett, *The Effective Invitation* (Old Tappan, NJ: Fleming H. Revell Company, 1984).

416 Palau's first public invitation occurred in Oncativo, a town of about twelve thousand in the province of Córdoba, Argentina, on May 25, 1960. More than three dozen people invited Christ into their hearts as their Savior and Lord on that night. Luis Palau and David Sanford, *Luis Palau: Calling America and the Nations to Christ* (Nashville, TN: Thomas Nelson, Inc., 1994; rev. 2000), 58–59.

417 Palau, *The Only Hope for America*, 135.

418 Palau, *Telling the Story*, 88.

419 Palau, "The Evangelist Has a Strategy," 234.

420 Palau, *Telling the Story*, 89.

421 Palau, *The Only Hope for America*, 81. According to Palau, instantaneous conversion was called "sudden conversion" by Calvin and also "instant salvation" by Moody. See also Palau and Sanford, *Calling America and the Nations*, 188.

422 Ibid.

423 Palau and Sanford, *Calling America and the Nations*, 21.

424 James D. Douglas, "God's Good Gaucho and Roundup Time in Glasgow," *Christianity Today*, 17 July 1981, 90.

425 Norman Lymberry, "Food for Thought," Hemel Hempstead Gazette, July 27, 1984; quoted in Holton and Jones, *Spirit Aflame*, 123.

426 Anne Townsend, "Luis Palau at Wembley," Church of England Newspaper, October 28, 1983, p. 1; quoted in Holton and Jones, *Spirit Aflame*, 163.

427 Holton and Jones, *Spirit Aflame*, 162.

428 Travis Dean Fleming, "An Analysis of Bill Bright's Theology and Methodology of Evangelism and Discipleship" (Ph.D. diss., Southern Baptist Theological Seminary, 2003), 125–26. See also David E. Aune, *Revelation 1–5*, Word Biblical Commentary, vol. 52 (Dallas, TX: Word, 1997), 254; Robert H.

Mounce, *The Book of Revelation*, The New International Commentary on the New Testament, rev. ed. (Grand Rapids: William B. Eerdmans, 1998), 113.

429 Perry and Strubhar, *Evangelistic Preaching*, 16.

430 Palau, *Telling the Story*, 86.

431 Ibid., 76.

432 Holton and Jones, *Spirit Aflame*, 29. Many others also acknowledged the plain, simple, and contemporary nature of Palau's language in preaching during Mission to London. See, ibid., 68, 71, 96.

433 William G. McLoughlin, *Modern Revivalism: Charles Grandison Finney to Billy Graham* (New York: Ronald Press, 1959), 429. See also Evans, *Profiles of Revival Leaders*, 85–88.

434 Sura Rubenstein, "Preacher to the World: Oregon's Luis Palau," *Northwest Magazine*, 15 September 1985, 6.

435 Ibid., 7.

436 Stewart Holloway, "Hit the Trail! The Life and Ministry of Billy Sunday" (seminar paper, EVANG 7642—The History of Spiritual Awakening, Spring 2003, photocopy), 18. Cf. According to William Evans, Billy Sunday's actions during his preaching were unique compared to those of other major evangelists. He observed, "Edwards read calmly, Finney reasoned with burning eyes, Moody dramatized energetically but restrainedly, and Billy Graham stands and preaches with intensity. But Billy Sunday, as Townsend says, 'is action incarnate.'" Evans, *Profiles of Revival Leaders*, 88–89.

437 While comparing Palau's preaching with Graham's, Sura Rubenstein observed that "In contrast to Graham, the forceful and decorous elder stateman of mass evangelism, Palau is casual, almost folksy, delivering his message with all the genuine concern, sincerity, good humor and familiar passion of one good friend cajoling another to do the right thing. At times, he is almost a Christian stand-up comic, using a sharp wit and the daily news to bring home his points about biblical living." Rubenstein, "Preacher to the World," 6.

438 Palau, *Telling the Story*, 87. Here Palau comments on Billy Graham's use of illustration: "Billy Graham often quotes from newspapers, citing events and personalities of the day, to highlight the urgency and relevance of his message." Ibid. A knowledgeable preacher will never ignore the culture of his audience. In fact, Billy Graham is a good example in this respect. Billy Kim, Graham's interpreter for his campaign in Seoul, Korea, in 1973, which had the largest single crowd in Graham's ministry with more than 1 million, recalled that Graham was very careful choosing the language and words for his message. Checking the validity of every illustration and allusion, Graham often asked Kim, "Will it fit the culture?" Pollock, *Billy Graham: Evangelist to the World*, 56.

439 For some examples of Palau's illustrations, see Luis Palau, "Illustrations Help Listeners See the Truth." *Preaching* 13 (November/December 1997): 54–56.

440 Palau, interview by the author, May 9, 2008.

441 Palau, "Our God Reigns," in *Our God Reigns*, 55.

CHAPTER 7

EVANGELISTIC STRATEGY: CAMPAIGNS, PART 1

In more than four decades Luis Palau has conducted more than 480 evangelistic campaigns and rallies, leading 1,080,079 people to profess Jesus as their Savior and Lord.[442] The evangelistic campaign is where Palau's heart and passion lies. Various issues pertinent to evangelistic campaigns are examined in this section.

Luis Palau Association

Importance of Team

Working as a team to fulfill the Great Commission is one of the vital strategies both in the New Testament and in subsequent Christian history.[443] Drawing attention to the facts that Jesus called the twelve disciples and worked with them as a team and that the apostle Paul always cooperated with other people for his evangelistic work, Luis Palau contends, "Throughout history, some of the most solid work has been done by people who worked as a team."[444] His statement at Amsterdam '86 is noteworthy in this regard:

> Sometimes financial or personnel problems tempt me to think, "I could do this on my own with far less stress." But the truth is, I need the wisdom, strength, and encouragement

> that come from a united team effort. … Ask God to give you a godly team. It may not be a very big team—you may not need a very big team. But as an evangelist, you need others to share your vision, your love for the lost and, quite frankly, your work load.[445]

For a successful evangelistic team there should be a clear purpose, a working strategy, and specific goals that are measurable as well as achievable.[446] In addition, according to Robnett, there should be at least three essential teams within the larger evangelistic team: prayer team, board of directors with senior advisors, and ministry team. Robnett also cautions, "Of course, none of these teams will experience healthy growth without a strong leader."[447]

Already in the early stages of his ministry, Palau recognized the value of teamwork. With some friends from his local church, Palau proclaimed the gospel through tent meetings in Córdoba, Argentina. Later on some American missionaries, including Bruce Woodman and Bill Fasig, joined his team.[448] But it was not until 1967 that Palau had his own evangelistic team with full-time staff. While working for Overseas Crusades, Palau conducted his first major campaign in Bogota, Colombia, in 1966, preaching to twenty thousand people. In the following year he formed his own evangelistic team within Overseas Crusades.[449]

Luis Palau Evangelistic Association (LPEA)

While serving as the president of OC International, Palau and his evangelistic team conducted many evangelistic campaigns. However, it became burdensome for Palau to manage his own team of thirty staff members while acting as the president of OC. At Palau's request, OC decided to separate Palau's evangelistic team from OC International. Finally, the Luis Palau Evangelistic Association was launched in October 1978 with its headquarters in Portland, Oregon.[450] Today it is one of the largest mass evangelism ministries in the world, with more than one hundred full-time staff members working at its headquarters in Oregon, as well as in its regional offices around the world. Today the ministry is known as the Luis Palau Association (LPA).

Like other organizations, the Luis Palau Association has greatly benefited from key team members who have played an important leadership role in shaping the ministry. Robnett mentions three such individuals, men who have been with Palau from the beginning and who still work with him today: Jim Williams, who directs Latin American ministries, having started working with Palau in 1968; David L. Jones, who oversees a variety of media, business, and operational issues and serves as vice president of corporate affairs; and Doug Steward, who oversees multi-media productions. Within the past two decades three of Palau's four sons—Kevin, Keith, and Andrew—also have served and continue to play a vital leadership role.[451] (In 2010 Kevin Palau was named President of the Luis Palau Association).

The threefold mission of LPA, drafted by Palau in the beginning, has not changed[452]: The ministry exists to proclaim the gospel, mobilize churches, and equip the next generation of evangelists. Palau has remained faithful to that mission.

Planning and Preparation

Palau is passionate about teamwork and preparation. People witness thrilling and moving moments when multitudes of people come forward to profess Jesus as their Savior and Lord during evangelistic campaigns. This exciting scene, however, cannot be created without a long period of planning.

Choosing the Location

Luis Palau normally targets big cities that are unevangelized. It was originally Graham's advice for him to aim at big cities. In their first meeting Graham directed Palau, "Go to the big cities, Luis, as Paul did. Leave the smaller towns to be evangelized by those who will be stimulated as they observe you preaching in the metropolitan campaigns."[453]

Targeting big cities for evangelization is both biblical and practical. It is biblical because it resembles the strategy of the apostle Paul. Many Pauline scholars support the idea that Paul had a strategy for selecting the locations for his missionary journeys. Paul deliberately focused his ministry on urban areas. Roland Allen observed that Paul visited the cities that were "centres of Roman administration, of Greek civilization, of Jewish influence, or of some commercial importance."[454] Michael Green also writes this:

> The Acts of the Apostles records his [Paul's] visit to city after city of importance: Antioch, the third city in the Empire; Philippi, the Roman *colonia*; Thessalonica, the principal metropolis of Macedonia; Corinth, the capital of Greece under Roman administration; Paphos, the centre of Roman rule in Cyprus; Ephesus, the principal city of the province of Asia.[455]

Targeting urban areas is practical as well. As Palau points out, more people are moving "from rural to urban areas," resulting in explosive population growth in big cities.[456] Palau also asserts that "the untouchables" in massive cities can be reached through campaigns: "High-rise apartment buildings are nearly impossible to enter for personal witness or the placing of gospel literature, much less a face-to-face presentation of the gospel itself. Coupled with the united action of believers throughout the city, modern mass campaign evangelism can have a penetrating effect."[457]

After receiving invitations from a host, Palau and his team determine "the worthiness and logical compatibility" of that region for conducting a campaign.[458] The most important criterion for deciding the locale has been the leading of the Holy Spirit.[459] Palau states, "Admittedly, sometimes our team's choices defy natural logic. … In my opinion, it's futile to even ask, *Shouldn't we wait to accept only the biggest and best possible crusade invitations?* [emphasis in original]. That's absurd. Our team's conviction is that we must make the most of every year the Lord gives us."[460]

Palau also maintains a prayer list of the cities for which he prays regularly. When an invitation comes from a city on his prayer list, he takes it very seriously and immediately responds, regardless of the size of the inviting body.[461] Besides these spiritual criteria, as a rule of thumb Palau has two other conditions: First, there should be more than one hundred churches that have signed on the invitation letter to host a campaign. Second, at least 10 percent of the total budget must be pledged from the beginning to test their degree of seriousness.[462] After receiving an official invitation from the local churches, preparation for an upcoming campaign ordinarily takes from twelve to eighteen months.[463]

Mobilizing Local Churches

Successful evangelistic campaigns require careful planning, involving as many churches as possible. Active participation, both of spiritual leaders and of local Christians, is vital in this process. If local churches are not actively engaged, the campaign will only be a waste of valuable time and money. While speaking of the importance of teamwork and cooperation in conjunction with local churches, Palau said this:

> Evangelists need other kinds of teams besides their immediate ministry team. We especially need to work with local churches. This is all part of the strategy for the harvest. An evangelistic event won't happen without the support and work and prayers of the local church. New believers need to be incorporated immediately and effectively into the Body of Christ. You'll need as many contacts as possible to do this.[464]

The first step of mobilizing local churches is building a partnership with local ministers.[465] The purpose of this partnership is manifold. In reference to the campaigns in Latin America, Palau states, "We meet with ministers to bring spiritual cleaning and awakening within the leadership, to give church-growth vision and goals, and to try to set up church-growth plans along with crusade evangelism."[466] Along with the spiritual preparation and strategic plans comes the formation of various committees. The traditional campaigns used to have more than a dozen committees. After changing the format of campaigns from traditional to contemporary style, however, LPA has reduced the number of committees by half for streamlined administration.[467]

The second step is mobilizing local believers. The success of an evangelistic campaign depends in large part on the successful recruitment of volunteers because a campaign requires thousands of helping hands. For instance, prior to Tampa Festival in 2006, about eleven thousand volunteers were trained.[468] As in the case of local pastors, the mobilization of believers is preceded by spiritual preparation and training. In Palau's view the spiritual awakening of believers should involve "at least a measure of cleansing and teaching on the indwelling Christ and the fullness of the Spirit among the Christians."[469]

Prayer

According to Sterling Huston, Billy Graham often emphasized that there are three important elements for evangelistic campaigns: "Prayer, prayer, and prayer."[470] Prayer is essential for any form of evangelism because evangelism is the work of the Holy Spirit. Huston asserts, "Effective Crusades are not built on persuasion, personality, or promotion. They are built by depending on the Holy Spirit to do a lasting work."[471] In fact, campaign evangelism needs more prayer than other evangelistic endeavor since the destiny of multitudes of souls is at stake.[472]

Prayer characterizes Palau's evangelistic campaigns as well; from beginning to end, prayer permeates each campaign. While describing prayer as the first step of evangelistic campaigns, Kevin Palau goes so far as to say, "Don't go to a place unless people have been praying to see God work in their area."[473] John McWilliam, who joined Palau's team in 1967 and has served as director of international crusades, explained the process and importance of forming prayer groups for campaigns:

> The most important element to start with is prayer. The first objective is to establish by faith with local pastors and leaders the number of prayer cells to be formed throughout the city. … Here they pray for the crusade, for non-Christian friends and for their community. The aim is to cover the whole city with prayer cells. Prayer is also carried out in nights of prayer as well as prayer chains. Once people sign up to lead prayer cells, they must receive periodic information from

> crusade headquarters via the prayer committee. There must be communication with these cells to keep track of how they are functioning. We have always seen the effect of prayer in our mass crusades and when it is lacking it is always felt.[474]

Mission to London is a good example of the pivotal role of prayer. Before the campaign began, Palau urged Christians around the world to pray for Mission to London, asserting, "Before we talk to London about God, we must talk to God about London."[475] As a result, Christians worldwide prayed for London, and prayer meetings throughout Britain were organized under a prayer committee.[476]

One of the most effective prayer strategies was "prayer triplets in which each individual prays regularly with two other Christians. After each shares the names of three friends with spiritual needs, the group prays for these nine friends, Mission to London, Luis Palau, Mission England, Billy Graham, and one another."[477] Various prayer strategies such as prayer triplets, prayer walking, a twenty-four hour prayer hotline, and others have been adopted and utilized by LPA for each campaign.

Promotion

Promotion is another essential part of the preparation for a successful campaign. Some people may feel uncomfortable with spending large sums of money for promotion.[478] To such individuals the following statement by Billy Graham about a half century ago is noteworthy: "I am selling the greatest product in the world; why shouldn't it be promoted as well as soap?"[479] About a year later Graham elaborated on this point in *Look* (7 February 1956): "In every other area of life we take for granted publicity, bigness and modern techniques. Why should not the church employ some of these methods that are used by big business or labor unions to promote their products or causes, in order to win men for Christ?"[480]

Luis Palau is well aware of the importance of promotion. In an interview with *Christianity Today* he pointed out lack of promotion as the reason for low attendance at the University of Wisconsin in Madison, saying, "I was the invited guest speaker, not the organizer.

... Therefore attendance was lower than I would have wished. To get the attention of 40,000 students, you've got to make a lot of noise, really shake it up. Next time I think we'd be more involved in the publicity."[481] Conversely, when 850,000 people attended Palau's two-day Buenos Aires Festival in 2008, the evangelist noted that the massive publicity had contributed to the record attendance. Some media reports even had the attendance exceeding one million. The publicity saturated the city.

Campaign promotion has two phases. First, promotion begins within the participating local churches. Kevin Palau points out that many Christians are not enthusiastic about evangelistic campaigns and that it takes a lot of effort to explain the benefits of a united, citywide effort. To stir their interest and passion for evangelism, LPA conducts many church presentations, urging every local church to present the upcoming events during its Sunday worship services. LPA also provides a brief video clip showing the actual scenes and excitement of campaigns.[482]

The second phase involves making the events known to nonbelievers. Individuals in participating churches spread the word and invite friends to the events.[483] In addition, the campaign is broadcast through various media, such as newspapers, television, radio, yard signs, bumper stickers, sign boards, and mailings.[484] Although public advertisements make people aware of the campaign, awareness alone does not necessarily bring them to the events. According to Huston, people are more likely to come to events on the basis of personal invitation, not publicity or advertising.[485]

The effective use of promotion in a Luis Palau campaign was researched by William H. Swatos, Jr., who conducted a telephone survey prior to, during, and after Palau's campaign in a Midwestern metropolitan area in 1990. The purpose of the survey was to determine the effectiveness of promotion for Luis Palau, who was not a well-known public figure at that time. The survey result confirmed the strategic role of promotion for campaigns. Swatos reported that "The findings show that the organizers of the event were successful in raising familiarity with Palau's name from less than ten to over forty percent of the population" and that among the most effective tools for promotion were "the newspapers, invitations hung on residence doors, and yard signs on supporters' homes and businesses."[486]

Mission to London is one of the best examples of promotion. In McWilliam's judgment, London is "one of the most difficult and cynical press areas of the world," but Mission to London received "the most extensive press coverage ever"[487] in Palau's ministry. The promotion was handled by a professional sales promotion agency, a subsidiary of Saatchi & Saatchi, which utilized every means available to communicate the campaign, including newspapers, posters, billboards, leaflets, and mass transit.[488] The promotion was so successful that the British weekly *Punch* reported, "One can hardly move around the City at the moment without being collared by bright-eyed strangers who try to persuade you that life cannot be worth living until one has heard the preachings of this evangelistic chappie, Luis Palau."[489]

Finances

One concern regarding evangelistic campaigns is the enormous amount of money they cost. The total budget for a Luis Palau campaign in the United States ranges from $700,000 to $3.5 million,[490] while most campaigns fall into the range of between $1 million to $2 million.[491] Campaigns in large cities, such as one in Washington, D.C., in 2005, cost $3.5 million,[492] while another in Tampa in 2006 cost $3 million.[493]

How does LPA raise the enormous amount of funds when no offerings are taken at the festival? First, Palau insists that at least 10 percent of finances for a campaign be pledged in advance from the participating churches—this tests the seriousness of churches for a campaign.[494] After changing the campaign format to festival style, LPA also accepts donations from corporate sponsors that are friendly to the Christian cause. In Kevin Palau's assessment, the involvement of corporate sponsors, such as Interstate Batteries, Thriftway Stores, Johnson & Johnson, and others "not only provides financial help, but also puts a 'civic' face on the event."[495] Contrary to popular belief, however, these donations consist of only 10 to 20 percent of the total budget. The rest of the funds, which represent the biggest portion, come from donations from individuals.[496]

More often than not finances have been a matter of faith. As McWilliam stated, "It has been our experience that when God's people are motivated and involved in God's work, they themselves will provide the resources needed to do the job."[497] One such case occurred during Palau's 1975 campaign in Nicaragua. Palau and his team had budgeted for only limited radio coverage. But with faith they enlarged the vision to utilize a satellite radio network and television broadcasting to reach twenty Spanish-speaking countries and 200 million Spanish-speaking people with the gospel. This plan cost them $200,000, but God answered their prayer and provided the finances.[498] Palau challenges other evangelists with confidence: "God will make a way, even though you may not have all the contacts and cash you think you need to do it. Just say, 'Lord, would you use me?' and take Jesus Christ to the city."[499]

Reaching Unbelievers Through Friendship Evangelism

Evangelistic campaigns can succeed only when believers are motivated and equipped to share the message of the gospel. Quoting Archbishop William Temple, "We cannot separate the evangelization of those without from the rekindling of devotion of those within." Leighton Ford put it this way: "Evangelism must begin among those within the framework of the church before it can spread to those without, and this is where mass evangelism can be uniquely useful."[500] Luis Palau and his team have been committed throughout their campaigns to the training of believers in personal evangelism. In Palau's view, evangelism training prior to and during evangelistic campaigns gives many Christians the first-time opportunity to lead someone else to Christ. His contention is this:

> During a crusade, a sense of spiritual power, the excitement, the harvest going on around them, and the unusual movement of God in the city causes even timid Christians to discover that personal evangelism is the most exciting experience in the Christian life. For many believers who were indecisive about sharing their faith, the crusade marks the beginning of a lifetime witness.[501]

As Robnett mentions, encouraging and motivating believers for evangelism must be accompanied by equipping them with the necessary tools to share the gospel.[502] Emphasis on evangelism normally begins five to eight months prior to campaigns. LPA asks participating churches to highlight evangelism one Sunday each month. The organization provides monthly bulletin inserts with different emphases, along with a tract by Luis Palau addressing a particular topic, such as "youth, adults, children, men, divorce, etc."[503]

The main thrust of evangelistic strategy for Palau's team has been friendship evangelism.[504] Effective evangelism is based on relationships. Most nonbelievers come to believe in Jesus because of the influence of a Christian friend or relative, and this has been true in campaign evangelism as well.[505] An LPA survey shows that more than 70 percent of inquirers who respond to the invitation have been invited to the campaigns by friends or relatives.[506] The best-known friendship evangelism program has been called Operation Andrew. Before a campaign launches, each friendship evangelist is challenged to pray for his or her family members, neighbors, friends, and colleagues and to invite them to evangelistic events. This method has been used powerfully for many years in the ministry of Luis Palau and his team around the world.[507] Although its name has been changed over time, first to Partners in Evangelism and later to Advocates, the concept and principles of friendship evangelism remain the same.[508]

Securing and training friendship evangelists is one of the key factors to the success of a campaign.[509] Statistics from the Church on the Way, which participated in Palau's campaign in Los Angeles's San Fernando Valley in 1994, confirms this point. Scott Bauer observed a striking difference in a rate of evangelism between two groups of people, both of whom participated in campaigns within the Church on the Way: "Those who committed to Friendship Evangelism partnership had a rate of evangelism which was .658 higher per person than the non-Friendship Evangelism individuals—65.8 more decisions per 100 Friendship Evangelism partners."[510] Thus participating churches in campaigns must attempt to enroll more believers in friendship evangelism programs. Furthermore, when the campaign is over the fruits of friendship evangelists must be preserved by connecting the converts to local churches.

Bridging New Converts to Local Churches

Critics of mass evangelism allege that the results of campaigns are short-lived. And indeed, without proper follow-up evangelistic campaigns will be only events. Due to much emphasis on and deliberate efforts to preserve new converts, many inquirers in Palau's campaigns have been successfully connected to and nurtured by local churches.[511] Following Leighton Ford's divisions in the campaign process, "preparation, penetration, and preservation," Palau clarifies, "The *preservation and continuation* [emphasis in original] phase seeks to edify, disciple, incorporate, and see spiritual reproduction in those who come to Christ during and immediately following the crusade."[512]

Palau's special concern for individual converts in mass evangelism coincides with that of some evangelists in previous generations. In his thesis on major vocational evangelists, Sung Ho Kang identified this concern for individuals as one of the great common methodologies among the celebrated evangelists in the past. He states, "Finney, for instance, invited individuals to the 'anxious bench,' Moody to the 'inquiry room,' and Sunday to the 'sawdust trail.' Chapman also had concern for the specialization of individuals."[513] Evangelists must strive to bridge new converts to local churches for nurture. Palau has been faithful to this principle. He has trained counselors and assimilated new converts into local churches through a carefully organized follow-up plan.

Training of Counselors

Counselors play a pivotal role in bridging inquirers to local churches. The goal of counselors is "To connect one-on-one with every Festival [campaign] inquirer onsite and refer them to an appropriate participating church who will follow up promptly and effectively."[514] LPA used to train local Christians who wanted to serve as counselors all together.

More recently, Palau's organization has been using a DVD kit and the internet for this purpose. Each participating church can train its own volunteers prior to a campaign in meetings facilitated by a pastor or small-group leader.[515] During the campaigns counselors distribute and collect response cards; confirm the decisions of inquirers; pray with them; and give new believers a booklet titled *Growing Faith*, which contains the Gospel of John, Bible studies for new believers, and an article by Palau, "What Is a Real Christian?"[516]

The process of follow-up used to begin with the formation of nurture groups prior to the launch of a campaign. According to McWilliam, nurture groups are "small Bible study or discipling cells formed throughout the city."[517] These groups provided the best environment in which new converts could get acquainted with other Christians and glean basic knowledge of the Christian faith. Since most churches today have their own small groups, nurture groups are no longer being formed, but decision makers are being encouraged to join established small groups.[518]

Assimilation of New Believers into Local Churches

After people invite Jesus into their heart by praying with Palau, the task of the campaign team is to build a bridge between inquirers and the local churches. As Robnett comments, "Our job as evangelists goes only so far, but the spiritual life of every individual who accepts Christ at one of our events has just begun."[519] During a campaign response cards are collected, counted, and sorted geographically each night, with the cards being broken into four categories: (1) churched inquirers or those who came with a friend from a participating church, (2) unchurched inquirers who have listed no friend, (3) out-of-town inquirers, and (4) incomplete cards for research.[520] Inquirers are referred to local participating churches according to their indication on response cards. If they are not related to any church, they will be referred to appropriate churches as judged by geographical and ethnic elements.[521]

After inquirers have been referred to local churches, the primary responsibility for follow-up rests with those churches. However, LPA continues to monitor the status of follow-up and sends inquirers helpful advice and materials for their growth in the Christian faith. The general follow-up timeline after an English-language campaign is as follows:[522]

Week 1

From LPA: Inquirers receive first email from Palau, with links to several websites, blogs, and devotionals that will help them begin to grow in Christ.

From Church: Churches call those referred to them.

Week 2

From LPA: Inquirers receive CD ROM containing MP3 Bible, video "First Steps of Faith Series with Luis Palau," and other articles for their spiritual growth.

From Church: Church follow-up courses begin.[523]

Week 3

From LPA: Follow-up team begins contacting churches to confirm follow-up. LPA re-refers inquirers if churches have not implemented their plans.

Week 4

From LPA: Inquirers receive "Healthy Habits" offer from LPA.[524]

By training counselors and making deliberate efforts for follow-up, Palau has connected inquirers to local churches and has thus preserved his evangelistic fruits.

Endnotes

442 LPA, "Ministry Impact Statistics." These statistics are as of September 2008.

443 For instance, the apostle Paul, as an evangelist and missionary, always worked with a group of people in carrying out God's call. According to Lucien Legrand, Paul usually mentions his co-workers as his apostolic team at the beginning of his letters (1 Cor. 1:1; 2 Cor. 1:1; Phil. 1:1; Col. 1:1; 1 Thess. 1:1; 2 Thess. 1:1). Lucien Legrand, *Unity and Plurality: Mission in the Bible*, trans. Robert R. Barr (Maryknoll, NY: Orbis Books, 1990), 111. Earl Ellis also observes that in the book of Acts and Paul's writings, some one hundred names are associated with the apostle, and most of them are coworkers within his mission network. E. Earle Ellis, *Prophecy & Hermeneutic in Early Christianity* (Grand Rapids: Baker Books, 1993), 11.

444 Luis Palau, "Missions to the End of the World," in *Global Crossroads: Focusing the Strength of Local Churches*, ed. W. Harold Fuller, World Evangelical Fellowship (Mandaluyong, Philippines: OMF Literature Inc., 1998), 287.

445 Luis Palau, "The Evangelist and the Ministry of the Holy Spirit," in *The Calling of an Evangelist*, ed. J. D. Douglas (Minneapolis, MN: World Wide Publications, 1987), 138.

446 Luis Palau and Timothy Robnett, *Telling the Story: Evangelism for the Next Generation* (Ventura, CA: Regal Books, 2006), 137–38.

447 Robnett, *Telling the Story*, 70. Robnett also stresses the importance of teamwork for evangelists, as follows: "Why does the evangelist need a team? Because while evangelists have great gifts, they also have glaring weaknesses. Many evangelists have great abilities to inspire but are weak in following through on the details. Many evangelists can challenge and create vision but are awkward at developing plans and processes. … Evangelists need teams around them to bring balance, wisdom and focus." Ibid., 123.

448 Luis Palau and David Sanford, *Luis Palau: Calling America and the Nations to Christ* (Nashville, TN: Thomas Nelson, Inc., 1994; rev. 2000), 54.

449 Ibid., 95.

450 Ibid., 138. Besides Palau himself, original board members included Paul Garza, Dr. Hillis, Milton Klausmann, Duane Logsdon, and Don Ward. After a while, Dr. Ted Engstrom, executive director of World Vision, and Dr. Walter Smyth, vice president of international ministries for BGEA, joined the board.

451 Robnett, *Telling the Story*, 123–24.

452 See appendix 2, "LPA Mission Statement."

453 Luis Palau, "The Future of Mass Evangelism," in *Evangelism: The Next Ten Years*, ed. Sherwood Eliot Wirt (Waco, TX: Word Books, 1978), 156.

454 Roland Allen, *Missionary Methods: St. Paul's or Ours: A Study of the Church in the Four Provinces* (New York; Chicago, IL: Fleming H. Revell Company, 1913), 13. See also Martin Dibelius, *Paul*, ed. W. G. Kummel (London: Longmans, 1953), 69.

455 Michael Green, *Evangelism in the Early Church* (Grand Rapids: Wm. B. Eerdmans Publishing Company, 1970), 262.

456 Palau, "Future of Mass Evangelism," 158.

457 Ibid., 160.

458 William K. Piotrowski, "Evangelism in a Chilly Climate," *Religion in the News* 4, no. 2 (Summer 2001), 26.

459 Palau and Sanford, *Calling America and the Nations*, 160.

460 Ibid.

461 Palau, interview by the author, May 9, 2008.

462 Ibid.

463 Kevin Palau, interview by the author, interview by telephone, August 8, 2008.

464 Luis Palau, "The Evangelist Has a Strategy for Harvest," in *The Mission of an Evangelist*, ed. J. D. Douglas (Minneapolis, MN: World Wide Publications, 2001), 234.

465 From his own experiences in campaigns with Palau, Robnett states, "It has been my experience that when we work together with local pastors, we maximize the effectiveness of any evangelistic event." Robnett, *Telling the Story*, 42.

466 "Luis Palau: Evangelist to Three Worlds," *Christianity Today*, 20 May 1983, 32.

467 Kevin Palau, interview with the author, August 8, 2008. Cf. For discussion of evangelistic campaign organization in general, see E. J. Daniels, "Organizing for the Evangelistic Crusade" in *Evangelism Today and Tomorrow*, ed. Charles L. Chaney and Granville Watson (Nashville, TN: Broadman Press, 1993): 154–71.

468 Michelle Bearden, "Man with a Message," *Tampa Tribune*, 19 November 2006. Mission to London also shows a good example of the massive need for volunteers for campaigns. Peter Meadows, executive director of the campaign, announced that the campaign would need "6,000 choir members, 2,000 ushers, 15,000 bridge builders, 600 advisers, 75,000 counselors, 16,000 church representatives, 2,000 task force members, 300 QPR-bound coaches (buses) filled with unbelievers each night, and volunteers to visit 4 million homes to extend personal invitations to the mission." Susan Holton and David L. Jones, *Spirit Aflame: Luis Palau's Mission to London* (Grand Rapids: Baker Book House, 1985), 85. Palau's campaigns do not have choirs any longer. For the list of volunteers for recent campaigns, see http://www.festivalvolunteer.com.

469 "Evangelist to Three Worlds," 32.

470 Sterling W. Huston, *Crusade Evangelism*, rev. ed. (Minneapolis, MN: World Wide Publications, 1996), 42.

471 Ibid., 45. See John 6:63 and 16:8. Huston goes on to say, "If we could organize or persuade people into the Kingdom, we could also organize and persuade them out again. This kind of evangelism would merely be human manipulation. … If our trust is in human resources alone, we will only reap that which is human. But if our trust is in God and His work, we will reap a rich spiritual harvest from the Holy Spirit." Ibid.

472 Cf. New Testament scholar A. B. Bruce aptly observed that due to the prayer of disciples for ten days, about three thousand souls were saved on the first Pentecost Sunday. Delos Miles, *Introduction to Evangelism* (Nashville, TN: Broadman Press, 1983), 220.

473 Kevin Palau, "Cooperative Evangelism," in *The Mission of an Evangelist*, ed. J. D. Douglas (Minneapolis, MN: World Wide Publications, 2001), 319. As a matter of fact, prayer often precedes the plan for campaigns. One such case was Palau's Aberdeen campaign in 1979. Three years prior to the campaign, a small group of believers began to pray for spiritual awakening. After two years, more than seventy prayer groups were meeting weekly in Northeast Scotland. David L. Jones and Luis Palau, *Scottish Fires of Revival* (Cupertino, CA: D.I.M.E. Publishers, 1980), 47. McBride also observed that Mission Maine in 1999 was born out of prayer eight years prior to the campaign, when a group of local pastors gathered together to pray. Kevin T. McBride, "Retaking the Village Green: Building Strategic Partnerships for Evangelism That Work in New England" (D.Min. project, Gordon-Conwell Theological Seminary, 2001), 156.

474 John McWilliam, "Mass Evangelism: Reaching Your City in the Eighties," *Urban Mission* 3 (September 1985): 8. McWilliam also gives an example of the powerful impact of prayer in the Rosario, Argentina, campaign in 1978. He states, "As sons found employment in answer to these prayers and sick relatives were healed, a great sense of awe and God-consciousness was created and thousands responded to the Gospel. Many of these cells continued on as house churches." Ibid., 8–9.

475 Holton and Jones, *Spirit Aflame*, 106.

476 Ibid., 108. Intercessors for Mission to London included Christians in Sweden, the Netherlands, Guatemala, Peru, Mexico, Argentina, and the United States.

477 Ibid., 110. For diverse prayer strategies during Mission to London, see ibid., 109–13.

478 For instance, it cost $300,000 for Graham's Mission England and $500,000 for Palau's Mission to London in advertising the campaigns. Both were handled by professional agencies. John Capon, "Billy Graham and Luis Palau: Fanning Revival Fires in England—Events and Strategies Behind a Remarkable Summer of Evangelism," *Christianity Today*, 13 July 1984, 52.

479 Malcolm Boyd, "Crossroads in Mass Evangelism?" *The Christian Century*, 20 March 1957, 359. This statement was originally made in an interview with British newspaper the *Observer* (24 April 1955).

480 Ibid.

481 "Evangelist to Three Worlds," 32.

482 Palau, "Cooperative Evangelism," 319.

483 For instance, during Mission to London, individual promotion was performed in three major ways: Operation Andrew, visitation, and saturation evangelism through media. For detailed information, see Holton and Jones, *Spirit Aflame*, 114–21. According to Sterling Huston, Operation Andrew has been "the most effective means of encouraging personal invitations" for Billy Graham's campaigns. Huston, *Crusade Evangelism*, 101. For discussion on promotion for campaigns, see also Sterling W. Huston, "Methods of Attracting a Larger Audience: Countries and Areas with Sophisticated Media," in *The Work of an Evangelist*, ed. J. D. Douglas (Minneapolis, MN: World Wide Publications, 1984), 503–13.

484 Both McWilliam and Huston point out the difference between publicity and advertisement. Publicity is information provided free, while advertisement is purchased. According to Huston, publicity includes posters in churches and public places, public service announcements, and bulletin inserts. Advertisement includes radio and television time, newspaper advertisements, billboards, and bus signs. McWilliam, "Mass Evangelism," 12; Huston, *Crusade Evangelism*, 96.

485 Huston, *Crusade Evangelism*, 99. Huston's conclusion is based on the practical experience of BGEA, as well as research done by Larry Caillouet, who conducted three surveys on promotion and its effects on Graham's campaigns. According to Caillouet, there are fundamental differences between awareness and attendance. He concluded, "*Awareness* of a Crusade in a community is influenced largely through the mass media and, in particular, through

newspapers which not only carry advertising, but extensive news coverage. However, *attendance* at the Crusade is influenced primarily by interpersonal factors" [emphasis in original]. Ibid.

486 William H. Swatos Jr., "Getting the Word Around: A Research Note on Communicating an Evangelistic Crusade," *Review of Religious Research* 33, no. 2 (December 1991): 176. The first survey was conducted two months prior to the event, and the last one was done about one month after the campaign. Ibid.

487 McWilliam, "Mass Evangelism," 12.

488 Holton and Jones, *Spirit Aflame*, 176.

489 "Oofy Prosser's city column," *Punch*, June 20, 1984; quoted in Holton and Jones, *Spirit Aflame*, 122–23. Holton and Jones also record that "Informal surveys found that almost everyone in London had seen the Mission to London posters and was aware of the meetings at QPR stadium." Ibid., 187.

490 Kevin Palau, interview by the author, August 8, 2008. Campaigns in Latin America cost much less than those in the States. According to Kevin, even campaigns in large cities in Latin America normally cost no more than $1 million. However, the ministry is looking at ways to trim its budgets and is exploring smaller markets and smaller budgets, in the range of $350,000 to $700,000.

491 Palau, interview by the author, May 9, 2008.

492 "Is Palau the Next Billy Graham?" *ABC News*, 8 October 2005 [online]; accessed 27 September 2007; available from http://abcnews.go.com/GMA/story?id= 1195278&page=1; Internet. Twenty percent of this amount was paid by corporations.

493 Bearden, "Man with a Message."

494 Palau, interview by the author, May 9, 2008. The finances for Palau's team and for a campaign are raised and managed separately.

495 Kevin Palau, "A New Look for Mass Evangelism," 2.

496 Kevin Palau, interview by the author, August 8, 2008. Cf. LPA has been a member of the Evangelical Council for Financial Accountability, which was established in 1979. Along with Graham, Palau has been a charter member of this organization, which has given him credibility with his financial supporters. Sura Rubenstein, "Preacher to the World: Oregon's Luis Palau," *Northwest Magazine*, 15 September 1985, 11–12.

497 McWilliam, "Mass Evangelism," 14.

498 Palau, *Telling the Story*, 55. Palau recalls, "In prayer, we committed the immense undertaking to God and asked Him to supply the finances we needed. We rose from our knees confident that He would provide. And He did! When the bills were in and the accounting completed, the needed $200,000 had come in, almost to the penny!" For other examples of faith finances, see also McWilliam, "Mass Evangelism," 14.

499 Palau, "The Evangelist Has a Strategy," 233.

500 Leighton Ford, *The Christian Persuader* (New York: Harper and Row Publishers, 1966), 86.

Luis Palau's first crusade took place in Bogotá, Colombia, in 1966.

Luis and Pat Palau during church planting days in Colombia, 1962.

Palau held four campaigns over 63 days in Guatemala during the 1970s, reaching 321,700 people with 8,426 registered commitments. Pictured is the 1977 crusade.

Palau with his good friend and mentor, Dr. Billy Graham.

Monterrey, Mexico, 1966 – one year after forming his evangelistic team.

Talking to teens during the 36-day Glasgow, Scotland, crusade in 1981. The crusade at Kelvin Hall drew 198,000 people.

The kickoff event at Trafalgar Square for the two-year Mission to London.

700,000 people attend the final day of Palau's 1982 Guatemala City crusade.

The 1984 Mission to London involved an award-winning promotional campaign.

QPR Stadium, London, 1984.

Team members in 1983. Citing the example of the Lord Jesus who had a team of 12, Palau believes every evangelist needs a team of faithful coworkers.

The seven-day Singapore crusade in 1986 drew 337,500 people with 11,902 registered decisions. The crusade was broadcast across Asia through a media campaign called "Asia 86."

The Hong Kong crusade in 1987 attracted 219,100 people with 31,268 registered decisions. It was Palau's first crusade with a Chinese audience.

Palau was one of the first evangelists to go into Eastern Europe during the fall of the Iron Curtain. Here, the evangelist is in Romania in 1990 where he visited three cities over nine days. He spoke to 215,000 people and 46,172 decisions were registered.

The team's modest first office building, 1979. Today the ministry makes its home in a 34,000 square foot building in Beaverton, Oregon.

The live TV call-in counseling program, "Night Talk" has been a key component of his ministry for five decades.

The 1999 crusade in Villahermosa, Mexico, was attended by 117,200 people with 4,236 registered decisions.

The Palau family left to right: Keith, Andrew, Luis, Pat, Kevin, and Steve at the Boise, Idaho, Festival in 2001.

The festival model of evangelism was launched along the Portland, Oregon, waterfront in 1999.

A two-day homecoming festival in Cordoba, Argentina, in 2001 was attended by 211,480 people with 6,284 decisions.

Palau took his festival model of evangelism and action sports outreach to Manchester, England, in 2003.

Following the September 11, 2001, terrorist attacks Palau held a festival in Santa Cruz, California.

The 2003 festival in Buenos Aires, Argentina, captured the attention of the country and a two-day crowd exceeding 850,000 people.

The largest USA festival to date took place in Ft. Lauderdale, Florida, in 2003 where the two-day "BeachFest" drew more than 340,000 people.

One of the outcomes of the Ft. Lauderdale "BeachFest" was an award-winning evangelistic national TV special.

Preaching in front of the U. S. Capitol during the 2005 Washington, D.C. Festival attended by more than 100,000 people.

Greeting festival volunteers helping renovate one of several Washington, D.C. schools. The Community Care Day effort provided the nation's capital with an estimated $1.2 million in repairs to inner-city schools.

Attending church services in Beijing, China, in 2005 with President George W. Bush and Mrs. Laura Bush.

Being interviewed on radio during the two-day 2004 Lima, Peru, Festival that was attended by 667,000 people with 42,200 registered decisions.

Relevancy and creativity have been vividly demonstrated in Palau's use of mass media for longer than five decades.

The 2006 Costa Rica Festival drew an audience of more than 410,000 people.

The 2006 Houston, Texas, Festival was attended by 225,000 people.

Palau preaches the Gospel with both passion and compassion, always giving an opportunity for his audience to respond to the message.

Luis' son Andrew is following his father's footsteps along with a growing group of Palau Association Alliance members.

Andrew Palau preaching in Romania in 2008.

Returning to Buenos Aires in 2008, Palau's two-day festival drew an estimated 850,000 to 1 million people.

Palau has held three festivals in his hometown of Portland, Oregon. The 2008 festival attracted 185,000 people to Waterfront Park.

Evangelistic campaigns can only succeed when believers are motivated and equipped to share the message of the gospel.

Street banners hang in Nashville, Tennessee, as part of a massive grassroots publicity campaign to call attention to Palau's two-day CityFest.

A festival counselor helps an inquirer understand her decision, as well as next steps in beginning a personal relationship with Jesus Christ. Friendship evangelism is the main thrust of evangelistic strategy for the Palau team.

Palau festivals employ a massive grassroots publicity campaign to capture the attention of the city and make it easier for people to invite their friends to the event.

Palau reaches out to the media in all of his campaigns in order to reach more people with the Good News message.

Andrew and Luis visit with President Bill Clinton in 2000.

Kevin Palau became the president of the Luis Palau Association in 2010.

Luis and Pat will celebrate 50 years of marriage in August, 2011.

501 Holton and Jones, *Spirit Aflame*, 40. In a promotional DVD for counselor training, a counselor testified that "I've been a Christian for so many years. This is the first time that I talked to someone about Christ directly." "Luis Palau Festivals: Friends of the Festival Counselor Training" (Portland, OR: LPA, n.d.), DVD.

502 Robnett, *Telling the Story*, 73.

503 McWilliam, "Mass Evangelism," 10. According to McWilliam, LPA also equips individual Christians with various evangelism training courses, "using materials from groups such as Navigators and Campus Crusade," as well as other ministry partners.

504 Friendship evangelism, which is also called lifestyle evangelism, has been popular among evangelicals in North America since the 1980s. The prominent figure in friendship evangelism has been Joseph C. Aldrich, former president of Multnomah School of the Bible. John Mark Terry, *Evangelism: A Concise History* (Nashville, TN: Broadman & Holman Publishers, 1994), 194. Cf. Tom Stebbins introduces a range of description on friendship evangelism, expressed by major proponents of friendship evangelism: "Joseph Aldrich, author of *Friendship Evangelism* and *Gentle Persuasion*, describes friendship evangelism as 'loving people until they ask why.' Rebecca Manley Pippert, in her book *Out of the Saltshaker*, suggests that it is getting the church out of the sanctuary and into the world. D. James Kennedy, author of *Evangelism Explosion*, calls it witnessing as a way of life. Jim Peterson in *Living Proof* writes about it in terms of engaging people 'on their own turf.'" Tom Stebbins, *Friendship Evangelism by the Book* (Camp Hill, PA: Christian Publications, 1995), vii–viii.

505 Joseph Aldrich observes that 80 percent of all new converts come to believe in Jesus because of their relationship with a believing friend or relative. Joseph C. Aldrich, "Lifestyle Evangelism: Winning Through Winsomeness," *Christianity Today*, 7 January 1983, 13.

506 LPA, "Festival Counseling and Follow-up," Microsoft PowerPoint File, 17. This statistic is similar to BGEA's survey report. According to Huston, more than 80 percent of inquirers are brought to campaigns by friends. Huston also reports, "One survey of those who claim a personal relationship with Jesus Christ revealed that 85 percent could identify a relative within their family circle who had been praying for them." Huston, *Crusade Evangelism*, 50.

507 For instance, during the campaign in Glasgow in 1981, one teenage girl led thirty-eight friends to the Lord through friendship evangelism. Palau and Sanford, *Calling America and the Nations*, 151. McWilliam also testified that "One man in London led thirty friends to Christ from his Operation Andrew lists before the crusade ever began. Another woman in a crusade in Mexico City rented a bus to the crusades to bring fifty relatives for whom she had been praying." McWilliam, "Mass Evangelism," 9–10.

508 According to McWilliam, Operation Andrew was also called Each One Bring One in Latin America. McWilliam, "Mass Evangelism," 9.

509 This has been true with BGEA as well. Sterling Huston, who worked with Billy Graham for a long time, testifies that "The secret to the harvest in Crusade evangelism is tens of thousands of Christians committing themselves to the

concepts embodied in the Prayer Triplet and Operation Andrew programs." Huston, *Crusade Evangelism*, 53.

510 Scott Bauer, "Crusade Evangelism" (D.Min. project, Oral Roberts University, 1995), 129.

511 See discussion on "Evangelistic Fruit" of Luis Palau in chapter 13.

512 Luis Palau, "Citywide Crusade Evangelization," in *Let the Earth Hear His Voice: International Conference on World Evangelism*, ed. J. D. Douglas (Minneapolis, MN: World Wide Publications, 1975), 610.

513 Sung Ho Kang, "Major Vocational Evangelists from Charles Finney to Billy Sunday and Their Development of Methods for Urban Mass Evangelism" (Th.M. thesis, Southwestern Baptist Theological Seminary, 1997), 79. Cf. According to Delos Miles, Finney's "anxious bench" or "anxious seat" was not his invention. He adopted it from the mourner's bench at Methodist camp meetings. Miles, *Introduction to Evangelism*, 235. It is also noteworthy that, in the words of Glyn Evans, Billy Graham is the one who adopted and "perfected the technique of follow-up beyond that of his predecessors." William Glyn Evans, *Profiles of Revival Leaders* (Nashville, TN: Broadman Press, 1976), 12.

514 LPA, "Festival Counseling and Follow-up," 2. After changing the campaign format to a festival style, counselors are now called "Friends of the Festival."

515 Ibid., 3.

516 Ibid., 10.

517 McWilliam, "Mass Evangelism," 12. McWilliam found that nurture groups are especially useful in Britain and other European countries where many large church buildings exist with deceasing membership. Nurture groups provide "a smaller, caring family in which to begin the nurturing discipling process." McWilliam attributed the success of Mission to London to two factors: Operation Andrew and nurture groups. Ibid., 13. For detailed discussion on follow-up of Mission to London, see Holton and Jones, *Spirit Aflame*, 166–72.

518 Timothy Robnett, interview by the author, interview over telephone, August 6, 2008.

519 Robnett, *Telling the Story*, 42.

520 LPA, "Festival Counseling and Follow-up," 16.

521 Ibid., 18–19.

522 Ibid., 20–25.

523 LPA also provides follow-up plans for local churches if they do not have one. LPA's recommendation includes: "Living Your Strengths Spiritual Journey" from the Gallup Organization, "The Alpha Course," "Luis Palau's Follow-up Materials," and "Seeker Small Groups" from the Willow Creek Association. Ibid., 20.

524 Palau's book, *Healthy Habits for Spiritual Growth*, deals with fifty-two habits to cultivate the Christian lifestyle. Luis Palau, *Healthy Habits for Spiritual Growth: 52 Principles for Personal Change* (Grand Rapids: Discovery House Publishers, 1994).

CHAPTER 8

EVANGELISTIC STRATEGY: CAMPAIGNS, PART 2

Reaching Affinity Groups Through Specialized Programs

During evangelistic campaigns the major events are conducted at the stadium.[525] Yet this is not the only place evangelism occurs. As a matter of fact, Luis Palau acknowledges that drawing people to the stadium is getting harder these days. He acknowledges, "The stadium is not the number one vehicle for leading people to Christ."[526] Most Palau campaigns supplement the main events with special affinity group events, which often include breakfasts, luncheons, dinners, and other special events for different groups of people, normally grouped by gender or age, such as children, youth, and senior adults. Palau has also reached some specific groups of people based on their needs and homogeneous nature. Three such people groups and Palau's strategies to reach them are examined in the following discussion.

Reaching the Brokenhearted Through Specialized Counseling

One of the vital ministries of Palau's team during past campaigns has been counseling people with various life issues in common. Jim Williams, who joined Palau's team in 1968, began the first counseling center at Palau's campaign in Costa Rica in 1972 and has been in charge of LPA's counseling ministry ever since.[527] According to Williams, counseling during campaigns originally began in 1965 with Palau's live television counseling program called "Luis Palau Responds," in which people called Palau on live television and asked for biblical answers for their life problems. Because it became impossible for Palau to talk to every caller on live television, counseling centers were born to facilitate counseling more people personally.

The counseling center was ordinarily located either on the campaign site or in some neutral location, including places such as "homes, restaurants, school buildings, doctors' or lawyers' offices."[528] As the demand for counseling increased, Williams began to train local believers at each campaign in biblical counseling so that they could also serve as counselors. People come for help for various reasons. During Mission to London, for example, Williams observed that some common and recurring problems included uncontrolled sexual lust and behavior, depression, homosexuality, alcohol, and drug addiction.[529]

Williams suggested a fourfold purpose for the counseling center:[530] The primary purpose was to win people to Christ. By visiting a counseling center, many people heard the gospel personally and came to believe in Jesus. Second, it provided an opportunity for local Christians to be trained in and to practice biblical counseling. With the knowledge and skill gained through training and experience during campaigns, they could provide valuable ministry in their own local churches even after the campaigns.

Third, counseling helped new converts solve problems in their personal lives according to biblical teaching and thus to grow in their Christian faith. Fourth, counseling helped believers who were struggling with chronic problems. In this case LPA staff members rather than local Christians normally counseled them. The benefits and impact of counseling during campaigns was manifold as well, as Williams asserts:

> The counseling center is not reaching the masses, but it does reach the person who does not feel comfortable in mass meetings; the person who feels the need to ask questions before making a decision; the person burdened with guilt about the past. It also adds credibility to the overall crusade

> effort, and silences the critics who want to complain about "mass psychology." And it gives the evangelist a place where he can refer those who want to speak with him individually.[531]

After changing the campaign format to a festival style, LPA no longer provides counseling centers. But counseling is still going on effectively via email.[532]

Reaching National Leaders Through Breakfasts and Luncheons

One of the benefits of evangelistic campaigns is a strategic outreach to people in leadership positions. Palau recognized in the early stages of his ministry the value of reaching the leaders of a society, and this has been his consistent strategy ever since. Palau explains:

> Sharing the love and claims of Jesus Christ with government leaders is one of the unique aspects of our ministry. Through the years, members of royalty, presidents, cabinet members, diplomats, congressmen, parliamentarians, and others have listened as we've opened God's Word and shared the Gospel.[533]

Nancy DeMoss, who has reached many business and political leaders with the gospel through outreach dinner parties, calls these leaders the "neglected minority." Contrary to popular perception, she has found them to be very responsive to the gospel when approached in a culturally relevant and nonthreatening way. They are also looking for genuine friends who can understand them because they "are frequently troubled with marriage and family difficulties, and are often confronted by pressure from special interest groups, labor disputes, [and] political uncertainties."[534]

Palau is convinced that mass evangelism provides an excellent venue for national leaders to hear the message of the gospel. He makes these observations:

> Mass evangelism arrests the attention of government and national leaders and gains a hearing for the Gospel in places otherwise not easily accessible. As governors (Acts 13) and kings (Acts 26) gave the apostle Paul a hearing, so today the leaders of nations ought to hear the Word of God. In many countries they ordinarily do not pay attention to our message; but when these leaders see a mass movement of people, or an impact made on the media, they usually begin to listen![535]

The power of mass evangelism to reach political leaders has been especially strong in some countries in Latin America. Of course, it is not hard to imagine that such leaders are looking to gain the popularity of the people. Palau recalls, "Some presidents were eager to be on the platform and we had to pointedly not invite them."[536] Nevertheless, Palau seizes these opportunities to share the message of the gospel with them.

A typical approach to reach people in leadership during campaigns has been inviting them to a breakfast or luncheon.[537] Kimberly Claassen described the breakfast meeting for elected officials that took place during Palau's campaign in Kansas City in 1997:

> U.S. congressmen, state legislators, mayors, judges, and nearly 200 other officials in Kansas City greeted each other as they arrived for breakfast at the Adam's Mark Hotel. They couldn't deny being a bit curious. Several months now they'd seen the speaker's picture on billboards and yard signs around greater Kansas City.[538]

Palau's strategy to reach national leaders has been effective in many countries. Reports on his campaign in Caracas, Venezuela, in 1979 are a good example:

> A key breakthrough for the evangelicals occurred the following morning when Palau and 75 church leaders joined Venezuelan President Luis Herrera Campíns and his aides

> for the nation's first Presidential Prayer Breakfast. During a brief speech Palau said that nations and men who fear God will be blessed by him; then he turned to President Herrera and said, "God will bless you because today you have publicly honored him."[539]

During his campaign in Costa Rica in March 2006, Palau met with the president, senators, judges, and other politicians both privately and publically. LPA reports that 40 of the 150 guests at a luncheon for government leaders expressed their decision to believe in Jesus after Palau's address.[540]

Moreover, sharing the gospel with top leaders of a country has often opened a door to proclaim the good news to the masses on a national level. One such case was the campaign in Bolivia in 1974, in which "Palau was specially invited by President Banzer to address the gathering of 125 cabinet members, military chiefs, and other prominent leaders of Bolivian industry, commerce, and government."[541] During the Presidential Prayer Breakfast, which was the first in the history of Bolivia, Palau declared, "Bolivia—or any nation—is ungovernable without God."[542]

Touched by Palau's address, President Hugo Banzer helped Palau proclaim the gospel to the people of Bolivia. At Palau's request, Banzer authorized ten nights of free air time on national television. Watching Palau counseling on television, he also requested 1 million copies of the New Testament to give away to students through the ministry of education. Although securing 1 million copies was challenging, this request was fulfilled with the help of the Bible League. Palau records, "Since 1975 every primary and secondary school child in Bolivia has studied the New Testament twice a week!"[543]

This incident clearly demonstrates the powerful impact of reaching top leaders of a country preliminary to saturating the whole nation with the gospel. When Palau came back to Bolivia in 1978 for another campaign, the people's response was overwhelming. Palau records, "The three weeks of meetings broke almost every crusade record we'd ever set—for attendance (180,000), decisions for Christ (18,916), and ratio of decisions to attendance (10.5 percent)."[544]

Certainly this remarkable outcome had something to do with Palau's previous visit and strategic outreach to Bolivia's political leaders.

During this campaign, Palau had the privilege to speak at another Presidential Prayer Breakfast to national leaders, including Bolivia's new president, General Juan Pereda Asbun. In a private meeting after the prayer breakfast, Palau explained the message of the gospel to President Pereda, who "bowed his head and gave his life to Christ."[545]

As already discussed in the context of Palau's theology, Palau's association with political dictators in Latin America has been one of the lingering criticisms against him. In the eyes of the public, Palau's decision to physically stand alongside these dictators may give the impression that he supports their political ideas and regimes. In this respect, Palau may not be able to escape criticism.

Nevertheless, using the explanation by which Palau defends himself, his motive in reaching national leaders has been evangelistic. He has not been engaged in any political campaigns, nor has he pursued political positions. Furthermore, the strategic role of reaching political leaders for the purpose of evangelism cannot be denied.

As demonstrated in Palau's ministry, friendship with political leaders has provided opportunities for more extensive ministry. As long as the evangelist's motive is pure and evangelical, reaching political leaders with the gospel can serve as an effective evangelistic strategy in any country.[546]

Reaching the Underprivileged Through Servant Evangelism

Steve Sjogren, the pioneer of servant evangelism, observes that "people don't necessarily remember what they are told of God's love, but they never forget what they have experienced of God's love."[547] Servant evangelism has been a vital part of Palau's ministry during his campaigns. As discussed in the section on Palau's theology, social reform is not the primary goal of his ministry. Yet he believes that Christians should work to rectify social problems and meet the needs of suffering people.

Although evangelism must take priority over social reform, it is still imperative for Christians to extend Christlike love to people.

During campaigns, the Palau team has shown God's love in practical ways to the unprivileged; these projects have included food drives, free medical check-ups, house construction, neighborhood and school renovation, community clean-up, and clothing giveaways.[548]

Recently Palau and his team have paid more attention to social concern than ever before. Palau's Portland "CityFest with Luis Palau" in 2008 incorporated a strategic form of servant evangelism called "Season of Service." As Palau explained, "Season of Service will address critical needs of the homeless, the hungry, the medically uninsured, the impoverished, the environment, and the public schools."[549] This project is historical and phenomenal in the fact that 625 churches, along with civic and corporate leaders throughout the area, joined this benevolent task. LPA expected fifteen thousand volunteers to join this project from May to August of 2008. However, the number of volunteers reached twenty-two thousand in August, and the Season of Service was extended through September.[550]

Today, under the leadership of Kevin Palau, Season of Service is a sustainable component of all Palau festivals.

Planting New Churches Through Evangelistic Campaigns

In his book *The Evangelization of the Roman Empire*, Glenn Hinson contended that "Christianity spread principally and normally, though not exclusively, through the planting of churches."[551] The prominent figure in church planting in the first century was the apostle Paul, whose mission was incomplete until the new converts had been brought into local churches.[552] Not only was church planting a vital strategy for evangelism in the first century, but its importance is growing even faster today. According to church-growth scholar Eddie Gibbs, church planting will be more and more important, due to the closure of many small churches that are no longer relevant for younger generations.[553]

Luis Palau has utilized this crucial strategy of evangelism in conjunction with his evangelistic campaigns. The combination of these two strategies is possible, says Palau, "because of the sheer volume of converts"[554] through campaigns. Palau's first involvement with church planting occurred early in his ministry in Argentina. While working for SEPAL in 1960, Palau, along with Ed Murphy and others, went to Oncativo, a town of about twelve thousand residents, which had not been evangelized at all. About seventy people who came to believe in Jesus on the basis of Palau's preaching formed a new church. Within the next couple of years this church planted several other churches in nearby towns.[555]

From the formation of LPA, church planting has been a part of Palau's vision.[556] John McWilliam testifies that "We [LPA] have seen hundreds of new churches begin as new believers have been brought into living congregations to be discipled and turned into reproducing Christians for God's honor."[557] The best example of church planting through an evangelistic campaign occurred during Palau's two-week, region-wide campaign in Rosario, Argentina's second largest city with a population of 1.6 million, in November of 1976.

The campaign "Rosario Plan" has been presented as a successful case study and encouraging model for connecting campaign evangelism with church planting. According to Palau, Edgardo Silvoso, along with church-growth experts such as Donald McGavran, Peter Wagner, and Leighton Ford, "developed a comprehensive plan that united church-growth principles with proved crusade evangelism strategies."[558] Peter Wagner remarked that the Rosario Plan had a twofold purpose from the beginning: (1) expansion growth—membership growth of participating churches, and (2) extension growth—strategic planting of new churches.[559]

The Rosario Plan was launched fourteen months before Palau's campaign and continued even after the campaign, with Palau's campaign providing "the dramatic focal point."[560] The Rosario Plan set up the goal before the start of the campaign of establishing sixty-nine new congregations, called "silos." These silos were formed to incorporate new converts so that they could grow into full-fledged churches. Although this goal was not reached, forty-two new congregations were formed, out of which twenty-seven had survived by April 1978.[561] This is a tremendous result when one considers the fact that only forty churches had been planted in the previous ninety years of missionary activity in this region.[562]

The effectiveness of church planting in conjunction with evangelistic campaigns has been carefully considered by William A. Giovannetti.[563] With Luis Palau's Say Yes! Chicago in 1996 as the background of his project, Giovannetti presents a strategy of evangelism by linking church planting with evangelistic campaigns.

> The objective is simple: when the Chicago Crusade is over and the LPEA has moved on to other places, a significant number of new churches will be in place, caring for new converts, continuing to multiply disciples, and providing a model for future attempts to link church planting to crusade evangelism.[564]

According to Giovannetti, combining the two methods of evangelism is conceivable and effective because of their "complementary weaknesses and strengths." He explains:

> Where church planting finds its greatest difficulties—making meaningful contact with potential members—crusade evangelism finds one of its greatest strengths. And where crusade evangelism finds its greatest difficulties—the gap in follow-up and the high attrition rate of converts—church planting finds its greatest strengths. The two methodologies are natural complements.[565]

Church planting in conjunction with a campaign is a corporate effort between the Palau team and local churches hosting the campaign. However, the responsibility of planting churches should lie with local leadership. Giovannetti's argument follows the indigenous principle espoused by Donald McGavran:

> It must remain crystal clear that the plan is not that the LPEA will plant churches in Chicago. Rather, the plan is that Chicago's pastors and leaders will cooperate in an effort to stimulate church planting in connection with the Chicago Crusade. The LPEA will help as a catalytic agent, but the burden of this plan rests on the shoulders of local leaders.[566]

Palau and his team no longer strategically link campaigns with church planting, although they do encourage it. In fact, however, the value of church planting has been diminished because many churches already exist in most regions. Rather than planting churches, the Palau team now encourages inquirers to join established, Bible-believing churches.[567] Another reason LPA is no longer actively involved in church planting is the denominational issue. There can be a spirit of jealousy and competition among the local churches when a church is planted through campaigns.[568]

Such reasons are understandable. However, if LPA can find a systematic way to avoid unnecessary conflicts and thus reduce the competing spirit among churches, planting churches in connection with campaigns could still be an effective strategy of evangelism in some regions.

New Forms of Evangelistic Campaigns

In recent years Luis Palau has radically changed the format of campaigns to adapt to changing cultures in a relevant and innovative way. The first of a series of these innovative campaigns, called "festivals," appeared in Portland, Oregon, in 1999.[569] Although a festival shares much in common with a traditional campaign, the approach is more contemporary and culturally sensitive.[570] In the words of Michelle Bearden of the *Tampa Tribune*, a festival "fuses old-time religion with 21st-century culture."[571]

According to LPA, a festival offers fun for the whole family, fantastic food, top Christian musicians, a Veggie Tales children's area complete with Bob and Larry, a community care area, and an impressive skate park featuring some of the best professional skateboarders, BMX and FMX riders.[572]

Kevin Palau, the main architect, in conjunction with his brother Andrew, of the festival style, explains several differences between current and previous campaign formats.[573] First, instead of enclosed stadiums and indoor arenas, a festival takes place in open areas outdoors. In 1999 and 2000 LPA used Tom McCall Waterfront Park for Portland Festival. In fact, preaching in open areas is not something new to Luis Palau, who says, "I started out preaching in the parks and streets of Argentina, so why shouldn't I bring it to America?" He contrasts the venues this way:

> The big difference is you are where the people are. You're not renting a stadium and surrounding yourself with four walls and a roof and shutting out the noise of the city. Downtown in the park you're really in the city, putting out the Gospel in the marketplace just as the apostle Paul did as he traveled from city to city.[574]

Second, while a traditional campaign "uses music to build up to a message," the new campaign model can be called "a music festival."[575] Portland Festival '99, for instance, featured top Christian singers such as "Bob Carlisle, Point of Grace, 4Him, Audio Adrenaline, dc Talk's Toby McKeehan, Third Day, Nikki Leonti, Dawkins & Dawkins, T-Bone, and The Tribe Called Judah."[576] Because music played a central role, the Portland festivals became known as the "Great music! Good News" festivals.

Unlike his approach with traditional campaigns, Palau typically presents the gospel at least a couple times throughout each day of the festival. In fact, there can be as many as ten evangelistic messages during a festival day from multiple evangelists including both Luis Palau and his son Andrew Palau.

Third, the atmosphere of a festival is quite different from that of a traditional campaign. A festival provides a comfortable atmosphere that is family and non-Christian friendly. Kevin Palau describes it:

> People sat on blankets with their family and friends, enjoying the sun and good music. Food was available from local vendors and restaurants. ... Children enjoyed the children's area, which featured face painting, a petting zoo, clowns, balloons, and other activities.

In his dissertation William Morrow acknowledges the value of this friendly atmosphere: "People are drawn to these festivals because they offer non-threatening entry points. People can enjoy live music, eat, and hear the gospel message."[577]

Fourth, a festival is financed by corporate sponsors as well as church and individual sponsors. Palau was a pioneer in bringing corporate sponsors into faith-based events. In Kevin Palau's judgment, the involvement of corporate sponsors makes these evangelistic events look more like normal events to non-churched people.

Finally, the festival model requires fewer committees for efficiency and a shorter lead time for local church leaders. And unlike Palau's past crusades, that ran anywhere from one to sixteen weeks in length, the festivals are usually just two-day events.

While the Palau sons helped their father reinvent his ministry through the festival model, the senior Palau was initially skeptical. A week before the Portland Festival, Luis Palau told a newspaper reporter, "If 10,000 people come, I'll be very happy. If 50,000 people come, I'll be out of my mind."[578] To Palau's surprise, however, 93,000 people joined the festival in two days, breaking the record at that time for the largest attendance for one of Palau's campaigns in the United States.

This is an astonishing result when compared to Palau's previous campaign, as Kevin Palau notes:

> With exceptions in Romania, Singapore, and Hong Kong, Luis Palau crusades outside of Latin America have attracted smaller crowds. In more than 30 crusades in the United States prior to 1999, for example, the largest crowd was about 18,000 at the Rosemont Horizon—and that for a Say Yes Chicago crusade youth night featuring a free concert by the Newsboys.[579]

But the new festival model has changed all of that.

After back-to-back years of festival success in Portland,[580] Luis Palau began to expand this model in other U.S. cities and regions around the world. Since 1999 more than six million people have participated in Palau's festivals worldwide. Some of the highlights include "Ft. Lauderdale, Florida (300,000), Nashville, Tennessee (90,000), Houston, Texas (225,000), Manchester, England (55,000), Lima, Peru (650,000), and

Buenos Aires, Argentina (850,000)."[581] After changing to a festival format, notes Palau, attendance has risen tenfold.[582]

LPA has recently created another innovative outreach for children and youth called "Livin It." Although he has not ignored people of other ages, children and youth have been Palau's strategic audiences, as he shares here:

> Youth, otherwise indifferent to the Christian message in many areas of the world, is [*sic*] often attracted by the mass crusade approach. ... Since over 50 percent of the world's population is now estimated to be under twenty five years of age, mass evangelization must be used to communicate Christ to this new generation.[583]

Livin It was birthed by Kevin Palau and a group of Christian action sports enthusiasts. Through Livin It, skateboarders and BMX riders capture the attention of youth by performing extreme sports and presenting the gospel. As their ministry began to grow, other Christian action sport ministries, including skating, BMX, FMX, surfing, and snowboarding, joined Livin It.[584]

These young athlete-evangelists have not only been a part of Palau's festivals but have also been conducting their own national tour. In addition, two DVDs have been recorded, "Livin It" and "Livin It LA," featuring skate and BMX athletes.[585] According to an LPA report, from 2005 to 2007 19.2 million people have been reached through the ministry of Livin It.[586] Today, Livin It and Next Generation Alliance (NGA) are part of Palau's Alliance Ministries, a focal part of the ministry's future.

Palau's new evangelistic campaign model has both strengths and weaknesses. To a large extent it has successfully overcome one of the setbacks of traditional mass evangelism: With the competition of booming entertainment, people are losing interest in mass evangelism. By engaging the culture in a relevant and innovative way, however, the festival style is appealing to more people. The result is astounding. The average size of the audience has grown tenfold from previous campaigns.

Yet the very strength of this new model can become its weakness. People come to the festival to enjoy music, food, playgrounds, extreme sports, and other entertaining programs. Such elements certainly achieve a goal, providing a bridge between the Christian and the secular world. But the real success of an evangelistic campaign cannot be measured solely by the number in attendance. In an atmosphere of loud music, food, and other entertaining elements, people are easily distracted.

A couple of cautions and suggestions must be introduced here. First, the evangelist must make elaborate efforts to draw people's attention from such an exhilarating atmosphere to spiritual reality. He or she must lead the audience to look deep within their hearts and encourage them to look up to God to find hope in Christ. This is not an easy task. Directing people's attention from a jovial festival mood to God requires much spiritual preparation and a careful plan. In addition, in such an atmosphere people may be tempted to make decisions not on the basis of the truth of the gospel but on their elevated emotional condition. To avoid this, the evangelist must clearly communicate the message of the gospel.

Despite some intrinsic weaknesses, the value of the new methodology should not be underestimated. If the evangelist and his or her team can overcome the vulnerabilities, Palau's new model can provide a new paradigm in mass evangelism and greatly advance the strategy.

Conclusion

The evangelistic campaign has been Luis Palau's most significant strategy to reach people with the gospel. With Billy Graham disappearing from the public scene, people are concerned about the future of campaign evangelism. However, Palau has proved that campaign evangelism is still effective when it adapts to the changing culture in relevant and creative ways. Successful campaigns must be preceded by fervent prayer, careful planning, and state-of-the-art promotion and followed by well-planned incorporation of inquirers into the local churches.

While keeping the traditional elements that are still vital, Palau has dramatically changed the format of campaigns. With festivals that are friendly to nonbelievers and families, Palau is reaching more people with the gospel by engaging the culture. The fact that the attendance rate has grown tenfold is sufficient evidence to prove that his new strategy is working. This result demonstrates the importance of developing a new strategy for a new generation.

While the evangelist, Luis Palau, has not changed, more people are coming to evangelistic events because of the new formats. Although his new model is not without pitfalls, it presents a significant paradigm shift in terms of the strategy for mass evangelism. Indeed, Palau has a history of knowing when to reinvent his ministry—always without changing the message.

Palau also has incorporated various evangelistic strategies into campaign evangelism. To reach nonbelievers he has utilized friendship evangelism, to reach the brokenhearted he has employed counseling, to reach the underprivileged he has adopted servant evangelism, and to establish new converts he has embraced church planting. In conclusion, Palau has utilized every possible means of evangelism in conjunction with his evangelistic campaigns to fulfill the Great Commission.

Endnotes

525 Cf. After changing campaign's format to a festival style, campaigns take place in open areas.

526 Luis Palau, "Whatever Happened to Evangelism? Luis Palau Wants to Rekindle Our Passion for the Lost," *Christianity Today*, 8 April 1996, 39. However, Palau argues that the stadium meeting is still a necessary and indispensable part of evangelistic campaigns: "But without the stadium, we wouldn't have the affinity groups, the luncheons, breakfasts, dinners. It would be much more difficult to buy television time, or to grab the attention of the media, or to attract the youth, if we didn't have the stadium events."

527 Susan Holton and David L. Jones, *Spirit Aflame: Luis Palau's Mission to London* (Grand Rapids: Baker Book House, 1985), 169.

528 James Williams, "Specialized Counseling During Evangelistic Campaigns," in *Work of an Evangelist,* ed. J. D. Douglas (Minneapolis, MN: World Wide Publications, 1984), 496. For more discussion on Palau's live television counseling, see "Mass Media as Evangelistic Strategy" in the next chapter.

529 Holton and Jones, *Spirit Aflame*, 170.

530 Williams, "Specialized Counseling," 495–96.

531 Ibid., 498.

532 James Williams, interview by the author, interview by telephone, August 8, 2008. Williams received approximately five thousand emails for counseling in 2007.

533 Luis Palau and David Sanford, *Luis Palau: Calling America and the Nations to Christ* (Nashville, TN: Thomas Nelson, Inc., 1994; rev. 2000), 63. Palau adds, "Such leaders, because of the pressures of their positions and the types of lives they feel they must lead to appear successful, seldom feel genuinely loved. Many of them shed tears when I say I want to pray for them, no strings attached."

534 Nancy DeMoss, "Reaching Business and Political Leaders," in *The Work of an Evangelist*, ed. J. D. Douglas (Minneapolis, MN: World Wide Publications, 1984), 647. Nancy DeMoss is chairman of the Arthur DeMoss Foundation. In this article she provides excellent details for planning, preparing, and conducting evangelistic dinner parties for business and political leaders.

535 Luis Palau, "The Future of Mass Evangelism," in Evangelism: *The Next Ten Years,* ed. Sherwood Eliot Wirt (Waco, TX: Word Books, 1978), 157.

536 "Luis Palau: Evangelist to Three Worlds," *Christianity Today*, 20 May 1983, 28.

537 Williams, interview by the author, August 8, 2008. In many cases, invitation is based on relationships.

538 Kimberly Claassen, "Reviving the Nations," *The Plain Truth* (March/April, 1998), 10.

539 Bill Conard and David L. Jones, "Uniting for Evangelization in Booming Caracas," *Christianity Today*, 4 January 1980, 57. During this campaign, Palau also hosted a tea time and luncheon: "[Palau] also spoke to 700 women at an afternoon tea sponsored by the congress. Wives of top government and military officials, as well as key businesswomen attended. A luncheon address by Palau drew 560 businessmen, high military figures, and a number of doctors and lawyers. At both affairs the evangelist gave an invitation." Ibid., 60.

540 "To Reach a Nation, Reach the Leaders!" *Proclaim!,* 2006, 7.

541 Gary Hardaway, "Bolivia: Prayer in a Time of Trouble," *Christianity Today*, 15 March 1974, 56.

542 Ibid. Concerning his private relationship with heads of state, Palau said, "I go as an ambassador of Jesus Christ. As respectfully as I can I try to present the Gospel clearly and honestly. So far, God has enabled me to do this with each of these men." Ibid., 56–57.

543 Palau and Sanford, *Calling America and the Nations*, 117.

544 Ibid., 139. When compared to the results of his previous campaigns in Bolivia in 1974, this is really astonishing. According to LPA's "Ministry Impact Statistics," Palau's campaign in 1974 for twenty days drew 82,400, and the number of inquirers was 9,210. LPA, "Ministry Impact Statistics."

545 Ibid., 140. Palau personally led some national leaders to accept Christ, including two presidents of Bolivia, Hugo Banzer and Juan Pereda Asbun.

546 For more discussion on this point, see "Criticisms of Theology and Philosophy of Evangelism" in chapter 5.

547 Steve Sjogren, *Conspiracy of Kindness: A Refreshing New Approach to Sharing the Love of Jesus with Others* (Ann Arbor, MI: Servant Publications, 1993), 30. According to Sjogren, servant evangelism consists of deeds of love, words of love, and adequate time. Ibid., 22.

548 For example, see Michelle Bearden, "Man with a Message," *Tampa Tribune*, 19 November 2006.

549 David Hardy, "A Season of Service," *Multnomah*, Spring 2008, 5.

550 Kevin Palau, interview by the author, August 8, 2008.

551 E. Glenn Hinson, *The Evangelization of the Roman Empire* (Macon, GA: Mercer University, 1981), 33. C. Peter Wagner also asserts, "The single most effective evangelistic method under heaven is planting new churches." C. Peter Wagner, *Church Planting for a Greater Harvest* (Ventura, CA: Regal Books, 1990), 11.

552 Pauline scholar Paul Bowers asserts, "The new believer implicitly becomes a believer-in-community, and Paul is concerned in his mission not only with the emergence of such believers but also with the emergence of such communities." Paul Bowers, "Fulfilling the Gospel: the Scope of the Pauline Mission," *JETS* 30 (1987): 187.

553 Eddie Gibbs, *Church Next: Quantum Changes in How We Do Ministry* (Downers Grove, IL: InterVarsity Press, 2000), 97. Societies are also becoming more and more diverse, resulting in diverse groups of people. There are different generations and ethnic groups even in the same society. People have different characteristics according to their interests, jobs, education, income, etc. It is, therefore, necessary to approach people according to their different characteristics. In the words of Larry Lewis, "New churches are needed to penetrate all people groups in societies." Larry L. Lewis, *The Church Planter's Handbook* (Nashville, TN: Broadman Press, 1993), 21.

554 Palau, "The Future of Mass Evangelism," 163.

555 Palau and Sanford, *Calling America and the Nations*, 57–59.

556 Jerry B. Jenkins and Luis Palau, *Luis Palau: Calling the Nations to Christ* (Old Tappan, NJ: Revell, 1978; Chicago, IL: Moody Press, 1980), 193. Palau's memo to the board of Overseas Crusades for the foundation of his own evangelistic team well reflects this vision.

557 John McWilliam, "Mass Evangelism: Reaching Your City in the Eighties," *Urban Mission* 3 (September 1985): 8.

558 Palau and Sanford, *Calling America and the Nations*, 129.

559 Peter Wagner, "Plan Rosario: Milepost for Saturation Evangelism," *Church Growth Bulletin* 14 (September 1977): 147. See also Edward F. Murphy, "Mass Evangelism Is Not Obsolete," *Christianity Today*, 28 February 1975, 9.

560 Wagner, "Plan Rosario," 146. The whole period had been from September 1975 to May 1977. According to Wagner, a total of 67,027 people, including

4,000 local Christians, attended fourteen nights of campaign meetings. Among them more than 3,100 made public decisions at Palau's invitation. He also reports, "Another 18,000 attended satellite crusades in three other cities with 1,400 making decisions for Christ." Ibid., 147.

561 Edgardo Silvoso, "In Rosario It Was Different—Crusade Converts Are in the Churches," *Evangelical Missions Quarterly* 14, no. 2 (April 1978): 84. According to Silvoso, "The highest percentage of incorporation is 85 percent and the lowest 4 percent, with the majority of churches in the 35 to 50 percent range."

562 Palau and Sanford, *Calling America and the Nations,* 129. For the process of the Rosario strategy, see also William W. Conard, "Principles Behind the Rosario Plan," *Latin America Pulse* XIII, no. 3 (October 1978), 2–8; Juan Carlos Miranda, "Rosario Came Just in Time," *Church Growth Bulletin* 14 (September 1977): 150–51.

563 For discussion on mass evangelism and church planting, see also William Brad Morrow, "Mass Evangelism and Its Effect on Church Planting: A Filipino Case Study" (Ph.D. diss., Southern Baptist Theological Seminary, 2003).

564 William A. Giovannetti, "A Strategy for Linking Crusade Evangelism with Church Planting" (D.Min. project, Fuller Theological Seminary, 1996), 3.

565 Ibid., 69–70.

566 Ibid., 89.

567 Williams, interview by the author, August 8, 2008.

568 Palau, interview by the author, May 9, 2008.

569 According to Kevin Palau, in Latin America and on several occasions in the States, the name "festival" had been used even before 1999, but the format had been the same as that of traditional campaigns. Kevin Palau, interview by the author, August 8, 2008.

570 Kevin lists some festival characteristics that have not been changed from previous campaigns: working through local churches, proclamation in unity, mobilizing and training believers, clear gospel message with opportunity to respond, follow-up of new believers through the churches, and extensive media coverage. Kevin Palau, "A New Look for Mass Evangelism," 2–3.

571 Bearden, "Man with a Message."

572 "What Is a Luis Palau Festival?" [online]; accessed 15 November 2007; available from http://www.palau.org/lpea/festivals/; Internet.

573 Kevin Palau, "A New Look for Mass Evangelism," 2.

574 "93,000 Attend Luis Palau's Portland Festival '99," *Proclaim!,* 2007, 28.

575 Kevin Palau, "A New Look for Mass Evangelism," 2. Cf. Music has been a vital part of campaigns. Since Charles Finney, most successful mass evangelists have been accompanied by great musicians as their "co-evangelists." For example, Finney had Thomas Hastings, Moody had Sankey, Sunday had Rodeheaver, and Billy Graham had Shea and Barrows. Delos Miles, *Introduction to Evangelism* (Nashville, TN: Broadman Press, 1983), 236. See also William G.

McLoughlin, *Modern Revivalism: Charles Grandison Finney to Billy Graham* (New York: Ronald Press, 1959), 87, 92–95, 98–99.

576 "93,000 Attend Luis Palau's Portland Festival '99," 28.

577 Morrow, "Mass Evangelism and Church Planting," 25.

578 Palau and Sanford, *Calling America and the Nations*, 208–9.

579 Kevin Palau, "A New Look for Mass Evangelism," 1.

580 Portland festivals in 1999 and 2000 drew 230,000 people in total.

581 "What Is a Festival?" [online]; accessed 11 August 2008; available from http://www.palau.org/festivals; Internet. The number in parentheses indicates attendance.

582 "Is Palau the Next Billy Graham?" *ABC News*, 8 October 2005 [online]; accessed 27 September 2007; available from http://abcnews.go.com/GMA/story?id=1195278&page=1; Internet.

583 Palau, "The Future of Mass Evangelism," 159.

584 In 2006, they formed "Livin It Alliance."

585 "Livin It" (Portland, OR: PalauFest Productions, 2004), DVD; "Livin It LA" (Portland, OR: Livin It Productions, 2006), DVD.

586 "Luis Palau Legacy Campaign," *Proclaim!*, 2008, 29. A total of 680,278 attended Livin It outreaches, and 46,931 made public decisions for Christ. The majority, 18.1 million people, had been reached through media.

CHAPTER 9

EVANGELISTIC STRATEGY: MASS MEDIA

Utilizing mass communication tools, such as the press, radio, television, films, and the Internet, has also proved to be very helpful to the process of presenting the message of the gospel.[587] While there can be no doubt that mass media cannot replace the community of faith, these tools have unique merits and, when properly used, can serve as a bridge between unbelievers and local churches.[588]

Mass Media as Evangelistic Strategy

From the early years of his ministry, Luis Palau has utilized many forms of mass media for evangelism, including radio, television, the press, books, tracts, films, and more recently the Internet. While some Christians regard the media as "a mortal enemy," Palau calls it "one of the greatest allies in communicating the Good News on a large scale."[589] He contends that mass media should be used as a means to communicate God's love to people:

> Properly utilized, mass evangelism places the media at the service of a sovereign Creator. God allowed the invention of modern means of communication, I believe, for the purpose

> of sharing his truth, not to corrupt humanity. Thus when films, telephones, radio, television and the press become God's instruments, they fulfill his holy purpose to redeem and bless humanity.[590]

At Amsterdam '86 Palau pointed out to other evangelists that "Utilizing mass media is certainly not an option for every evangelist. But for some of us it's territory we need to claim for God and possess for His glory and for the spreading of His Kingdom."[591]

Palau's conviction in terms of the use of mass media for evangelism stems from his belief that while the message is sacred, the method is not. For Palau, using mass media for evangelism is like applying the first-century principle of mass evangelism to today's milieu. He explains:

> The Apostle Paul went to the marketplace where they sold vegetables and started talking about the Gospel. He got a riot going, and he got attention from the people. In today's time, going to the television is going to the marketplace. That's where the action is, that's where most people pay attention.[592]

When asked whether Jesus would be on television if He were here, Palau responded with an unequivocal yes. He also believes that the apostle Paul would have scheduled a press conference to draw the attention of people.[593] There are some practical reasons behind Palau's passion for utilizing mass media for evangelism. More than anything else, mass media makes it possible to saturate a city with the message of the gospel.

Media coverage during evangelistic campaigns stirs people's interest in the Christian faith and creates "God-consciousness" in a city. It also draws the attention of political leaders and other influential people and gives them an opportunity to hear the gospel.[594]

Palau has utilized both secular and Christian mass media. Using secular media for evangelism is strategic. In fact, some question the effectiveness of Christian media in terms of evangelism. For example, Don Cox made these observations:

> By and large, the non-Christian society is not being reached through media evangelism.... Religious broadcasting is primarily reaching insiders. ... The primary role of the mass media could be characterized as providing some Christian nurture to people who are already Christians.[595]

In the same vein, Rusty Wright states this:

> In the United States, religious programs on radio and television reach only 9.2 percent of the total population. And 84 percent of those who view religious shows in the United States are already born again. This means that Christian programs are largely reaching Christian audiences. But secular shows can have a much greater percentage of non-Christians watching them.[596]

These statistics clearly show that utilizing secular media for evangelistic purposes is far more effective and extensive in its influence than using Christian media. Aware of this, Luis Palau has utilized secular TV and radio for his ministry, sometimes even in an aggressive and forceful way.[597]

Palau makes use of the secular public media whenever he holds evangelistic campaigns. A glimpse of his appeal to the public media can be found in his comment at a press conference in Kansas City in 1997. To a group of reporters from television, radio, and newspapers, he invited, "Help us with the reporting. Don't talk too much about me—talk about Jesus Christ. That's the best thing you can do. I can't do the job in one week to let all of Kansas City hear the voice of God without the help of the media, so give me a hand."[598]

In many cases, the media coverage has been positive and supportive of Palau and his ministry. But sometimes it has been cynical and critical. Nevertheless, as McWilliam observes, even an unfavorable report plays a positive role overall for the campaign, drawing people's attention and stirring people's interest in spiritual matters.[599]

McBride's observation during Palau's Mission Maine supports this idea. He records, "Even [to] the most antagonistic media, the message of Christ was still being presented. What they intended to be a satire, turned out to be a positive article proclaiming the gospel."[600] Such a report illustrates the strategic value of utilizing secular mass media for the cause of the gospel. When utilized properly, mass media can be a valuable tool to reach more people with the good news.

Radio and Television Broadcasting

Luis Palau's vision to preach the gospel through mass media began when he first heard Billy Graham preach on the radio in 1952. Palau prayed to God to use him on the radio to bring people to Christ, and his prayer has been answered, no doubt beyond his wildest imaginings.[601] LPA estimates that "Today he [Palau] can be heard daily by millions of people on more than 2,600 radio stations broadcasting in forty-two countries in both English and Spanish."[602]

Radio has been one of Palau's passionate and favorite methods of evangelism. Commenting on Palau's view, Robnett acknowledges, "If he had only one means of preaching the gospel, he would use radio."[603] Although radio is an old technology, it still holds certain merits, especially for evangelistic purposes. First, in many respects radio has no limitations in its coverage. In the words of John Fear, "radio knows no geographical, social, political, or ideological boundaries."[604] It can reach even countries where religious freedom is forbidden. Second, as Palau observed, radio "is still the only technology available in some parts of the world."[605]

Palau's first use of radio for evangelistic purposes occurred while he was living in Colombia in 1964. In the same year Palau began two radio programs, "Luis Palau Responde" and "Cruzada," both for Spanish audiences. "Responde" is Palau's five-minute question-and-answer program that provides biblical answers to life's questions, and "Cruzada" is a fifteen-minute Bible teaching program designed to help people grow in their faith. According to LPA's estimation, today these programs are heard daily by 22 million people in the Spanish-speaking world.[606]

Another daily radio program, "Heartbeat with Luis Palau," was launched in 1991 for English audiences. This was similar to its Spanish counterpart, "Cruzada," in its nature. In 1993 LPA also started a two-minute daily program, "Luis Palau Responds." Like "Luis Palau

Responde," it was a question-and-answer program for English speakers.

Since the year 2000 LPA has aired another English program, "Reaching Your World with Luis Palau"; this is the only English radio program still running today.[607] According to LPA the program is a "one-minute and two-minute daily English feature that provides listeners with practical encouragement on how to share their faith."[608] The program airs in forty-two countries.

Palau also has utilized television to share the gospel. In 1965 he launched his first live television counseling program in Quito, Ecuador; it is now called "Night Talk with Luis Palau."[609] During this live program, which is aired on local stations during campaigns, people call in to Palau with various life issues, to which Palau provides biblical answers. This live counseling on television, originally suggested to Palau by one of his key team members, seems to be his unique contribution to evangelism methodology. As far as he knows there was no precedent for evangelists to counsel people live on television in North America.[610]

Palau's live question-and-answer program has been popular and effective, leading many people to Christ. A survey during Palau's campaigns in El Salvador in 1970 shows that over a two-week period his live broadcast captured more than 66 percent of the national viewing audience each night.[611] Concerning Palau's live counseling during the campaign in Guayaquil, Ecuador, in 1980, McWilliam comments: "People literally were flying in from various cities for counseling, as well as traveling many hours by bus as their spiritual needs were aroused through seeing the TV programs."[612]

In 1985 Palau conducted six live counseling programs during the campaigns in Argentina. People's response was so overwhelming that he recalls, "We were dumbfounded when hundreds of viewers kept calling in for hours after we went off the air. ... Biblical counselors trained by Dr. Williams were still leading callers to Christ all day long and halfway through the night a week later!"[613]

This live call-in counseling on television has some unique advantages. As Palau observes, although he counsels one person at a time, the effect is multiplied since a multitude of people in the audience with similar situations or problems will sympathize with the counselee and find answers to their own problems. People also feel intimacy when Palau counsels each person individually. Unlike watching Palau preaching to a crowd, they feel that he is speaking to them directly and personally. In addition, Palau can identify in these conversations what is troubling people and demonstrate that the Bible is relevant to all of life's problems.[614]

Besides live counseling programs, LPA has produced TV specials based on the ministry's "Great music, Good News" festivals, which have been aired throughout North and South America.[615] Beachfest Fort Lauderdale in 2003, for example, was broadcast as a television special, "Beachfest with Luis Palau," that received the "Television Special of the Year" award from the National Religious Broadcasters.[616]

Another milestone in LPA's media ministry was a one-hour TV documentary, "Livin It: Unusual Suspects," produced in 2005 by PalauFest Productions. Four individuals—Stephen Baldwin, Chynna Phillips, Christian Hosoi, and Luis Palau—are featured in this documentary, each telling from their own unique perspective how they came to know Christ. People's response was so overwhelming that this program aired across the States, in Russia, and in the Netherlands and was nominated for an Emmy award in 2006.[617]

Publications, Internet, and Other Electronic Media

Books, articles, and other forms of literature have played a part in Palau's evangelistic strategy. Palau himself has authored more than fifty books and booklets, including his most recent book, *A Friendly Dialogue Between an Atheist and a Christian*, which was authored with a Chinese government official and scientist, Zhao Qizheng. Palau's career as a writer began with his first book, *Walk on Water, Pete*, published both in English and in Spanish in 1974. While his books have been written originally either in Spanish or English, some of them have been translated into several other languages, including Dutch, Swedish, German, Portuguese, Finnish, Afrikaans, Chinese, and Korean.[618]

Palau and his team have published several magazines over the years. The first was *Cruzada*, a quarterly news magazine in Spanish, first published in 1972. In 1978 they added a Spanish magazine for pastors and Christian leaders in Latin America, titled *Continente Nuevo*. They also oversaw the editorial content of the Spanish magazine for pastors called *Apuntes Pastorales*. *Briefing*, the Palau team's news reports for English-speaking readers, was first published in 1979.[619] Its name has been modified to *Heartbeat* in 1988 and again to *Proclaim!* in 1994, under which title it is still being published today.

Through evangelistic campaigns LPA has also distributed millions of evangelistic booklets and tracts to new converts. In addition, Palau has contributed many columns and articles to leading magazines and newspapers, both Christian and secular. Recently, for instance, he has been featured in such magazines as "*Christianity Today*, *World*, *New Man*, *Daily Bread*, *Charisma*, *Outreach*, *Portland Monthly*, and *Texas Monthly*."[620]

Along with the development of new technology, Palau has utilized the latest mass communication techniques available. These include films, videos, CDs, DVDs, the Internet, blogs, and podcasts. In 1972 LPA produced its first evangelistic film in both Spanish and English.[621] Since then, many of Palau's sermons have been produced as videos and CDs. LPA has also produced several DVDs that feature Palau's festivals.

More recently, Palau has been a regular contributor to some Internet blogs covering topics on faith, Christianity, and evangelism. According to LPA, "Some of his [Palau's] most recent contributions can be found on the *Newsweek/Washington Post* blog site known as *On Faith*."[622] In addition, Palau's monthly audio blog, *Growing Faith*, can be heard "through iTunes, Yahoo! Podcasts, iPodder.com, Podcast Alley, Podcast.net, Odeo, Podcast Pickle, and Podnova."[623] Palau understands the importance of social media in engaging people in conversations about Jesus Christ.

Saturation Evangelism Through Mass Media

During evangelistic campaigns Luis Palau utilizes mass media to saturate a city or region with the message of the gospel. Although Palau makes use of media to varying degrees in all of his campaigns, some have employed mass media more strategically than others. Some of the highlights are Continente '75, Commonwealth '84, Continente '85, Asia '86, and Continente '98.

The first of a series of these major media outreaches was Continente '75 during a campaign in Managua, Nicaragua, which lasted for twenty-two days. Using a COMSAT satellite and other technology, Palau and his team communicated the message of the gospel in twenty-three countries in the Americas via fifty-six radio stations and more than one hundred television stations.[624] Difusiones InterAmericanas (Inter-American Broadcasting), a Costa Rica–based organization, estimated that about 80 million people were reached with the gospel through this event.[625]

Commonwealth '84 was a landmark media outreach in 1984. During the last week of Mission to London, Palau's preaching was aired via radio and television in more than fifty English-speaking countries on five continents. Commonwealth '84 used the same technology as Continente '75, sending airwaves via satellite signals. The response was so overwhelming that LPA received testimonies from people around the world even months after the mission.[626]

Compared to Continente '75, which was broadcast for three weeks, Commonwealth '84 was relatively short, being broadcast for only six days. In the view of Holton and Jones, however, "the latter extended the Gospel to a much larger audience and geographical area, reaching cultures new to the Palau team's ministry."[627] They estimated that around 175 million people listened to Palau's preaching worldwide, many in the Third World.[628]

Another massive media outreach took place in Latin America in 1985. Over Easter Palau's team covered Latin America with the message of the gospel. Known as Continente '85, this media outreach reached twenty-two countries of Latin America. Continente '85 was five times larger in terms of the number of stations than Continente '75; more than 330 radio and 480 television stations broadcast the message of the gospel.[629]

Palau has also reached Asia with the gospel through media. During the first Asian campaign in Singapore in 1986, Palau and his team decided to reach all Asian countries with the gospel. Thus Asia '86 was born in cooperation with many broadcast companies, such as Far East Broadcasting Company, Trans World Radio, HCJB, and other radio and television networks. Palau's five campaign messages were translated into eight Asian languages and broadcast across the continent. Along with radio and television broadcasts, they distributed Palau's booklet *What Is a Real Christian?* in sixty nations through about 300 distributors. Asia '86 was historical. Palau comments, "Never before had so many ministries worked hand in hand to reach so many Asian people in one fell swoop."[630]

In North America, Palau's Say Yes Chicago in 1996 utilized media effectively. Many of Palau's twenty-seven one-hour live television programs broadcast in Chicago were aired nationwide by national cable networks. Beachfest Fort Lauderdale in 2003, the largest festival to date in the United States, was another highlight of media outreach. It was broadcast live on more than twelve hundred radio stations, and its television special, *Beachfest with Luis Palau*, was designated "Television Special of the Year" by the National Religious Broadcasters.[631] Palau's live call-in counseling program, "Night Talk," was televised locally by PAX and broadcast nationwide by "satellite and cable via Sky Angel, iLife, and FamilyNet."[632]

Continente '98 was Palau's third continent-wide media outreach in Latin America. During his campaign in Argentina in 1998, approximately 500 stations broadcast Palau's recorded messages. Palau's first Middle East campaign also impacted multitudes of people through media. During the campaign in Cairo, Egypt, in 1998, Palau's message was recorded and distributed the following day to 585 churches. Approximately 110,000 people watched the videos each night, and more than 30,500 people made public decisions for Christ.[633]

Conclusion

Mass media have been a significant aspect of Palau's evangelistic strategy from the early years of his ministry. He has utilized literature, radio, television, the Internet, and other technologies to spread the gospel. During his evangelistic campaigns Palau makes strategic use of both secular and Christian media. This draws people's attention to the Christian faith and ultimately results in saturation of a region with the gospel. Among his achievements, Palau's live counseling on television seems to be his unique contribution to evangelistic strategy using mass media.

Although Palau has spread the gospel on virtually every continent through mass media, the Spanish-speaking world has been most affected. Palau's goal to reach 250 million Spanish-speaking people in the world with the gospel through media was very ambitious. Echoing John Wesley, he even declared that "The twenty-three Spanish-speaking countries of Latin America are our parish."[634]

God has honored Palau's faith and fulfilled his vision. By the end of the 1970s, Palau could boldly claim that his team had already saturated Latin America with the gospel through media. He stated, "We had broadcast the Gospel via television and radio to at least one out of every three Spanish-speaking people in the world."[635] Now through the worldwide web most of Palau's campaigns can be either seen or heard live on the Internet.

Endnotes

587 Mass media has become an important tool of evangelism from the early twentieth century. According to John Mark Terry, utilization of radio for preaching began in 1921, and TV broadcasting with religious purpose was started in 1952 by Catholic bishop Fulton J. Sheen. Use of TV for evangelism reached its climax in the 1970s and 1980s, until the scandals of some televangelists broke out. John Mark Terry, *Evangelism: A Concise History* (Nashville, TN: Broadman & Holman Publishers, 1994), 199–210. For a brief historical sketch of mass media for evangelism, see also Delos Miles, *Introduction to Evangelism* (Nashville, TN: Broadman Press, 1983), 244–48, 269–85.

588 See "Is TV Appropriate for Mass Evangelism?" *Christianity Today*, 16 October 1987, 50; "Televangelism, Pro and Con," *Home Missions*, June 1973, 8–9.

589 Luis Palau, "The Evangelist Has a Strategy for Harvest," in *The Mission of an Evangelist*, ed. J. D. Douglas (Minneapolis, MN: World Wide Publications, 2001), 233.

590 Luis Palau, "The Future of Mass Evangelism," in *Evangelism: The Next Ten Years*, ed. Sherwood Eliot Wirt (Waco, TX: Word Books, 1978), 162.

591 Luis Palau, "The Evangelist and the Ministry of the Holy Spirit," in *The Calling of an Evangelist*, ed. J. D. Douglas (Minneapolis, MN: World Wide Publications, 1987), 140.

592 Luis Palau and Rusty Wright, "Getting on Secular Television and Radio Talk Shows," in *The Work of an Evangelist*, ed. J. D. Douglas (Minneapolis, MN: World Wide Publications, 1984), 839.

593 Luis Palau and Mike Umlandt, *The Only Hope for America: The Transforming Power of the Gospel of Jesus Christ* (Wheaton, IL: Crossway Books, 1996), 78.

594 Palau, "The Future of Mass Evangelism," 157, 160.

595 Don Cox, "Evangelism and the Mass Media," *Evangelism in the Twenty-First Century: The Critical Issues*, ed. Thom Rainer (Wheaton, IL: Harold Shaw Publishers, 1989), 67. Cf. A survey also reveals that most viewers of Christian broadcasts are older Christian women. Jeffrey K. Hadden and Charles E. Swann, *Prime Time Preachers* (Reading, MA: Addison-Wesley Publishing Co., 1981), 61–62.

596 Palau and Wright, "Getting on Secular Television and Radio Talk Shows,", 834.

597 For a couple of episodes in which Palau urged secular media to cover his campaigns in a forceful way, see Palau and Wright, "Getting on Secular Television and Radio Talk Shows," 840.

598 Kimberly Claassen, "Reviving the Nations," *The Plain Truth* (March/April, 1998), 11.

599 John McWilliam, "Mass Evangelism: Reaching Your City in the Eighties," *Urban Mission* 3 (September 1985), 12.

600 Kevin T. McBride, "Retaking the Village Green: Building Strategic Partnerships for Evangelism that Work in New England" (D.Min. project, Gordon-Conwell Theological Seminary, 2001), 112–13.

601 Luis Palau and David Sanford, *Luis Palau: Calling America and the Nations to Christ* (Nashville, TN: Thomas Nelson, Inc., 1994; rev. 2000), 37. Some of the radio networks through which Palau has preached include "HCJB, Far East Broadcasting Company, Moody Broadcasting, Trans World Radio, and hundreds of other Christian radio networks and stations."

602 "Radio," LPA [online]; accessed 28 July 2008; available from http://www.palau.org/media/radio; Internet.

603 Luis Palau and Timothy Robnett, *Telling the Story: Evangelism for the Next Generation* (Ventura, CA: Regal Books, 2006), 102.

604 John Fear, "Strategy Report Mass Media," in *Let the Earth Hear His Voice: International Conference on World Evangelism*, ed. J. D. Douglas (Minneapolis, MN: World Wide Publications, 1975), 598.

605 Palau, "The Evangelist Has a Strategy," 233.

606 LPA, "An Overview of Luis Palau's Life and Ministry," October 2007, 2.

607 Ibid., 4, 6. Sarah Bruce, interview by the author, interview by telephone, July 31, 2008. Sarah Bruce is producer of *Reaching Your World with Luis Palau.*

608 "Radio," LPA [on-line]; accessed 28 July 2008; available from http://www.palau.org/media/radio; Internet. According to LPA, "For his persistence in sharing

the Good News worldwide on radio, the National Religious Broadcasters (NRB) presented Luis with its Milestone Achievement Award in 2002."

609 The latest live call-in counseling was produced during the campaign in Fort Lauderdale, Florida in 2003. Bruce, interview by the author, July 31, 2008.

610 Palau, interview by the author, May 9, 2008.

611 Palau and Sanford, *Calling America and the Nations*, 101. According to Palau, this survey was performed by an independent polling agency at the request of the station owner.

612 McWilliam, "Mass Evangelism," 12. Concerning this live counseling, *Christianity Today* reported, "The nation's largest television network, 'Telecentro,' broadcast Palau's live question-and-answer program for 12 nights, and radio station HCJB in Quito transmitted Palau's crusade messages into at least 10 countries in Central and South America." "Television and Radio Made the Greatest Impact During Evangelist Luis Palau's Recent Two-week Crusade in Guayaquil, Ecuador," *Christianity Today*, 24 October 1980, 74.

613 Palau and Sanford, *Calling America and the Nations*, 169.

614 Palau, interview by the author, May 9, 2008.

615 "Television," LPA [online]; accessed 28 July 2008; available from http://www.palau.org/media/television; Internet. According LPA, "These 'Great music, Good News' specials have been widely acclaimed for their quality, entertainment value, and positive evangelistic message as evidenced by a 2001 Emmy nomination."

616 LPA, "Overview of Life and Ministry," 5. "Luis Palau Festival: Live from Fort Lauderdale, FL" (Portland, OR: PalauFest Productions, 2003), DVD.

617 Ibid. LPA also produced the nationally syndicated radio special "Livin It: Unusual Suspects," which aired on 10,744 stations across the country in 2006. "Radio," LPA [online]; accessed 28 July 2008; available from http://www.palau.org/media/radio; Internet.

618 Susan Holton and David L. Jones, *Spirit Aflame: Luis Palau's Mission to London* (Grand Rapids: Baker Book House, 1985), 63. Chinese and Korean are not listed in the reference, but *Friendly Dialogue* was first published in Chinese prior to the English version, and three of Palau's books have been translated into Korean so far.

619 Ibid. According to Palau, the purpose of *Continente Nuevo* has been to "feed the shepherds who feed the flock of God." More than 40,000 leaders have subscribed to this magazine. Palau and Sanford, *Calling America and the Nations*, 34.

620 "Print," LPA [online]; accessed 28 July 2008; available from http://www.palau.org/media/print; Internet.

621 Palau and Sanford, *Calling America and the Nations*, 113.

622 "Blogs" LPA [online]; accessed 28 July 2008; available from http://www.palau.org/media/blogs; Internet.

623 Ibid.

624 Palau and Sanford, *Calling America and the Nations*, 122. Radio programs aired live, while television aired taped programs.

625 Luis Palau, "Evangelism in the Future," in *Evangelical Missions Tomorrow*, ed. Wade T. Coggins and E. L. Frizen (South Pasadena, CA: William Carey Library, 1977), 173. See also Edward Murphy, "Continente '75: Evangelism in Ripened Fields," *Church Growth Bulletin* 12 (January 1976): 507–9.

626 Holton and Jones, *Spirit Aflame*, 11, 164. See ibid., 191-92 for some testimonies sent from people around the globe.

627 Ibid., 194–95.

628 Ibid., 192. Holton and Jones also record that "Participants in Commonwealth '84 included Bible Literature International, ELWA Radio, Far East Broadcasting Association, Far East Broadcasting Company, HCJB in Ecuador, Trans World Radio, Moody Broadcasting Network, Northwestern College Radio Network, Trinity Broadcasting Network, and WTKK-TV in Washington D.C." Ibid., 193.

629 Palau and Sanford, *Calling America and the Nations*, 167.

630 Ibid., 170.

631 LPA, "Overview of Life and Ministry," 5.

632 Kimberly Claassen, "Luis Palau Beachfest: Taking the Good News to the People," *Wireless Age*, January/February 2003, 30.

633 LPA, "Overview of Life and Ministry," 5–6.

634 Palau and Sanford, *Calling America and the Nations*, 109.

635 Ibid., 144.

CHAPTER 10

EVANGELISTIC STRATEGY: EQUIPPING NEXT-GENERATION EVANGELISTS

Christian A. Schwarz, the renowned church-growth strategist, uses the analogy of an apple to stress the importance of church planting, saying, "Just as the true fruit of an apple tree is not an apple, but another tree … the true fruit of a church is not a new group, but a new church."[636] The same analogy may apply to an evangelist: The true fruit of the evangelist is not converted souls, but another evangelist who will lead many others to Christ. Luis Palau offers a good example in this respect; he has committed his life to mentoring and equipping evangelists from upcoming generations.

Mentoring Young Evangelists

The importance of raising new evangelists cannot be overemphasized. In fact, this method is practical as well as biblical. In his seminal book *Master Plan of Evangelism*, Robert Coleman insists that making disciples was the most important strategy of Jesus Christ on Earth. Coleman notes, "His [Jesus'] concern was not with programs to reach the multitudes, but with men whom the multitudes would follow."[637] Perhaps this statement best describes Luis Palau's passion and vision for future evangelists. Following the example of his Master, Jesus Christ, Palau has helped to equip many as evangelists.

From his own experiences, Palau knows the value of mentoring. As he acknowledges often, he has been mentored by such people as Billy Graham, Dick Hillis, Ray Stedman, and Keith Bentson. Palau asserts, "Thanks to their mentoring, I was spared a lot of unnecessary grief and dead ends."[638] He also honestly acknowledges that evangelists have a tendency to hinder the success of younger evangelists for fear that they might outgrow and overtake them.[639] However, he strongly believes that mentoring and equipping young evangelists is the ultimate strategy of mass evangelism. At Amsterdam 2000 Palau advocated for this:

> Evangelists need other evangelists. We need each other all the time. Build partnerships. Invest in the lives of other evangelists. My team and I currently work with 10 partner evangelists. We offer training and resources to many other evangelists who are just getting started. Someone needs to carry on the work after you're gone. Show them how! It's the ultimate harvest strategy.[640]

As early as 1972 Palau began to invest in the lives of younger evangelists. He mentored and trained associate evangelists on his team. Many of them have grown up to be successful evangelists and have their own evangelistic ministries today.[641] Palau does not regard them as his helpers but as God's servants, working together with him for God's kingdom and glory. His respect for and companionship with associate evangelists is confirmed by his own words. Referring to Dan Owens, a member of Palau's Alliance Ministries, Palau notes, "I always like to make it clear that Dan doesn't work for me, but with me, as God's evangelist."[642]

One of the most significant fruits of Palau's mentoring is his own son, Andrew Palau. Andrew departed from God during his college years at the University of Oregon, but God brought back the prodigal son in 1993. During Palau's campaign in Kingston, Jamaica, Andrew yielded his life to Jesus and soon joined his father's evangelistic team.[643] Since 2006 he has been working as an evangelist alongside his father, preaching in many festivals and Livin It rallies in the States and around the world, including Poland, Romania, India, Jamaica, Mexico, Egypt, Argentina, and parts of Africa.[644]

Next Generation Alliance

Formation of NGA

As Palau has received guidance from several spiritual mentors, he is now paying back the debt to young evangelists. This has been achieved in many ways. He has lived an exemplary life as an evangelist, spoken in many evangelism leadership conferences, and written books and articles on the ministry of the evangelist. As Palau recalls, however, "Still, we felt an urgency to do more."[645] Palau and his team were looking for more effective and specific ways to help young evangelists for world evangelization. This vision came true with the formation of the Next Generation Alliance (NGA) in 1998.

Palau envisioned NGA, based on his appreciation for his mentors in the past, as an organization committed to passing down what he has learned to "younger, gifted evangelists."[646] The vision of NGA was spawned during the Say Yes Chicago campaign in 1996, during which a team of evangelists, along with Palau, presented the gospel throughout the city. Palau notes, "Out of that experience God cemented plans for our evangelistic association to more formally and more aggressively ensure that a new generation of evangelists carries the banner of evangelism well into the 21st century."[647] Palau also pronounces, "America is not going to be evangelized by a few 'famous' evangelists. God didn't plan it that way. He has given the gift of evangelism to thousands."[648]

Ministry of NGA

According to LPA, "Next Generation Alliance exists as a global network to identify, affirm and equip evangelists worldwide to complete the Great Commission in our generation."[649] Palau had three specific goals for NGA from the beginning.[650] First, it exists to "serve a small network of independent partner evangelists."[651] Since most evangelists lack the resources for large campaigns, NGA shares its know-how from decades of experience and mentors a selected group of evangelists. More specifically, Palau states, "We help them establish a strong board of directors, pursue open doors for crusade invitations, mobilize and train a broad cross-section of the church for evangelism, and raise the prayer and financial support they need to keep preaching the Gospel."[652]

Second, NGA endeavors to "present medium-sized intensive training conferences." These conferences provide invaluable information for evangelists, covering topics such as "the role and work of an evangelist, how to set up strict guidelines for accountability, how to do Christian fund-raising, how to work with the secular media, how to evaluate crusade invitations, how to do friendship evangelism and counselor training, etc."[653]

Third, NGA also provides "seminary-level evangelism training" in conjunction with Multnomah Biblical Seminary. Today NGA, along with several seminaries, offers internships to future evangelists. Young evangelists learn important lessons for mass evangelism, in practice as well as in theory.[654]

Currently NGA hosts a large evangelism conference every three years in America and a couple of conferences for evangelists around the world every year. It also conducts numerous in-depth seminars on various issues pertinent to evangelism. Besides these conferences and seminars, young evangelists also learn by participating in campaigns,[655] through which they achieve "a new level and new maturity in their own ministry."[656] They gain firsthand experience in preaching the gospel to the masses, learn to better understand their role as evangelist, and acquire essential skills.

In addition, mentoring is an integral part of NGA's ministry to young evangelists. Robnett, the director of NGA and LPA's Alliance Ministries, describes the importance and mechanism of mentoring in NGA:

> Effective evangelists also find great wisdom and encouragement by seeking out older, experienced evangelists as

mentors. Next Generation Alliance exists to connect evangelists in these relationships. When Mike Silva first began serving the Lord as an NGA partner evangelist, Dr. Bill Thomas came alongside to support and mentor Mike's growing ministry. Dr. Thomas's extensive knowledge and experience in international evangelism allowed Mike to learn about preaching the gospel in underdeveloped countries, and over time, those countries became the focus of Mike's ministry. Now that Mike himself mentors newly emerging evangelists, Dr. Thomas has taken three more young servants under his wing to teach them about international evangelistic ministry.[657]

Fruits of NGA

NGA's ministry for the past ten years has borne much fruit. Beyond the mentoring and equipping of young evangelists, multitudes of people have come to know Christ through campaigns. In some cases a team of evangelists from NGA has worked with Luis Palau. Statewide campaigns such as Mission Maine (1999) and Mission Connecticut (2001) are highlights in terms of this strategy.

On the other hand, NGA has launched its own campaigns around the world independently from Palau. Multiple evangelists saturate a city, a region, or even a nation with the message of the gospel through such campaigns. In addition to proclaiming the gospel, they share the love of Christ in concrete ways: "They serve hands-on through medical camps, drilling wells, holding conferences, trainings, teaching, planting churches, participating in feeding programs, providing life-saving essentials such as mosquito nets, blankets, and more."[658]

NGA's ministry has extended to virtually every continent, with particularly notable achievements in Asia and Africa.[659] In Uganda alone, from 2004 to 2007 more than 610,000 people heard the gospel through NGA events, with 66,000 responding to the message in public.[660]

Through NGA dozens of smaller ministries have been born as well.[661] NGA also estimates, "More than 17 million people have been reached with the Good News, and more than 792,000 have made documented, public commitments to Jesus Christ through the work of NGA. In ten years the alliance has grown from only a handful of evangelists to more than 200 evangelists and ministries."[662] Robnett expects that number to grow to over 500 by 2013. As a result of the Alliance Ministries, festivals, and media, Palau sees a great future for the ministry he launched nearly five decades ago.

Having been mentored by several spiritual advisors, Luis Palau has known the value of mentoring and equipping evangelists. His vision for raising evangelists to preach the gospel to future generations has been accomplished with the formation of NGA. Through the ministry of NGA and Alliance Ministries, young evangelists have been trained and continue to be trained in knowledge and practice, and multitudes of people have come to believe in Jesus. Among the many evangelistic strategies Luis Palau has utilized, perhaps NGA is the most significant and effective in the long run. Even after Palau finishes his mission on Earth, his influence will continue through those who have learned from him.

Final Thoughts on Evangelistic Strategy

Flowing from his theological convictions in evangelism, Luis Palau has reached people with the gospel throughout his ministry, using every means available. The last five chapters have addressed Palau's four representative strategies for evangelism: preaching, evangelistic campaigns, mass media, and the equipping of future evangelists.

A couple of common characteristics can be observed in his approaches. First, his strategies resemble those of preceding evangelists in many respects. Building upon the methods of his predecessors, he has continued to develop new strategies. Second, each approach is marked by relevancy and creativity. These have been key principles of Palau's strategy.

Each strategy has its unique features. First, his preaching has been biblical and Christ-centered, employing a problem-solution approach. In these respects, his approach resembles Graham's. On the other hand, his message is similar to Moody's in that he emphasizes God's love rather than His judgment. Second, in evangelistic campaigns Palau, while adopting the methodologies of previous evangelists, has moved beyond their ideas. Like Finney and Moody, Palau has developed culturally relevant and innovative strategies. The successes of the new models of campaigns, such as festivals and the action sports ministry Livin It, confirm this point.

Third, Palau has employed mass media tactically to saturate a region, a country, or even a continent with the gospel. His live call-in television counseling is noteworthy because of its effectiveness and uniqueness. Finally, Palau's commitment to future evangelists has borne much fruit through the ministry of NGA. His evangelistic ministry will be continued by those so trained until Christ comes.

Luis Palau's ministry showcases the importance of strategy in mass evangelism. The fact that his audience has grown tenfold after he altered the format of his evangelistic campaigns provides valuable insight. For mass evangelism to be viable and effective for world evangelization, its approach must be continually modified by adopting and developing new strategies in a relevant and creative way. Because of his willingness to adjust his strategy, Palau's ministry has grown tremendously, touching individual lives and transforming society. The following chapters will examine his evangelistic fruits around the world.

Endnotes

636 Christian A. Schwarz, *Natural Church Development: A Guide to Eight Essential Qualities of Healthy Churches* (Carol Stream, IL: ChurchSmart Resources, 1998), 68.

637 Robert E. Coleman, *The Master Plan of Evangelism*, 2nd ed. (Grand Rapids: Spire, 1994), 27.

638 David Sanford, "Luis Palau: Calling America and the Nations to Christ," *Life Wise* (December/January 2002), 9. For the influence of Palau's mentors on himself, see chapter 2.

639 Luis Palau and Timothy Robnett, *Telling the Story: Evangelism for the Next Generation* (Ventura, CA: Regal Books, 2006), 132.

640 Luis Palau, "The Evangelist Has a Strategy for Harvest," in *The Mission of an Evangelist*, ed. J. D. Douglas (Minneapolis, MN: World Wide Publications, 2001), 234.

641 Luis Palau and David Sanford, *Luis Palau: Calling America and the Nations to Christ* (Nashville, TN: Thomas Nelson, Inc., 1994; rev. 2000), 112–13. These

evangelists include Galo Vazquez, Edgardo Silvoso, Carlos Quiroa, Marcelino Ortiz, and others.

642 Ibid., 171–72.

643 Mike Umlandt, "A Father's Passion," *New Man: Proclaiming Life to Men* (June 1997), reprinted from LPA.

644 "Andrew Palau Festivals," *Proclaim!,* 2008, 22–23.

645 Palau and Sanford, *Calling America and the Nations*, 204.

646 Sanford, "Calling America and the Nations," 9.

647 Palau and Sanford, *Calling America and the Nations*, 203.

648 "Evangelism in the New Millennium," *Proclaim!,* September 1999, 4.

649 "Next Generation Alliance," LPA [online]; accessed 6 August 2008; available from http://www.palau.org/nga; Internet.

650 Palau and Sanford, *Calling America and the Nations*, 204.

651 There were nine partner evangelists in the network in the beginning: Haje Andraus, Kelly Green, Frank Harber, Dimitris Iliadis, Steve Jamison, Dan Owens, Mike Silva, Bill Thomas, and Steve Wingfield. "Announcing: Next Generation Alliance," *Proclaim!*, March 1998, 4.

652 Palau and Sanford, *Calling America and the Nations*, 204.

653 Ibid.

654 Robnett, interview by the author, via telephone, August 6, 2008.

655 Ibid.

656 "Passion for Madurai Brings Luis Palau's Next Generation Alliance to India," *Proclaim!,* vol. 4, 2006, 14. The specific campaign in this comment was in Madurai, India, in 2006. In eighteen festivals, NGA evangelists presented the gospel to more than 110,934 Indian people and led 20,281 of them to Christ. Ibid., 13.

657 Robnett, *Telling the Story*, 43.

658 "Next Generation Alliance Is Thriving," *Proclaim!,* 2008, 31.

659 Robnett, interview by the author, August 6, 2008.

660 "Arise Uganda and Beyond," *Proclaim!,* 2008, 30.

661 "Introducing the Luis Palau Association's Innovative Evangelism Conference," *Proclaim!,* vol. 4, 2006, 15.

662 "Next Generation Alliance," LPA [online]; accessed 6 August 2008; available from http://www.palau.org/nga; Internet.

CHAPTER 11

GLOBAL IMPACT: LATIN AMERICA AND EUROPE

Toward the end of his ministry the apostle Paul declared, "So from Jerusalem all the way around to Illyricum, I have fully proclaimed the gospel of Christ" (Romans 15:19). In modern terms, states Soards, Paul claims to have preached the gospel from Israel through Lebanon, Syria, Turkey, and Greece, as far as portions of Bulgaria, Albania, and Yugoslavia.[663]

Like the apostle Paul, Luis Palau has been a global evangelist. For more than four decades he has preached the gospel around the world. This chapter analyzes his evangelistic impact from different perspectives. First, it examines the geographical expansion of his ministry, moving from Latin America to Europe, North America, and other parts of the world. The second part verifies the fruits of Palau's ministry in individual lives, local churches, and local communities. Each section contains specific examples to validate his impact.

The Global Ministry of Luis Palau

Luis Palau was once dubbed by *Christianity Today* as the "evangelist to three worlds."[664] This title illustrates Palau's ministry in Latin America, Europe, and North America. At the time this report was written, these three continents had been Palau's focus of ministry. Yet his ministry was not limited to these areas. Although this section is arranged by order of Palau's geographical influences, it nearly coincides with the chronological sequence of his ministry.

Palau once commented that "Part of our responsibility as evangelists is to be aware of spiritual trends in nations around the world."[665] Such spiritual trends, as Palau has perceived and described, will be discussed with regard to each continent, on conjunction with consideration of the prevailing social conditions. Knowing the social and spiritual backgrounds of each region increases one's awareness of the gravity of Palau's ministry. Specific events highlighting his worldwide ministry and unique contributions to global evangelism are examined.

Latin America: Shining the Light in the Darkness

Social and Spiritual Conditions

The social and spiritual conditions of Latin America in the second half of the twentieth century were depressing. Most countries had gone through political revolutions and turmoil. Socially, many people were living an immoral and squandering lifestyle. Problems such as dishonesty, infidelity, drinking, and gambling had penetrated societies. Commenting on United Nations statistics, Palau stated that "In some areas of Latin America up to 70 percent of the population is illegitimate."[666]

The escalating social and political problems also divided religious groups according to their responses to the depressing social conditions. Liberation Protestants and Catholics acted aggressively and violently in an effort to rectify the social injustices of Latin America. On the other hand, evangelicals maintained that change must begin with individual lifestyles, spurred by regeneration rather than social structure.[667]

In the midst of this political and social unrest, the spiritual hunger of people had grown more desperate. At Amsterdam '86 Palau remarked that "In Latin America, people are begging to hear the Gospel. A spiritual hunger and openness exist that are giving an unprecedented place for preaching God's Word."[668] It was against this backdrop of social darkness and spiritual hunger that Luis Palau first shined the light of God's love by proclaiming the message of the gospel to the multitudes of Latin America.

Evangelistic Ministry

It stands to reason that, since Palau was born in Argentina, Latin America has been his primary ministry field from the beginning. As one can ascertain from the phrase "the Billy Graham of Latin America," God has used Palau powerfully as His harvester of souls in that continent. Palau's evangelistic fruits have been most plentiful in Latin America. Ever since he began to preach on the streets of Córdoba, Argentina, at the age of nineteen,[669] Palau has been preaching the gospel through evangelistic campaigns and mass media reaching every country in Latin America.

Palau's first large-scale campaign in Latin America was conducted in Bogota, Colombia, in 1966. This campaign is unforgettable to Palau not only because it was his first large campaign but also because it was a historic event for Christians in Colombia, who had often been persecuted and even stoned to death because of their faith in Christ.

In the face of persecution against Christians, seven thousand young people decided to risk their lives by parading through the city. They held Bibles over their hearts and carried transistor radios while listening to and singing along with Christian songs. Palau's biographer records, "Posters and banners bearing the words 'Jesus Saves' filled the street. The singing grew louder and the people watching smiled. When the columns of marchers surged forward, many older Christians, including missionaries and national pastors, joined the parade."[670] By the time Palau was ready to preach, about twenty thousand people had gathered at Bolivar Plaza. Palau preached from John 8:36 under the banner "Christ the Liberator." Palau later recalls that "It was an historic moment for Colombia and indeed for all of Latin America."[671]

In 1970 Palau conducted a ten-day campaign in Mexico City, with more than 106,000 in attendance and 6,675 public decisions. Through this campaign Palau was assured of God's calling as an evangelist and earned international attention throughout Latin America. One journalist reporting this event called Palau "the Billy Graham of Latin America." The word spread quickly, and more opportunities began to open for Palau to hold mass evangelistic events throughout Latin America.[672]

Palau's campaign in Managua, Nicaragua, in 1975 was another breakthrough in his ministry. For twenty-two days 187,000 people participated in the campaign. Furthermore, approximately 80 million people throughout Latin America were reached with the gospel via radio and television broadcasting; this media campaign became known as Continente '75.

In 1976, Palau's campaign in Paraguay doubled the size of the evangelical church in that country, with a reported 5,000 new converts. Another meeting in 1982 was much more successful; 10,250 people made their public profession in Jesus from the total of 155,000 people in Asunción, Paraguay's capital city.[673]

On November 28, 1982, Palau preached at Guatemala City's Campo Marte Parade Grounds, celebrating Guatemala's centennial anniversary of an evangelical church.[674] There were 700,000 people in attendance, the largest single audience in Palau's ministry. According to historian Virgil Zapata, this was the largest Christian gathering not only in Guatemala but also in the history of Latin America.[675]

After changing the format to a festival style, Palau's campaigns began to draw more people in Latin America. According to Jim Williams, who spent four decades directing LPA's ministries in Latin America, a festival style of evangelism appeals to Latin Americans because of their love for such *fiesta*.[676] The size of the audience on average has grown by three to four times in each campaign, but when compared for each day the attendance rate has grown more than ten times.

A couple of simple comparisons confirm this point. For instance, Palau's campaign in Monterrey, Mexico, in 2007 drew 401,950 people over two days. In contrast, his campaign in 2000 had seen a total attendance of 94,872 over six days.[677] So the audience for the whole campaign had grown about four times, while attendance for each day had grown almost thirteen times.

Another example is his campaign in Lima, Peru. In 2004 he preached to 667,000 people for two days, in comparison to the 240,750 people who had gathered in 1984 over a period of nine days. That's an attendance rate almost three times larger in total and close to twelve times larger for each day.

Palau saw the largest audience of his lifetime after changing to a festival style. His festival in Buenos Aires, Argentina, in 2003 drew 851,942 people over two days. His previous campaign in that city had occurred in 1977, with 81,500 people in attendance over five days. The attendance had grown more than ten times in total and more than twenty-six times for each day.[678]

Evangelistic Contributions to Latin America

Luis Palau's evangelistic contributions in Latin America are manifold. More than any other single factor, he has preached the gospel through campaigns and mass media and has led multitudes of people to believe in Christ. Roman Catholics comprise the vast majority of Latin Americans. Although they claim to be Christians, many of them do not have assurance of salvation or a personal relationship with God. In his preaching to Latin Americans Palau deliberately emphasizes that faith is having a personal relationship with God through Jesus Christ. "And then," Palau emphasizes, "many people begin to realize what is missing in their faith."[679]

The most significant theological contribution of Luis Palau in Latin America is his defense of the pure gospel against the ideas of liberation theology. The twentieth-century Latin America had experienced a wave of social upheaval and had witnessed the rise of liberation theology, along with communist reformation. By the end of the 1970s, while rejoicing over the tremendous evangelistic fruits in Latin America, Palau lamented that "the same doors that had been open for the Gospel the past decade had also remained open for the Marxists and other enemies of the Gospel. The battle for the heart and soul of Latin America was far from over!"[680] In the context of Marxist revolution on the one side and liberation theology on the other, Palau preached the gospel as the sole answer to the problems of Latin America.

Liberation theology in Latin America departed from biblical teachings on some of the most important theological concepts, including sin, redemption, and regeneration.[681] The menacing influence of liberation theology was not limited to Catholics but had drawn in a disturbing number of evangelicals. In his interview with *Christianity Today* Palau identified the sources of liberation theology among evangelicals: "Basically it's been disseminated by the faculty and graduates of two seminaries. The Methodist seminary in Buenos Aires got into trouble with revolution, and the Latin American Biblical Seminary in San José, Costa Rica, taught it and spread it."[682]

In April of 1982 Palau, along with evangelical theologians of Latin America who were alarmed about the growing and ominous influence of liberation theology among the evangelicals, formed the Confraternity of Evangelicals in Latin America (CONELA).[683] In his foreword to the book *People of the Mandate*, Palau briefly introduces the background of CONELA, in the formation of which he had played a leading role:[684]

> At the time, it was hard to overemphasize the importance of CONELA's task. Leftist ideologies were penetrating the Latin American church, and there was no united defense of the biblical gospel, nor offensive as to how Christians should apply biblical principles in their churches. ... CONELA played a significant role in shepherding the shepherds who led the flock of God through this rocky political and socio-economic moment.[685]

Thus Palau has not only shined the light of the gospel into the darkness but also has protected the integrity of the gospel against the forces of darkness in Latin America. History may prove this to be Palau's greatest legacy to the Church in Latin America.

Europe: Waking Up Sleeping Churches

Social and Spiritual Conditions

Europe was once known as the land of Reformation and great revivals. Individuals such as John Wycliffe, Martin Luther, John Calvin,

Ulrich Zwingli, John Wesley, George Whitefield, and Charles Spurgeon, among others, had been great spiritual leaders, shaping and promoting the Christian faith around the world. Today, however, Christianity is losing ground in many European countries. According to research by Ed Vitagliano, news editor for the AFA Journal, the percentage of people attending church on an average Sunday had been decreasing in most countries in the 1990s. The figures stand currently at: England (27 percent), West Germany (14 percent), Denmark (5 percent), Norway (5 percent), Sweden (4 percent), and Finland (4 percent).[686]

Palau has visited Great Britain more often than any other country in Europe, although Britain's spiritual condition has not been much different from that of the rest of Western Europe. In Palau's judgment, "For all but a small percentage of the people in Britain and Western Europe, Christianity is ancient history, not a living relationship."[687] From the late nineteenth century Britain has witnessed a great decrease in its Christian population, affecting all denominations. During his Our God Reigns evangelistic tour of England in 1980, Palau lamented the devastating spiritual condition of England:

> Churches by the hundreds were closing, often being converted into mosques or Hindu temples. Every year, British companies were shipping hundreds of tons of obsolete, often ornate church furnishings to America, Japan, and Western Europe for auction to antique dealers.[688]

According to *Christianity Today*, in England "[Church] Attendance has dropped from 45 percent of the population in 1851 to 15 percent in 1979."[689] Its reporter John Capon pointed out some possible factors in this decline:

> The decline can be attributed to a number of factors: the secularist view of the elite, whose opinions are heard on television and read in the press; the cumulative effect of two major wars within a lifetime, which destroyed whole communities and caused major social upheaval; the lack of a clear, confident, and consistent proclamation of the gospel by Christians.[690]

Even though 27 million people, who comprised 58 percent of the whole population, claimed to be members of the Church of England, most of them were nominal Christians. Less than 6 percent of those baptized took Communion on Christmas or Easter, when the highest attendance had ordinarily been seen.[691]

The depressing spiritual condition also affected British society. During Mission to London Palau remarked on the results of rejecting God the population was experiencing, which included: "A rising violent crime rate, an increase in sexual immorality, a glut of pornography, and escalating drug and alcohol abuse. Quieter results—but just as fatal—are divorce, single-parent families, and loneliness."[692] Thus the spiritual and social conditions of England have been hopeless and gloomy. But Palau has not lost hope, as he proclaimed at Amsterdam '86:

> When it comes to the Gospel, Europe is hard and cynical. To me, that's all the more reason to preach there frequently and fervently. Nothing will give me greater joy than to see that hard shell of a continent cracked wide open for Jesus Christ. I hope to see millions of the younger generation truly humble themselves before God so that the Holy Spirit can move with power in Europe.[693]

In conclusion, most European countries have been in deep spiritual lethargy and are facing its bitter consequences. Yet through mass evangelism Luis Palau has attempted to wake up what once had been the center of the Christian faith.

Evangelistic Ministry

Palau's first European campaign was conducted in Sevilla, Spain, in 1973, at the invitation of six churches.[694] Compared to his campaigns in Latin America, its scale was small. But it was successful, with 350 public decisions in an area where there had been fewer than 500 professed Christians.[695] A couple of years later Harvey Thomas, a member of the Graham team, helped open the door for Palau to preach in Western Europe; Palau was invited to preach at Eurofest

'75, a youth congress in Brussels, Belgium, as well as at the "Ministry of Thanks" tour of Britain the following year. Palau called this invitation "a clear-cut Macedonian call to minister in Europe."[696]

Palau's full-scale campaign in Europe did not happen until 1977, when he held campaigns in Germany for ten days, along with his first British campaign, Jubilee '77 Christian Festival in Cardiff, Wales. Since Jubilee '77, Britain has become Palau's frequent campaign site. In 1979 he conducted a series of campaigns in Scotland for twenty-nine days. According to *Christianity Today*, in Aberdeen, where Palau had spent the last ten days, "There had not been a unified evangelistic effort for an entire generation."[697] About three thousand people gathered each night, and a local newspaper reported Palau's campaigns to be "The Miracle in the Rain."[698]

The next year Palau had another opportunity to preach in ten cities of England for ten days and six cities of Scotland for four weeks. The cumulative attendance was 92,500 people, with 4,700 making public professions.[699] Another big campaign took place in Glasgow, Scotland's largest city, in 1981. More than six hundred churches participated in the campaign for five weeks.[700] The total audience reached 200,000, and 5,300 people professed their faith in Jesus.[701]

Besides these, Palau conducted numerous other campaigns and rallies in Britain, the longest and largest of which was the one in London in 1983 and 1984, known as Mission to London.[702] Mission to London had two phases: Phase 1 proclaimed the gospel in Greater London in September and October of 1983 for fifty days, and phase 2 reached Londoners with the gospel at QPR stadium for forty days in the summer of 1984. More than 1,700 churches from all denominations united for Mission to London, and 15,000 Christians volunteered to serve for the campaigns. The result was tremendous: Phase 1 drew more than 210,000 people, with 8,000 publicly professing Christ as their Savior and Lord. Around 280,000 people attended phase 2, of which approximately 19,000 made public decisions for Christ.[703] In addition, more than fifty English-speaking countries heard the gospel through the media outreach, Commonwealth '84.[704]

Palau's other campaigns in Europe have included Sweden, Switzerland, Denmark, France, the Netherlands, Norway, Italy,

Finland, Ireland, Portugal, Belgium, and others. He also conducted an evangelistic campaign in Poland in 1987, his first in Eastern Europe. This was followed by a series of campaigns in that region, including Hungary, the Soviet Union, Czechoslovakia, Bulgaria, Romania, and Latvia.[705]

Moreover, Palau's campaigns in five cities behind the Iron Curtain of the old Soviet Union in September 1989 were historic events. Just a few weeks before the collapse of communism in Eastern Europe, Palau preached the gospel to crowds in Moscow, Leningrad, Kiev, Riga, and Kishinev by official invitation.[706] The spiritual hunger of people was immense, Palau records, recalling that "During each meeting there were moments when people would be suddenly weeping, sobbing, [and] shaking almost uncontrollably. It was a very moving and soul-searching experience."[707]

Among Palau's campaigns in Eastern Europe, the most fruitful were in Romania in 1990 and 1991. The spiritual vacuum in that country, after forty-five years of communism's reign, followed by its collapse, was undeniable. Palau recalls that during his last meeting in Romania 8,200 people—almost 80 percent of the audience—lifted their hands to declare their faith in Jesus.[708] In total, 340,900 people had attended the campaigns, and 85,618 people had made public decisions.[709]

Evangelistic Contributions to Europe

Besides leading multitudes of people to Christ—without doubt the most important outcome—Palau made a couple of notable evangelistic contributions to European countries. First, he awakened sleeping churches and rekindled passion for evangelism among Christians. As discussed previously, the Christian population has been dwindling in most countries in Western Europe, and most Christians have been nominal and lethargic in their spirituality. Through evangelistic campaigns Palau has challenged their lukewarm attitude and equipped them to share the gospel effectively.

Second, Palau's evangelistic campaigns have often brought churches together for evangelistic purposes. For instance, disunity had been prevalent among the various denominations in England before Palau launched his Mission to London campaigns. John Capon reported that the younger school of Anglican evangelicals was more concerned with internal affairs; free church evangelicals preferred smaller scale evangelistic methods; the separatists had doctrinal doubts about ecumenical involvement; and the charismatics were busy with their own exuberant worship.[710]

However, Mission to London united more than seventeen hundred churches under the umbrella of evangelism, transcending their denominational differences.

Third, Palau's most significant theological contribution in Europe, and in Great Britain in particular, has been reclaiming biblical authority.[711] During his campaigns in Great Britain, inerrancy of the Bible was often the focus of debate. Many pastors and theological students did not believe in the inerrancy of the Bible. On the first day of his Glasgow campaign, Palau declared that "It's either back to the Bible or back to the jungle for Britain."[712] During Mission to London Palau strongly contended that many churches in London were empty because they did not regard the Bible as the Word of God, inspired by the Holy Spirit.[713] Palau's resolute stance cannot be compromised, because it is the Bible that contains the message of salvation.

Palau continues to carry a burden for evangelism in Western Europe, the homeland of his ancestors. The evangelist acknowledges that Western Europe is one of the most difficult places in the world in which to preach the gospel. He sees apathy, passivity, and humanism killing the church. As he often states, "God has no grandchildren. The church is only one generation away from extinction if we don't evangelize."

Endnotes

663 Marion L. Soards, *The Apostle Paul: An Introduction to His Writings and Teaching* (New York: Paulist Press, 1987), 28.

664 "Luis Palau: Evangelist to Three Worlds," *Christianity Today*, 20 May 1983, 28.

665 Luis Palau, "The Evangelist and the Ministry of the Holy Spirit," in *The Calling of an Evangelist*, ed. J. D. Douglas (Minneapolis, MN: World Wide Publications, 1987), 139.

666 "Evangelist to Three Worlds," 31.

667 David Stoll, *Is Latin America Turning Protestant? The Politics of Evangelical Growth* (Berkeley and Los Angeles, CA: University of California Press, 1990), 19.

668 Palau, "Evangelist and Ministry of the Holy Spirit," 140.

669 Luis Palau and David Sanford, *Luis Palau: Calling America and the Nations to Christ* (Nashville, TN: Thomas Nelson, Inc., 1994; rev. 2000), 41. Even though his team was small and the meetings were often unsuccessful from human standards, young Palau learned the basics of evangelism through this experience. Palau later recounts that "Although we saw few conversions, I began to learn the basics of evangelism. We ran into everything: laughter, scorn, questions that required quick answers, questions that required diplomacy, you name it."

670 W. Terry Whalin, *Luis Palau* (Minneapolis, MN: Bethany House Publishers, 1996), 10.

671 Palau and Sanford, *Calling America and the Nations*, 94.

672 Ibid., 101–2.

673 Randy Frame, "Palau Holds Mass Crusades Throughout Paraguay: Encouraging Results Are Reported in This Emerging South American Nation." *Christianity Today*, 12 November 1982, 72, 76.

674 "Evangelist to Three Worlds," 29. As acknowledged by Palau himself, however, this rally was "more a celebration than an out-and-out campaign." He also states, "From the believers' standpoint it was called 'Gratitude '82'." Ibid.

675 Palau and Sanford, *Calling America and the Nations*, 158.

676 Williams, interview by the author, August 8, 2008.

677 The festival style was not implemented for this campaign. The first festival in Latin America was conducted in Rosario, Argentina, in 2000. LPA, "An Overview of Luis Palau's Life and Ministry," October 2007, 6.

678 The statistics are from "Ministry Impact Statistics" by LPA. One must consider the growing fame and popularity of Luis Palau in Latin America as a variable factor. Yet the growth rate is still astonishing.

679 Palau, interview by author, May 9, 2008.

680 Palau and Sanford, *Calling America and the Nations*, 144.

681 "Evangelist to Three Worlds," 30. Palau summarizes the basic doctrines of liberation theology as follows: "Basically liberation theology says that sin is in the institutions and in the structures.... Redemption, for the liberation theologian, is found in revolution: change the structures of the institutions and you will eliminate the sin that oppresses and you will have a free society. ... As for regeneration, basically, the idea of liberation theology is that the new man will emerge when institutions and structures are liberated from sin." Ibid.

682 Ibid.

683 Palau's resolution for such a united organization against liberation theology was formed during his participation in the second Latin American Conference on Evangelism (CLADE II) in Lima, Peru, in 1979. He was disappointed by the nature of its meeting. He recalls, "Incredibly, biblical evangelism was

about the last thing anyone talked about during the conference. Much of the program stressed the temporal, rather than the spiritual. Many delegates complained about what they called the 'socio-political content' of the majority of messages." Palau and Sanford, *Calling America and the Nations*, 143.

684 Palau and Sanford, *Calling America and the Nations*, 149. Palau served on the advisory board of CONELA, and two of his staff members, Marcelino Ortiz and Bill Conard, served on the ad hoc committee.

685 Luis Palau, "Foreword," in *People of the Mandate.* W. Harold Fuller, *People of the Mandate: the Story of The World Evangelical Fellowship* (Grand Rapids: Baker Book House, 1996), xii. [This book is about the history of the World Evangelical Fellowship.] See also Palau and Sanford, *Calling America and the Nations,* 149.

686 Vivian S. Park, "Scholars Find Decline of Christianity in the West," *The Christian Post*, 6 March 2004 [online]; accessed 20 August 2008; available from http://www.christianpost.com/article/20040306/scholars-find-decline-of-christianity-in-the-west.htm; Internet. Park continues, "However, according to Gene Edward Veith, culture critic for World magazine, attendance of the more conservative Catholic Church is far higher than that of liberal Protestant churches: Ireland (84%), Poland (55%), Portugal (47%), and Italy (45%)."

687 Luis Palau, "Which Part of the Great Commission Don't You Understand?" *Christianity Today*, 16 November 1998, 74.

688 Palau and Sanford, *Calling America and the Nations*, 145.

689 John Capon, "Billy Graham and Luis Palau: Fanning Revival Fires in England—Events and Strategies Behind a Remarkable Summer of Evangelism," *Christianity Today*, 13 July 1984, 28. It also states, "Some put the current figure at 11 percent or less." London was the worst in the decline of church attendance. According to a Bible Society survey, "it was falling by 3 percent a year, and in 1979 dropped below 200,000 for the first time." Ibid., 52.

690 Ibid., 28.

691 Ibid.

692 Susan Holton and David L. Jones, *Spirit Aflame: Luis Palau's Mission to London* (Grand Rapids: Baker Book House, 1985), 43.

693 Palau, "Evangelist and Ministry of the Holy Spirit," 140.

694 Palau and Sanford, *Calling America and the Nations*, 119.

695 Ibid.

696 Ibid., 122.

697 Forrest Boyd, "Luis Palau in Aberdeen: Melting Scottish," *Christianity Today*, 20 July 1979, 42.

698 Ibid.

699 LPA, "Ministry Impact Statistics."

700 *Christianity Today* reported that "Palau preached in Glasgow Cathedral, spoke at universities and colleges, visited pubs, talked with teen-agers on the street and shipyard workers on Clydeside, was a guest of the duke of Argyll in his castle, and participated in many TV and radio programs and newspaper interviews." James D. Douglas, "God's Good Gaucho and Roundup Time in Glasgow," *Christianity Today*, 17 July 1981, 90. For more on this campaign, see James D. Douglas, "Luis Palau Returns for Glasgow Crusade." *Christianity Today*, 29 May 1981, 34–35.

701 Holton and Jones, *Spirit Aflame*, 67.

702 Cf. In 1984 Billy Graham also preached the gospel in six British cities. His Mission England drew more than 1 million people, and 96,982 people reportedly registered public decisions. Holton and Jones, *Spirit Aflame*, 11.

703 Holton and Jones, *Spirit Aflame*, 85, 137, 175, 190.

704 See "Saturation Evangelism Through Mass Media" in chapter 9.

705 See appendix 3 for the full list of campaigns with year, location, length, attendance, and number of inquirers.

706 Luis Palau, "Is God Relevant?" *The Plain Truth* (March/April 1998): 59. See also Terry C. Muck, "An Open-air Crusade in the Soviet Union? Believe It!" *Christianity Today*, 20 October 1989, 36–37.

707 Palau and Sanford, *Calling America and the Nations*, 184.

708 Ibid., 187–88.

709 LPA, "Ministry Impact Statistics."

710 Capon, "Billy Graham and Luis Palau," 30.

711 For more discussion on Palau's view on the Scriptures, see "Evangelism and the Bible" in chapter 3.

712 Holton and Jones, *Spirit Aflame*, 69. This was originally Billy Graham's statement. Holton and Jones record that Palau's remark was reported in the press and that "the authority of the Bible suddenly became a public issue."

713 Ibid., 52.

CHAPTER 12

GLOBAL IMPACT: NORTH AMERICA AND BEYOND

North America: Calling America to Christ

Social and Spiritual Conditions

America has been blessed spiritually and economically, having become the leading world power. However, according to Palau's assessment, America is "in the 'transition generation' between the mid-century revival of Christianity and total secularism."[714] Palau states, "Everything began to change during the Vietnam War."[715] Today America is in a state of hopelessness, suffering from racial and generational conflicts, sexual impurity, and an ungodly lifestyle.[716]

Palau's concern for the spiritual and moral decline in the United States is serious. He solemnly warns the nation:

> We still think we're a superior nation, not realizing the glory is departing. We're almost as bad off now as Latin America was in the 1960s. The only difference is countries like Colombia and Guatemala are on the way up and America is passing them on the way down. As a nation, we need to

> honor the Lord once again and change direction—fast!—before God abandons us to judgment.[717]

Palau also observes that in the United States religious hypocrisy and sectarianism among Christians are deeply rooted. At Amsterdam '86 Palau observed this:

> When I look at the United States, I am appalled by the spiritual confusion and sectarianism I see. ... And while I hate to say it, it's true that if you could scratch beneath all the plastic smiles and positive thinking for which Americans are known worldwide, you'd often find arrogance, self-righteousness and divisiveness. If there is one country that has spread sectarian denominationalism in the world, it is the United States of America.[718]

In his interview with *Christianity Today* in 1996, he also remarked, "America is the toughest country in the world to get denominations to work together."[719]

Furthermore, America is losing its passion for evangelism. Palau laments that in North America, "while there is much discussion about evangelism, real evangelism is hard to detect."[720] And "Most churches devote very little time to evangelism of *any* [emphasis in original] kind."[721] Consequently, America is departing from God morally and spiritually, and Palau has taken up the challenge to call America back to God.

Evangelistic Ministry

After marrying Patricia Marilyn Scofield, Luis Palau became an American citizen in 1962. But it took a while for him to actively pursue mass evangelism in North America. The reason for the delay was his misplaced notion that the USA was Billy Graham's parish. Although Palau had great success and earned renown as an evangelist in Latin America and Europe, he was hesitant to launch his evangelistic ministry in the States in full scale because Graham was still vigorously involved in his ministry.

Palau states, "For twenty-nine years, however, I clearly felt the restraint of the Holy Spirit. Until Billy Graham's crusade ministry slowed down in the United States, I believe God was leading our team to concentrate our crusades in Latin America, Europe, and Asia."[722] Finally, in 1989, Palau asked Graham's blessing for his ministry in North America.[723] With the permission and blessing of Graham, Palau at that time began to expand his ministry in North America in full force.

Palau's ministry in the United States may be divided into three phases. First, before 1990 Palau was hesitant to launch campaigns without the blessing of his mentor, Billy Graham. Since 1970 Palau had periodically preached the gospel in various evangelistic rallies in America. His first full-scale campaign, conducted in Los Angeles in 1980, was directed toward Spanish-speaking people.[724] In 1981 the first English campaign took place in San Diego. About forty thousand people attended the campaign during its twelve days, and around twelve hundred people made public decisions. Several other evangelistic campaigns followed. Yet it seems that Palau had difficulties catching the public's attention during this period.

Reporting on Palau's campaign in Colorado Springs in 1984, Sura Rubenstein observed, "They love him in Latin America, and they love him in Europe. … But here in the United States, the Luis Palau Evangelistic Team is hardly known."[725] Moreover, the Palau team lacked sufficient support from local churches, as Rubenstein reports:

> A key part of Palau's strategy—strong support and outreach by local churches—was absent in Colorado. … Lack of local church support also was a factor in a recent team decision to postpone indefinitely a long-planned crusade in Dallas, Texas, that was to be held in the fall of 1986.[726]

The second phase of Palau's ministry in North America began in 1990, with Graham's approval, encouragement, and blessing. Palau began to focus as much as 50 percent of his ministry on re-evangelizing North America.[727] Some of the campaigns prior to the creation of the festival model included Palm Springs, California (1991); McAllen, Texas, and Reynosa, Mexico (1992); Phoenix, Arizona (1992); Ft. Worth, Texas (1993); Grand Rapids and Holland, Michigan (1994); Miami, Florida (1995); Chicago, Illinois (1996); Kansas City, Missouri (1997); Olympia, Washington (1998); multiple cities across Maine (1999), North Dakota (2000) and Connecticut (2001).

Among them, Palau's Say Yes Chicago campaign was his biggest in the United States to that moment. Palau recounts, "After four years of preparations, our ministry was ready to embark on what to that point was by far our most ambitious U.S. campaign."[728] The Chicago campaign had come into the spotlight because of Palau's new strategy. Instead of preaching at one location, Palau divided the greater Chicago area into nine sectors[729] and employed a group of evangelists to preach the gospel. From this experience he envisioned the formation of NGA.[730]

Say Yes Chicago lasted for fifty-seven days, as reported in *Christianity Today*:

> He [Palau] preached 26 night meetings, including 17 in the city. In all, Palau spoke at 75 meetings in 57 days. The 55 specialty events—businessmen's breakfasts, women's luncheons, youth nights—drew the most receptive audiences, including 18,000 at the Rosemont Horizon to hear the Newsboys, an Australian Christian band.[731]

The total attendance was 129,615, with 10,112 people making public decisions to follow Jesus.

The final phase of Palau's ministry in the United States began with the new festival format.[732] This change started with the Portland festival in 1999, after which the situation began to change dramatically. Palau's ministry in the United States has been thriving ever since he changed to a festival style. As discussed previously, attendance has increased to ten times what it had been before.[733] U.S. festivals have included Portland, Oregon (1999 and 2000); Fort Lauderdale, Florida (2003); Washington, D.C. (2005); Houston, Texas (2006); Tampa, Florida (2007); and Nashville, Tennessee (2007).

Among these, Beachfest in Fort Lauderdale drew the largest audience to date in Palau's ministry in the United States. This festival was aimed at reaching college students during their spring break. Although the main festival was conducted in Fort Lauderdale, it was broadcast live on more than twelve hundred radio stations and linked via satellite to more than twenty mini festivals in major cities across America.[734] Beachfest was successful, with 340,375 in attendance and 7,968 registered decisions.[735] To Palau, this campaign had a special meaning; it confirmed his confidence in the use of a festival style.[736]

Evangelistic Contributions to North America

As discussed before, Palau perceives that moral and spiritual decline is prevalent in America because people have departed from God. Through his mass evangelistic efforts he has been calling America back to God. He insists that the only way to restore America is "Good News, not good advice."[737] Thus, he asserts that presenting the gospel is the only hope for America:

> The resurrected Christ has power to change America, where 80 percent of the people claim to be Christians, but few live any differently from pagans or atheists, as though God has no claim on their lives. Their hearts have not been changed, and unless Jesus Christ changes their hearts, they never will be any different from those outside the Christian faith.[738]

Palau's preaching to Americans emphasizes love and forgiveness. In his view, American evangelicals have "a reputation as harsh, unloving, bitter people, condemning to hell pregnant young women at abortion clinics and homosexuals marching in Washington."[739] What people need is the message of forgiveness, and this has been the major theme of his preaching in America.[740]

Palau has also emphasized the importance of evangelism to American Christians who have lost their passion. That lack of passion has been the major problem affecting his ministry; his team often has difficulty gaining united support from local churches. Palau even remarks, "In each one, [campaign] evangelism has been warfare, and too many of its most vehement opponents have been Christians."[741]

In spite of such bleak situations, Palau's message has been positive. He declares, "My dream is this: that a massive wave of evangelization restores America's days of glory, those spiritual days when joy pervaded the land. America was once young in spirit, vibrant, and full of hope. It can be again."[742]

The Ends of the Earth

In 1983, in his interview with *Christianity Today*, Palau expressed his vision to reach America and Europe.[743] His dream not only has come true, but he has gone further. In fact, his evangelistic ministry has expanded to virtually every continent. Some of his important achievements are discussed in this section.

Palau's first evangelistic campaign in Asia was held in Singapore in 1986. The result was tremendous. About one third of a million people attended the campaign, and 11,902 people made public decisions. In addition, people throughout Asia heard the gospel through the media outreach called Asia '86.[744] Following the Singapore campaign Palau received invitations from "Hong Kong, India, Indonesia, Japan, the Philippines, Thailand, and other Asian nations."[745]

Among them, his campaigns in Hong Kong in 1987 and 1997 were historic. In the first campaign 219,100 people were in attendance, with 31,268 making public decisions.[746] Then in 1997 Palau preached in Hong Kong for a few weeks before that city returned to Chinese rule. This was supposed to have been the last evangelistic campaign of old Hong Kong, but Palau declared, "We call it the first crusade of the new China."[747]

China has since that time been a priority for Palau's ministry. There are two reasons for this: First, 20 percent of the world's population resides in China. Second, Palau has been praying for China from his boyhood.[748] His dream to preach in mainland China was fulfilled in 2000 when he preached the gospel in Shanghai and again in 2004, when he proclaimed the gospel in Beijing for nine days, with a total attendance of 9,663 people.[749] Since 2000 Palau has won over the friendship of many of China's national leaders and enjoys favor with the China government afforded to few Western evangelical leaders as evidenced by his numerous preaching engagements, media appearances and official state visits.

In November of 1988 Palau had an opportunity to reach Hindus with the gospel for the first time. He proclaimed the good news in Cuttack, East India, which had three thousand Hindu temples and fewer than three thousand Christians. Within five days more than forty-one hundred people made public decisions to follow Jesus.[750] Encouraged by this surprising result, the Palau team launched a twelve-year plan to saturate major cities across India with the message of the gospel.[751]

Besides these locations, Palau has preached the gospel in Auckland, New Zealand (1987); Kathmandu, Nepal (1995); Cairo, Egypt (1998); Istanbul, Turkey (1999); and other major cities around the world.

While his ministry in Latin America and Europe has thrived, for a while Palau had difficulty in the United States. After changing the campaign format to a festival style, however, he has been reaching the United States and other countries more effectively. Furthermore, his ministry was not limited to North America, Latin America, and Europe. He has been preaching the gospel to the ends of the Earth, making a significant impact on the eternal destiny of multitudes and advancing God's kingdom on Earth.

Endnotes

714 Luis Palau and David Sanford, *Luis Palau: Calling America and the Nations to Christ* (Nashville, TN: Thomas Nelson, Inc., 1994; rev. 2000), 180.

715 Luis Palau and Mike Umlandt, *The Only Hope for America: The Transforming Power of the Gospel of Jesus Christ* (Wheaton, IL: Crossway Books, 1996), 48. Palau goes on say, "Near the end of the war, I remember saying to my wife, 'It seems like the demons of hell have invaded the United States.'"

716 Ibid., 49–52.

717 Palau and Sanford, *Calling America and the Nations*, 90.

718 Luis Palau, "The Evangelist and the Ministry of the Holy Spirit," in *The Calling of an Evangelist*, ed. J. D. Douglas (Minneapolis, MN: World Wide Publications, 1987), 140.

719 Luis Palau, "Whatever Happened to Evangelism? Luis Palau Wants to Rekindle Our Passion for the Lost," *Christianity Today*, 8 April 1996, 39.

720 Luis Palau, "Which Part of the Great Commission Don't You Understand?" *Christianity Today*, 16 November 1998, 74.

721 Palau, *The Only Hope for America*, 17.

722 Ibid., 48.

723 Palau and Sanford, *Calling America and the Nations*, 181. Graham told Palau, "Well, you don't need it. But if you want it, you've got it. Get on with it! Everybody talks about evangelizing America. Now let's really do it."

724 See John Maust, "Palau Spanish-Language Crusade Pulls L.A. Hispanics Together for First Time," *Christianity Today*, 8 August 1980, 38–40.

725 Sura Rubenstein, "Preacher to the World: Oregon's Luis Palau," *Northwest*, 15 September 1985, 6.

726 Ibid., 12. Whether Palau would succeed in the United States as he had in Latin America and Europe was uncertain. Rubenstein remarks, "Things are looking good for Luis Palau. But whether the Latin American hot gospeler really can take over where Billy Graham leaves off is still uncertain. The answer, both Palau and Graham would say, is in God's hands."

727 Kimberly Claassen, "Reviving the Nations," *The Plain Truth* (March/April 1998): 13.

728 Palau and Sanford, *Calling America and the Nations*, 202.

729 John Kennedy and Bradley Baurain, "Palau Preaches to a Preoccupied Metropolis," *Christianity Today*, 16 July 1996, 68.

730 Palau and Sanford, *Calling America and the Nations*, 203. A similar strategy was employed during the statewide campaigns in Maine in 1999. See ibid., 208.

731 Kennedy and Baurain, "Palau Preaches to a Preoccupied Metropolis," 68. Although some of the meetings drew a large audience, many of them were not that successful in terms of attendance. According to Kennedy and Baurain, "The stadiums and auditoriums for the crusade, which came in under budget at $2 million, usually were far from full."

732 See "New Forms of Evangelistic Campaigns" in chapter 8.

733 "Is Palau the Next Billy Graham?" *ABC News*, 8 October 2005 [online]; accessed 27 September 2007; available from http://abcnews.go.com/GMA/story?id=1195278&page=1; Internet.

734 Todd Hertz, "Beach Blanket Rebirth: Luis Palau to Take Fort Lauderdale Spring Break Festival Nationwide," *Christianity Today*, 2 February 2003, 25.

735 LPA, "Ministry Impact Statistics."

736 Palau, interview by the author, May 9, 2008.

737 Palau and Sanford, *Calling America and the Nations*, 193.

738 Palau, *The Only Hope for America*, 10.

739 Ibid., 54.

740 Ibid., 53.

741 Luis Palau and Timothy Robnett, *Telling the Story: Evangelism for the Next Generation* (Ventura, CA: Regal Books, 2006), 107.

742 Palau, *The Only Hope for America*, 55.

743 "Luis Palau: Evangelist to Three Worlds," *Christianity Today*, 20 May 1983, 33.

744 Palau and Sanford, *Calling America and the Nations*, 170. For more information on Asia '86, see "Saturation Evangelism Through Mass Media" in Chapter 9.

745 Ibid., 170–71.

746 LPA, "Ministry Impact Statistics." The 1987 Hong Kong campaign also recorded the highest number of inquirers on a single night in Palau's ministry. On November 15, 1987, 3,984 people made public decisions out of 31,268 people—14.2 percent of those in attendance. LPA, "Overview of Life and Ministry," 3.

747 Claassen, "Reviving the Nations," 13.

748 Palau, interview by the author, May 9, 2008.

749 LPA, "Ministry Impact Statistics."

750 Palau and Sanford, *Calling America and the Nations*, 179. Palau shares about the spiritual warfare that he experienced during this campaign. He recounts, "Demonic activity was almost palpable at times during the festival. On one occasion, I felt either Satan was at work or some of the professing Christians there were secretly living in serious sin. I've seldom had to stop in the middle of my message, as I did then, to address this issue. The result was incredible. The spiritual atmosphere around us was instantly cleared and purified." Ibid.

751 "Evangelism: The Best Form of Social Action," *Christianity Today*, 17 February 1989, 51.

CHAPTER 13

EVANGELISTIC FRUIT

Luis Palau's global ministry has been fruitful in at least three areas: He has led many individuals to Christ; mobilized Christians, bringing about spiritual and numerical growth to local churches; and, ultimately, transformed society as a whole. Palau's fruit in each area is discussed, citing specific examples in this section.

Conversions and Transformed Lives

The fruit of any evangelist is most apparent in the conversion and transformation in individual lives. Through Luis Palau's evangelistic campaigns and rallies, as of September 2008 "1,080,079 people (Inquirers) have made documented decisions for Jesus Christ."[752] As pointed out by Henry Schmidt, however, a question arises as to the meaning of "documented decisions."[753] Many people may assume that "decisions for Christ" means "conversion decisions." LPA's decision card, however, includes three categories: conversion, rededication, and request for more information.[754] Among them the first two are counted as "documented decisions."[755]

In the case of Palau's campaign in Fresno, California, in 1986, the decisions were categorized by salvation, rededication, and assurance. According to the follow-up committee's statistics, the total decisions made were 2,980, with the breakdown of decisions by category as follows: salvation (1,761), rededication (576), assurance (352), and unknown (291).[756] Thus, "salvation" comprises 59 percent of total decisions. Palau's Mission to London in 1983 and 1984 shows a similar ratio. The survey by Missions Advanced Research and Communications Center (MARC) shows that profession of faith in Christ among decisions comprised 55 and 57 percent for each phase of Mission to London.[757] Based on this data, it appears that at least half of the total decisions in Western Europe and North America are first-time decisions for salvation.

But even taking this into consideration, the number of conversions through Palau's proclamation of the gospel is enormous, and the eternal status of those who have been converted has been altered forever. Furthermore, there are a couple of other factors to be considered. As Jim Williams observes, based on many years of counseling new believers, "It seems that many people do not come forward at the invitation, even though they come to believe in Jesus during campaigns."[758]

In addition, according to research by Scott Bauer, during campaigns evangelism takes place outside the campaign venue. Citing the example of his own church that participated in Palau's campaign in San Fernando Valley in 1994, Bauer states, "Over 80 percent of all evangelism related to the crusade participation of The Church On The Way took place outside the crusade events."[759]

This figure cannot be generalized, but it still suggests the possibility that many have been reached outside the main events during evangelistic campaigns. Finally, one must consider the impact of the converted on his or her family, friends, and neighbors. With changed hearts and inspired by the joy found in the gospel, new Christians enthusiastically share the good news with people around them. As a result, many others come to believe in Jesus.[760]

Numerous lives have been converted and transformed through Palau's ministry.[761] One astounding characteristic is the diversity of people whose lives have been changed. The list of converts reveals a broad spectrum. They include top leaders of society, including two presidents of Bolivia, Hugo Banzer and Juan Pereda Asbun, as well as the former president of Latvia, Guntis Ulmanis.[762] There are also some unlikely candidates who have been converted and changed, as Palau testifies:

> I know [thousands of people] whose lives have been dramatically changed: a drug dealer who once made thousands of dollars a week now gladly living for Christ while working a regular job; adulterous husbands and wives who now honor their marriage vows; lonely, withdrawn teenagers who now can't stop talking about Jesus at home and school; drug-addicted celebrities who now testify of deliverance and host Bible studies in their homes.[763]

One such case was Nick, a drug dealer bringing in ten thousand dollars or more each week. Although he made a lot of money, his life was miserable and lonely; his wife and three children had left him, his brother was in jail, and two of his friends and a cousin had died. When he called Palau during "Night Talk with Luis Palau," thinking that Palau might be a psychologist, he was on the run, about to end his life with a gun. Through his phone conversation with Palau, Nick accepted Christ into his heart, threw his gun into the river the following day, and came to Palau's campaign that evening, "saying he felt like a new man."[764]

During Mission to London many testimonies of conversions and transformations of lives were reported, Palau recalls:

> People of every creed, color, religious background, and walk of life trusted Jesus Christ—a member of the royal family, a top rock star, a famous actress, a disillusioned policeman, a car dealer, a truck driver, a bus driver interviewed that same night by BBC Radio, at least one member of the BBC staff, the official crusade photographer, an Australian soccer player, a young businesswoman, a gentleman whose wife had prayed for his salvation for twenty-one years, twenty-five boys at a British boarding school, a young gang member who had helped disrupt the meeting earlier that same evening, a runaway teenager, and more than a few religious ministers. What a dream come true![765]

Matt Redman, who was later to become a renowned British Christian songwriter, was one of the converts during Mission to

London. His songs, which include "Blessed Be Your Name," "You Never Let Go," "The Heart of Worship," and others are loved by Christians around the world today. But his life before his conversion was terrible. His father had committed suicide when Matt was only seven years old, leaving the impressionable boy to grapple with questions like "Was it anything to do with me? Did he not love us enough to stay around?"[766]

Things had become worse when his mother remarried an abusive man. The situation began to change, however, when Redman heard Palau preach at QPR during Mission to London, when he was ten years old. Although he knew about God, he had never had a personal relationship with Him. When Palau preached that God is the perfect Father, in contrast to human fathers with their failings, Matt's young heart was touched and he dedicated his life to Jesus.[767]

Growth and Renewal of Local Churches

The importance of the Church cannot be overemphasized, since it has been God's main agency of salvation throughout its history. Speaking of the evangelist's role, Palau insists that "Our goal should be to work with the Church, through the Church and for the Church as we seek to obey Christ's Great Commission."[768] Palau's campaigns not only bring sinners to God but bring spiritual renewal and growth to local churches. Such growth can be measured from two viewpoints: spiritual and numerical. The following segment will examine Palau's ministry as it relates to these two perspectives.

Spiritual Renewal of Local Churches

Evangelistic campaigns bring about spiritual renewal in local churches. According to Palau, the mission of LPA is not limited to reaching the lost; it serves "also to stimulate, train, and mobilize the church to continuous, effective evangelism, follow-up, and church growth. A crusade helps to renew churches to be more effective in their evangelistic ministries."[769] The spiritual renewal and growth of the local church can be assessed from several angles.

First, evangelistic campaigns ignite passion for evangelism and compassion for souls. Most churches are lukewarm before becoming engaged in campaigns, but their passion for evangelism is rekindled through the process. During Mission to London, Les Ball, Clapham Mission chairman and minister at Clapham Park Baptist Church, noted that "Mission to London made us focus much more sharply on how committed we really were to evangelism. It challenged us and exposed how much lip service we pay to evangelism in contrast to our actual involvement in evangelism."[770] After Palau's campaign in San Fernando Valley in 1994, Scott Bauer observed that "Without the focus of the crusade, there would not have been a way to raise the level of evangelism consciousness among the believers of the San Fernando Valley."[771]

Second, believers are mobilized and equipped for effective sharing of the gospel through evangelistic campaigns. Many volunteers for campaigns, including friendship evangelists and counselors, are spiritually awakened and equipped to share the gospel while receiving training and availing themselves of the opportunity to practice what they have learned. According to the survey by Schmidt, pastors who participated in Palau's Central California campaign in 1986 indicated "good training for counselors" as the greatest strength of the campaign.[772] In the words of Robnett, "By training the Church to present the life-changing gospel of Jesus Christ, we reap a greater harvest before, during and after public evangelistic events."[773]

Third, churches are united through their involvement with the campaign. As Jesus underscores in John 17, unity among Christians is one of the most important marks of spiritual maturity. Many leaders have identified unity among Christians as one of the most exciting results of campaigns. Gilbert Kirby, chairman of Mission to London's executive committee, observed, "It has been exciting to see people from different churches working together. ... If no other good came from Mission to London, it has done amazing good by bringing local Christians together and breaking down denominational barriers."[774]

Scott Bauer's research corroborates this idea. His survey during Palau's campaign in San Fernando Valley in 1994 reflects that unity among all participating churches was the most important single benefit of the campaign. Unity ranked even higher than "new people coming to the Lord."[775] Palau's campaign has often provided the first opportunity for local churches to be united and to work together in evangelism. McBride presents Mission Maine as such a case. Mission Maine was the first ever attempt at united evangelistic effort among the churches in the history of Maine. He announces, "Never before in the history of the church in Maine had such an all encompassing effort been launched."[776]

Numerical Growth of Local Churches

Critics of campaign evangelism often complain that evangelistic campaigns do not contribute to the growth of local churches. After surveying twelve hundred pastors who participated in Graham's campaign in Seattle in 1976, Win Arn comments:

> The results of this particular crusade appear to have made a more substantial impact on the Christian community than on the non-Christian community. With over half of those who respond already claiming to be Christians (53.7%), and another 15.7% uncertain as to why they responded, might mass evangelism in this and many other cases be more accurately termed "mass revival"?[777]

In his assessment of Graham's ministry, Mark Terry also indicates doubts concerning the long-term effectiveness of mass evangelism:

> Careful studies of Graham's crusades reveal that most of those making decisions were already members of a local church. Of course, this does not mean they were born again. It does mean, though, that very little church growth occurs as a result of a Billy Graham crusade.[778]

Evangelists and local church leaders must pay heed to such analysis. And this naturally leads one to ask the question, "What contribution does a Palau campaign make to the numerical growth of local churches?"

While negating the popular idea that public decisions made during the campaign do not continue afterward, Luis Palau boasts a high percentage of incorporation of inquirers into local churches. He states, "Actually, research of several of our festivals has shown that more than 70 percent of those who make a decision to follow Christ are active members of a local church six months after the festivals."[779] To support his idea Palau recommends three studies by parties independent of LPA.[780]

A close analysis of these studies, however, reveals that, as in the case of Graham's campaigns, many decision-makers in Palau's campaigns are already affiliated with the church in some way. For instance, Mission to London phase 1 shows a 74 percent rate of active membership of inquirers after one year.[781] Although this rate is very high, the Bible Society's survey of inquirers shows that "only 13% of the respondents did not attend church before they went to the area missions."[782] Furthermore, only 3 percent of inquirers had never been to church prior to the campaign. Accordingly, 97 percent of inquirers, "almost all who came forward, had attended or were attending church."[783] Thus, Pointer concludes, "Some unchurched are undoubtedly reached, even converted and added to churches, but very few."[784]

Palau's campaign in Fresno, California, in 1986 provides another good example. Six months after the campaign the follow-up committee surveyed inquirers from the campaign. According to the finding, "73.1% of the inquirers who had been 'unchurched' previous to the crusade were actively participating in Fresno area churches, and overall, 89.9% of the adult inquirers were actively participating in local churches."[785] The inquirers' survey also reveals that 72 percent of them had attended the church prior to the campaign. Among decisions for salvation, 53.4 percent of inquirers had a church background.[786] Based on these data, Schmidt concludes, "The role of crusade evangelism will probably be more effective in revitalizing the church than in reaching the lost in a mass context. ... Because the crusade style is more informational oriented and monological, it will not be as effective in reaching the thinking, religiously pluralistic pagan."[787]

Based on the research done by both Pointer and Schmidt, it seems reasonable to conclude that Palau's campaigns primarily reach church members or those already affiliated with a church. Accordingly, decisions made during Palau's campaigns have little impact on the numerical growth of local churches. However, this conclusion appears premature. There are several points to be considered before making a final judgment.

First, as pointed out by Glenn Firebaugh, critics of mass evangelism tend to evaluate evangelistic efforts solely from a church-growth perspective, as Win Arn did with Graham's campaign in Seattle in 1976.[788] Yet the fact that many decision-makers during campaigns are already church members does not reduce the importance of evangelistic campaigns; many churchgoers may attend the church without a true experience of conversion and assurance of salvation. Through campaigns such nominally religious people can become genuine followers of Christ. In the words of Leighton Ford, the campaign facilitates "the conversion of persons already identified in some way with the churches."[789]

Second, some of Palau's campaigns do show incredible rates of conversion of nonbelievers and consequently of the growth of local churches. This typically happens in unevangelized countries. The Rosario campaign is such a case. This campaign lasted for fourteen days and yielded 3,127 public decisions. According to Edgardo Silvoso, "Six months after the crusade, 57 percent of those who made a decision are attending church regularly, 26 percent have already been baptized and another 14 percent are in line for baptism."[790]

Furthermore, William Conard reports that twenty local churches, with a total membership of 1,799, participated in the campaign. Six months after the campaign, "these 20 churches had grown to 2,564—a 42.5% increase in 17 months, or an annual growth rate of 25.3%."[791] This is an astonishing rate of growth, considering the fact that their average growth rate had been only 1.4 percent over the previous ten years.[792]

Palau's campaign in Asunción, Paraguay's capital city, in 1982 offers a convincing example. Randy Frame indicates some phenomenal growth of local churches through this campaign, explaining, "Even before the crusade had ended, Baptist minister José Missena had welcomed 300 new members into his fellowship, more than doubling the size of his congregation. ... The pastor who supervised the crusade in the city of Encarnación reported that one of the walls of his church was knocked down to make room for 200 new believers."[793]

In 1984, Palau held a campaign in the southern town of Arequipa in Peru, which had only about one thousand Christians. According to Anselmo Rios, the leader of an Assemblies of God church, six thousand people—six times the previous number of Christians in the city—made decisions to follow Christ.[794] More recently, NGA's ministry has spawned phenomenal church growth. According to LPA's report, for instance, "In villages like Kariapatty [in Madurai, India], the church grew by more than 50 percent in four days."[795]

Third, Palau's campaigns have often facilitated the planting of new churches. Although church planting does not contribute to the numerical growth of existing churches, it does grow the Church of God. Palau insists, "Mass evangelism causes existing churches to face their responsibility for planting new congregations when the geographical and population configuration calls for it."[796] Many churches have been started through Palau's ministry.

The Rosario Plan in 1976 is the best-known campaign in this regard. Although the program did not reach its goal of starting sixty-nine new congregations, forty-two churches were formed, of which twenty-seven had survived by April 1978.[797] A pastor named Bruno Radi, who had to that point seen little fruit in his ministry, was ready to leave the church in defeat. While attending the conference for ministers during the Rosario Plan, however, his attitude began to change. In the following eighteen months he launched six new congregations.[798]

McWilliam cites another episode of church planting that happened in Uruguay:

> In a city of forty thousand people there were three evangelical churches. Two of the pastors had quarreled years earlier and had not talked since. In a pastor's conference, they confessed their sin and cleared up their relationship. God blessed with several thousand accepting Christ and several new churches were established.[799]

Church planting has occurred in many countries of Latin America, but the success is not limited to that region. During Palau's campaigns in Romania in 1990 and 1991, more than 85,600 people made public decisions to follow Jesus. According to the Lausanne Committee report, more than one thousand churches were planted as a result of Palau's ministry in Romania.[800] Furthermore, NGA also reports the formation of many new churches through its ministries. In Uganda, for example, from 2005 to 2007 about one hundred churches were started.[801] The organization also reports that, as of 2007, more than four thousand churches have been started through its ministries around the world.[802]

Finally, one must remember that the growth rate of a local church as the result of an evangelistic campaign differs significantly from one participating church to another. The most decisive factor is the level of involvement of a given local church. Palau explains:

> Our team's own post-crusade research has shown that if a church is actively involved in one of our crusades, it will receive seven times more growth afterward than a church that holds back and doesn't train its people to be friendship evangelists, counselors, and follow-up workers.[803]

Considering all the aspects discussed above, it seems appropriate to conclude that Palau's evangelistic campaigns have contributed to the numerical growth of local churches. Although some outstanding cases may not be generalized, they are still convincing enough to prove that his ministry has brought growth to local churches. His ministry has spurred church growth primarily in three ways: conversion and assurance of salvation on the part of nominal churchgoers, conversion of nonbelievers, and establishment of new congregations. Such fruits persuasively refute the claims that mass evangelism does not contribute to the growth of local churches. Thus, Palau's ministry verifies that mass evangelism is still vital to the spiritual and numerical growth of the Body of Christ.

Transformation of Society

In addressing the question of why evangelicals are flourishing in Latin America, even though they show little interest in social issues as compared to liberation theologians, David Stoll explains, "For people surviving on the margin of society, reforming one's day-to-day practices can offer immediate results of the kind often lacking in ambitious collective projects."[804] Although Stoll criticizes evangelicals in Latin America for their lack of social concern, such statements seem to at least acknowledge that people's lives have been changed immediately after their conversions. Actually, "ambitious collective projects" to change the world may not be possible without the transformation of individual lives.

Luis Palau strongly believes that the salvation of individuals will positively affect their lives and will in turn improve the society as a whole. This is possible because changed individuals permeate and penetrate every area of society, living out their lives as salt and light in the world. Palau infers, "Evangelism saves people not only from dying without Christ, but also from living without Him. And as they live with Him and for Him, they become salt and light in a world lost in darkness, sorrow, conflict, violence, and fear."[805] Palau cites the example of Guatemala, which as of 1989 had some 3 million Christians out of only 7 million people:

> As the Christians penetrate economic institutions, the military, education, politics, as they live out the biblical ethic, you can even begin to feel the changes coming along, and we should pray that this would happen. Rather than by violent revolution, by hatred, by bloodshed, why can't we dream that reformation could occur peacefully? Those of us from Latin America want to believe—and we may be naïve—but we would love to believe that if enough people who are converted really live out the biblical ethic, the nations could change, bringing blessing to the land. And that's the dream of nation after nation in the Third World.[806]

Palau's proclamation of the gospel with such conviction has brought substantial fruit. John McWilliam, for instance, described the fruits of Palau's ministry in society as follows:

> I personally have witnessed the impact of Christ on society as fathers ceased spending their meager incomes on drink and loose living and began to spend it on the clothing, education and well being of their families as a result of their conversion in a crusade. Through one crusade in Paraguay we saw a number of prostitutes come to Christ and then bring the owner of the establishment to hear the Gospel and turn his life over to Christ. Through the years the Luis Palau Team has seen countless cities and even nations and whole continents come under the powerful presentation of the Gospel of Christ.[807]

Although the transformation of society will be the ultimate fruit of the gospel, this outcome will be much slower in coming than the changes in individuals. In the words of Palau, "Total transformation of a life may have a sudden beginning, but its outworking is a long-term process."[808] Palau's forty-year co-worker Jim Williams supports this observation. While Palau's team was visiting some of the countries where they had conducted campaigns more than twenty years earlier, Williams met many people who had been converted as a direct result of the campaigns. After their conversion and changes in lifestyle, they had raised and educated their children with Christian values and worldviews. Twenty to twenty-five years later, Williams testifies, their children are penetrating and transforming every level of society with the gospel.[809]

A couple of real-life stories provide proof of the power of the gospel to transform society. The first happened early in Palau's ministry. Palau's encounter with Maria Benitez-Perez occurred during his live call-in counseling program in Ecuador in 1965. Maria, who had been raised in a wealthy and religious family, had rebelled against her parents as a teenager and joined a welcoming group of communists. Later she had become the secretary of the Communist Party in Ecuador.

By the time Maria met Palau she was a bitter and angry person, especially toward pastors and priests. She also had committed many evils in her life; she had married three times; had been adulterous; had stabbed a comrade; and had led student riots that had resulted in injury and death to many people. Although she had done such horrible things in anger, she could not rid herself of the guilt feelings. Through his counseling Palau assured her of God's love and forgiveness by repeating Hebrews 10:17, which promises, "Their sins and their lawless deeds I will remember no more" (NKJV).

When Maria finally accepted Christ, she became a totally different person. She broke away from the Communist Party, in spite of beatings and death threats, and even led some of her former communist friends to Christ. Furthermore, a communist revolution that had been in the planning stages for months failed to succeed because of Maria's intervention. On the morning of the planned revolution she led the Communist Party leader, who was slated to become the new ruler of the country, to her father's farm so that he could read the Bible and Graham's book *Peace with God*. Palau confidently asks, "Was Maria's conversion to Christ effective social action? Her changed life altered the course of national events—events that would have killed and oppressed the masses."[810]

Another story of conversion also illustrates how personal transformation can bring about social change. Rosario Rivera was a Marxist in Peru and an assistant of Che Guevara, the famous revolutionary. Palau recounts her story:

> Rosario had experienced one of the saddest childhoods I've ever heard of. Later she slipped into immorality, turned to violence, and became bitter toward God. After Guevara's death Rosario went to Lima, Peru's capital, where I happened to be preaching. She came to the stadium angry enough to kill me, but the Lord touched her heart. Early the next morning she trusted Jesus Christ, who completely transformed her. Instead of resorting to violence to bring about social change, Rosario began to give bread and milk to the poor and provided

> practical help to hundreds of families living in Lima's slums. Countless thousands have benefited from her ministry, and scores have found new life in Christ. And her story has been published now in Russian, German, and English.[811]

Rosario herself later pronounced, "If my heart burned for the revolution in the past, then it burns even more now, and if I did a lot for the poor before, then I do more now."[812] Such stories demonstrate the powerful impact of the gospel upon society. Thus, as Palau assertively declares, "Conversion leads to the greatest social action."[813]

Conclusion

In Matthew 7:16–20 Jesus explains the simple way to recognize whether a tree is good or bad: A good tree bears good fruit and a bad tree bears bad fruit. The last three chapters have examined the fruits of Luis Palau's evangelistic ministry around the world from various perspectives. Luis Palau is truly worthy to be called "a global evangelist." He has virtually traveled around the globe to proclaim the gospel, affecting hundreds of thousands of people's lives for eternity. Moreover, his global ministry is expanding today through the ministry of NGA.

Just as each continent has unique social and cultural backgrounds, Palau's evangelistic approach and contribution have varied. In Latin America he has preached the gospel as a light in the context of social darkness. He has been waking up the spiritually sleeping churches of Western Europe, and in the midst of spiritual and moral decadence he also has been calling North America back to God.

Luis Palau's ministry and life have substantially affected the world, and the seeds he has planted are still producing fruit. The impact of his proclamation of the gospel on people's lives, on local churches, and on society is certainly enough to verify the value and authenticity of his ministry. He has won many souls to Christ, brought spiritual and numerical growth to local churches, and ultimately changed society with the gospel message.

Palau's evangelistic fruit provides significant confirmation to the validity of mass evangelism when it is carried out in the power of the Holy Spirit. As discussed earlier, negative views are dominant among evangelicals concerning the role of mass evangelism for the evangelization of the world. However, Palau's evangelistic fruit provides credible evidence that mass evangelism is not obsolete, as some claim, but remains effective and strategic for world evangelization.

Palau persuasively refutes critics' claims that mass evangelism is a thing of the past that is no longer effective for today's world. Although some of the criticisms are valid, the strategic value of mass evangelism must not be obscured by them. A new age demands a new paradigm. When mass evangelism adopts and develops other new strategies for the changing world, it will still serve as a powerful means of proclaiming the timeless message of the gospel.

Endnotes

752 LPA, "Ministry Impact Statistics."

753 Henry J. Schmidt, "Crusade Decisions: Counting and Accounting for Lost Sheep," *Church Growth Journal of the North American Society for Church Growth*, 1 (1990): 28. While acknowledging Palau's integrity, Schmidt comments on the general tendency of most evangelists: "Itinerant evangelists are frequently stereotyped for 'over-stating, over-selling, and over-promising' good news."

754 LPA, "Guest Information Card." The card has three categories: "I prayed and invited Jesus Christ into my life today; I have received Jesus Christ as my Savior previously, but I rededicated my life to Him today; I listened to the message and would like more information." Cf. While acknowledging that "Luis Palau is a gifted evangelist and an articulate communicator," Schmidt observes, "However, there was fuzziness on the part of decision makers regarding what commitment was really being asked for." Schmidt, "Crusade Decisions," 29.

755 Kathy Chastain, interview by the author, via telephone, August 27, 2008. Kathy Chastain is media coordinator of LPA. She is in charge of updating "Ministry Impact Statistics."

756 Schmidt, "Crusade Decisions," 30, 39. The number in parentheses indicates the number of decisions. Other surveys show different outcomes; pastors' survey shows that "salvation" comprises 33 percent of the total decisions, while it was only 17.7 percent in the survey of decisionmakers. Ibid., 30.

757 Roy Pointer, *Crusade Evangelism: The Fruit That Remained; A Discussion Arising from Mission to London* (Bromley, Kent [England]: MARC Europe, 1988), 3. According to the Bible Society's survey of inquirers, 43 percent of the

total decisions are first-time decisions for salvation. This figure is lower than MARC's record that surveyed counselors.

758 Williams, interview by the author, August 8, 2008.

759 Scott Bauer, "Crusade Evangelism" (D.Min. project, Oral Roberts University, 1995), 139.

760 For example, Palau shares a letter he received from a convert who led his whole family to God after Mission to London: "Mission to London is not over, not by a long way. The QPR statistics will show that 'x' number of people gave their lives to Jesus on June 15th, 1984, but multiply that figure by five and it will be more accurate." Luis Palau and David Sanford, *Luis Palau: Calling America and the Nations to Christ* (Nashville, TN: Thomas Nelson, Inc., 1994; rev. 2000), 164.

761 For some examples, see Ibid., 83–89, 99–100, 128, 202.

762 Guntis Ulmanis, ex-president of Latvia, yielded his life to Christ at Palau's invitation during the campaign in Latvia in 1999. Palau also led Princess Alexandra, the Queen's cousin, to Christ. In America, the former Missouri senator, James M. Talent, came to believe in Jesus through Palau's ministry. Palau, interview by the author, May 9, 2008. Palau's influence on the leaders of society has been very strong. He has interviewed and counseled many presidents through personal appointments and occasions such as a presidential prayer breakfast. In Latin America, Palau counseled people such as Bolivian presidents Hugo Banzer and Juan Pereda Asbun, Ecuador's president, General Guillermo Rodriguez Lava, Paraguay's president, Alfredo Stroessner, and Venezuela's president, Dr. Luis Herrera Campins. See Palau and Sanford, *Calling America and the Nations*, 127, 144.

763 Palau, *The Only Hope for America*, 7.

764 Palau and Sanford, *Calling America and the Nations*, 196–98.

765 Ibid., 163. For more detailed testimonies of conversion and changed lives during Mission to London, see Susan Holton and David L. Jones, *Spirit Aflame: Luis Palau's Mission to London* (Grand Rapids: Baker Book House, 1985), 17, 19, 105, 137–38, 154–56, 189–90, 198–204.

766 "The Heart of a Singer/Songwriter: Matt Redman," *Proclaim!,* 2008, 10.

767 Ibid. Matt's testimony is also available in DVD. "Matt Redman: Modern Psalmist" (Portland, OR: LPA, n.d.), DVD.

768 Luis Palau and Timothy Robnett, *Telling the Story: Evangelism for the Next Generation* (Ventura, CA: Regal Books, 2006), 30.

769 Palau, *The Only Hope for America*, 19.

770 Holton and Jones, *Spirit Aflame*, 140.

771 Bauer, "Crusade Evangelism," 138.

772 Schmidt, "Crusade Decisions," 22.

773 Robnett, *Telling the Story*, 73.

774 Holton and Jones, *Spirit Aflame*, 94.

775 Bauer, "Crusade Evangelism," 121. "New people coming to the Lord" was ranked as the second, with 33 percent, while "Unity with other parts of the Church in the Valley" was rated highest, with 46 percent.

776 Kevin T. McBride, "Retaking the Village Green: Building Strategic Partnerships for Evangelism That Work in New England" (D.Min. project, Gordon-Conwell Theological Seminary, 2001), 83. McBride also points out that this event was the first statewide evangelistic campaign for Palau in the United States.

777 Win Arn, "Mass Evangelism: The Bottom Line," in *Pastor's Church Growth* (Pasadena, CA: Church Growth Press, 1979), 99–100.

778 John Mark Terry, *Evangelism: A Concise History* (Nashville, TN: Broadman & Holman Publishers, 1994), 170. To support his conclusion Mark Terry presents a couple of examples given by McLoughlin. He states, "For example, in 1956 Graham preached a crusade in Glasgow, Scotland, and the team announced 52,253 decisions for Christ. However, only 3,802 people (7 percent) actually joined a local church as a result. After the Toronto crusade, the Evangelistic Association reported that 902 out of 8,161 inquirers had joined a church or intended to do so. The Graham team admits that 60 percent of their converts are already church members. They attribute the dismaying results to poor follow-up by local churches." See William G. McLoughlin, *Modern Revivalism: Charles Grandison Finney to Billy Graham* (New York: Ronald Press, 1959), 516–18.

779 Palau, *Telling the Story*, 109. See also Palau and Sanford, *Calling America and the Nations*, 164. In the case of the campaign in Leeds in Yorkshire, England, in 1982, after several months 82 percent of decision-makers had been in the church. Furthermore, 100 percent of university students were still attending church. Holton and Jones, *Spirit Aflame*, 67. See also Palau and Sanford, *Calling America and the Nations*, 157.

780 Three studies include Pointer, *Crusade Evangelism*; Peter Brierley, *Mission to London: Phase 1, Who Responded?* (London: MARC Europe, 1984) and *Mission to London: Phase 2, Who Went Forward?* (London: MARC Europe, 1984); Schmidt, "Crusade Decisions."

781 Pointer, *Crusade Evangelism*, 5. Roy Pointer served on the executive committee of Palau's campaign in London. His study integrates two previous follow-up studies on Mission to London by Peter Brierley, European director of MARC Europe, and Lynda Barley, a research officer with Bible Society. Ibid., 1.

782 Pointer, *Crusade Evangelism*, 18.

783 Ibid.

784 Ibid. Roy Pointer supposes that Mission to London phase 2 at QPR should have had more people without any church background because of its massive public advertisement. Holton and Jones report that "many churches reported 25 percent increases in the size of their congregations, and some churches even doubled in size." Holton and Jones, *Spirit Aflame*, 16. For specific examples of church growth, see ibid., 146, 204–10.

785 Schmidt, "Crusade Decisions," 24. See also Palau and Sanford, *Calling America and the Nations*, 174. In the case of churched inquirers, the rate was 71.3 percent. Ibid., 28. Schmidt, however, raises suspicion on such data. After his own survey with local pastors who participated in Palau's campaign, Schmidt states, "The results of the Fresno adult inquirers' survey appears to completely contradict what Fresno pastors reported." Ibid., 24. According to Schmidt's survey, the number one problem with Palau's campaign rated by local pastors was "Problem with follow-up (delay, inadequate or misinformation, mismatched referrals)." Ibid., 22. The survey also shows that only 2.5 percent of referred inquirers to local churches were actively involved in the church. Schmidt reports, "In actuality of the 60 Fresno churches surveyed pastors reported: 12.4% initial attenders; 7.4% present attenders; 1.4% baptisms; 2.4% joined the church and 2.5% are actively involved." Ibid., 28. See ibid., 28-29 for Schmidt's plausible explanation for such discrepancy.

786 Ibid., 31.

787 Ibid., 32.

788 Glenn Firebaugh, "How Effective Are City-wide Crusades?" *Christianity Today*, 27 March 1981, 28. Firebaugh states, "The 1977 Arn study defines effectiveness in terms of direct numerical church growth. As Dr. Arn puts it, church growth (which he measures solely in terms of growth in church membership) is the 'bottom line.'"

789 Leighton Ford, "The Strategic Role of Mass Evangelism," *Christianity Today*, 24 November 1961, 32. According to Win Arn, "The church growth definition of evangelism is 'to proclaim Jesus Christ as God and Savior, to persuade people to become His disciples and responsible members of the Church.'" Arn, "Mass Evangelism: The Bottom Line," 98.

790 Edgardo Silvoso, "In Rosario It Was Different—Crusade Converts Are in the Churches," *Evangelical Missions Quarterly* 14, no. 2 (April 1978): 83.

791 William W. Conard, "Principles Behind the Rosario Plan," *Latin America Pulse* XIII, no. 3 (October 1978), 2.

792 Ibid. Silvoso suggests a higher average growth rate than Conard's figure. Silvoso reports, "The membership increase rate from 1964–1969 was 3.4 percent annually, and from 1970–1974 it was 9.8 percent." Silvoso, "In Rosario It Was Different," 83.

793 Randy Frame, "Palau Holds Mass Crusades Throughout Paraguay: Encouraging Results Are Reported in This Emerging South American Nation." *Christianity Today*, 12 November 1982, 72.

794 John Maust, "Terrorist Death Threat Fails to Force Palau Out of Peru," *Christianity Today*, 18 January 1985, 51. Another phenomenal rate of growth occurred in Chiclayo, Peru, in 1976. According to Palau, "A new church that already had one hundred fifty members grew seven hundred percent in less than a week through a carefully planned church growth effort." Palau and Sanford, *Calling America and the Nations*, 124.

795 Sandra Barrett, "Arise Uganda!" *Proclaim!*, vol. 1, 2004, 20.

796 Luis Palau, "The Future of Mass Evangelism," in *Evangelism: The Next Ten Years*, ed. Sherwood Eliot Wirt (Waco, TX: Word Books, 1978), 163.

797 Silvoso, "In Rosario It Was Different," 84. For more information on the Rosario Plan, see "Planting New Churches Through Evangelistic Campaigns" in chapter 8.

798 Luis Palau, "Working Together," in *Believing and Obeying Jesus Christ: The Urbana '79 Compendium*, ed. John W. Alexander (Downers Grove, IL: InterVarsity Press, 1980), 123.

799 John McWilliam, "Mass Evangelism: Reaching Your City in the Eighties," *Urban Mission* 3 (September 1985): 10.

800 Palau and Sanford, *Calling America and the Nations*, 188.

801 "Arise Uganda and Beyond," *Proclaim!*, vol. 1, 2008, 30.

802 Ibid., 31.

803 Palau and Sanford, *Calling America and the Nations*, 165.

804 David Stoll, "A Protestant Reformation in Latin America?" *The Christian Century* 107 (January 17, 1990): 46.

805 Palau, *The Only Hope for America*, 42.

806 Luis Palau, "Fear Not," in *Proclaim Christ Until He Comes: Calling the Whole Church to Take the Whole Gospel to the Whole World*, ed. J. D. Douglas (Minneapolis, MN: World Wide Publications, 1990), 369. Cf. Luis Palau, "Evangelist Luis Palau: Changing the World from the Inside Out," *World Vision* (April/May 1990), 8.

807 McWilliam, "Mass Evangelism," 8.

808 Luis Palau, "You Can Change the World," *Discipleship Journal* 33 (May/June 1986): 37.

809 Williams, interview by the author, August 8, 2008.

810 Luis Palau, "Evangelist Luis Palau: Changing the World from the Inside Out," *World Vision* (April/May 1990), 5 7. Maria's story is also found in Palau and Sanford, *Calling America and the Nations*, 83–87.

811 Palau, "Changing the World," 7.

812 Palau and Sanford, *Calling America and the Nations*, 106.

813 Palau, "Changing the World," 5.

CHAPTER 14

SUMMATION AND ANALYSIS

This research began with the premise that mass evangelism has throughout Christian history been one of the most effective means of proclaiming the gospel, but there have been uncertainty and a gloomy perception regarding the future of mass evangelism. In the midst of the growing concern, this writer has sought to find the possible solution for the impasse of mass evangelism through a study of the life and ministry of the evangelist Luis Palau. This final section will briefly reiterate some of the most important findings of this study, along with lessons for contemporary and future evangelists and local churches.

Integrative Summary

Many scholars have expressed pessimistic views about the future of mass evangelism. Some argue that this approach is theologically flawed, while others claim that mass evangelism is unappealing to people because it is culturally outdated. Still others point out the lack of credibility of evangelists, based on some much-publicized ethical blunders.

For more than four decades, however, Luis Palau has advocated the vital roles of itinerant evangelists and mass evangelism for world evangelization. He has substantiated his claim through significant accomplishments in his ministry and has provided a role model for itinerant evangelists, along with establishing some invaluable benchmarks for mass evangelism.

To evaluate Palau's impact on mass evangelism, this researcher has examined Palau's life, theology, and strategy, as well as the results of his ministry. Palau's life has been shaped by godly individuals he met along his spiritual journey. Through their help Palau gained a vision for the evangelization of the world and was equipped spiritually and intellectually for the work of an evangelist. Among those mentors, Billy Graham stands out. Through his example, advice, encouragement, prayer, and financial help, Graham has provided invaluable assistance to Palau.

Palau's evangelistic theology and philosophy, both of which are central to his evangelistic ministry, have been discussed in this study. His theology is grounded in the Scriptures and reflects the theology of preceding evangelists in many respects. He has been a strong supporter of biblical authority and has advocated the validity of campaign evangelism for contemporary and future generations. Through his theology Palau provides both biblical and practical guidelines for mass evangelism.

Palau's evangelistic strategy also resembles that of preceding evangelists. Learning from evangelists of the past, Palau has developed his own strategy. The two most important hallmarks of his approach have been relevancy and creativity. Palau's proclamation is marked by relevancy. He is a down-to-earth preacher who understands the life of his audience and employs relevant topics and illustrations.

Relevancy and creativity have also been vividly demonstrated in his use of mass media. Palau's live call-in television counseling has been notable in this regard. Moreover, these principles have been best illustrated in his recent changes in the format of the campaigns. Along with Livin It, which aims at reaching youth, Palau has changed the style of campaigns to family- and nonbeliever-friendly festivals. The fact that the average attendance at a campaign has grown tenfold since the adoption of that change indicates clearly the effect of this new strategy. The success of this new model also testifies to its importance.

Palau's evangelistic impact is felt literally in every continent. Theologically, he has been a defender of the pure gospel against the threat of liberation theology in Latin America; an advocate of biblical authority in Europe; a champion for moral and spiritual renewal in North America; and, more recently, an apologist of the gospel through friendly conversation with atheists in China.

Through his preaching, writing, and broadcasting, Palau has reached multitudes of people with the message of the gospel. Through evangelistic campaigns and rallies alone, he has led more than one million people to make decisions for Christ. His ministry has also brought remarkable results in terms of both Christian maturity and the numerical growth of local churches.

The impact of his preaching on society may be slow, but this is probably the most effective form of social reform. Individuals changed by the gospel will ultimately transform the world in which they live.

Finally, through the ministry of NGA and Alliance Ministries, Palau has mentored many evangelists and is expanding his evangelistic ministry to the ends of the Earth. The impact of his preaching is not limited to his own time but will continue into the following decades through those open to learning from him and his evangelistic team.

Lessons for Evangelists and Local Churches

The knowledge and experience gleaned from Luis Palau provide valuable insights into the field of evangelism. The implications of Luis Palau's evangelistic ministry for current and future evangelists are manifold. The most important factor for any successful mass evangelism is the evangelist himself. The moral lapse of some famous evangelists has fostered criticism and distrust against evangelists. Unless evangelists can restore the trust and honor of the populace, they will be unable to serve as faithful witnesses of the gospel.

Thus, the evangelist must be a man of integrity. Palau has set a good example in this regard. Particularly notable in this regard is the fact that even though some criticize his theology and methodology, no one seems to question his integrity. Evangelists must develop certain qualities that are essential and pertinent to their role and mission; these include vision, passion, compassion, boldness, and holiness. They must emulate in their lives and ministries those traits exemplified in the life of Luis Palau.

Second, evangelists must hold unswervingly to the theological convictions that are vital to their ministries. Most important is the conviction of the inerrancy of the Bible. The Bible is the perfect Book, which alone contains the message of salvation for human beings. Palau's other theological convictions and evangelistic strategies flow naturally from this powerful conviction.

Third, evangelists must learn from other evangelists. In fact, mass evangelism itself has evolved over time, building upon the methods of previous generations. Palau is no exception. He has learned and adopted essential strategies and skills for mass evangelism from his predecessors, men such as Charles Finney, Dwight Moody, and his mentor Billy Graham. His preaching and evangelistic efforts all reflect their influences. Along with "using all available means to communicate" and "using a team," Palau insists on "learning from the masters" as the most effective criterion for mass evangelism.[814]

Fourth, evangelists must acquire knowledge of the culture of their audience and employ culturally relevant and creative strategies. Although theologically conservative, Palau has been innovative in evangelism. One must remember that no method is sacred or unchangeable. While the message cannot be altered, the method should be flexible enough to respond to the changing culture and needs of people. Thus it is the responsibility of evangelists to present the timeless message of the truth in a time-sensitive way. Evangelists should not simply clone the methods and skills of Palau or of any other evangelist. Rather, they need to understand the culture of their audience and implement what they have learned in their contextual situations.

Last but not least is the importance of teamwork. As Palau acknowledges, working as a team is one of the most constructive ways to reach people. Many of Palau's evangelistic successes have been the product of teamwork. Without faithful coworkers, Palau would have achieved much less. When contemporary and future evangelists implement the lessons they can glean from Luis Palau, they will be better equipped and serve as more effective witnesses of the good news of Jesus Christ.

The findings of this study will help local church leaders and congregations to understand the strategic role of the evangelistic campaign and will enable them to work with evangelists efficiently by avoiding unnecessary confusions and conflicts.

First, spiritual preparation is a must for successful campaigns. Prayer must permeate the evangelistic campaign, with pastors and local congregations praying fervently and with great expectation that God will save as many sinners as possible. It is also imperative that they pray for the evangelists, various committees, those in leadership positions, and volunteers who serve during the campaign.

Second, key people for the success of any evangelistic campaign are the local pastors. When they fully understand the value of campaign evangelism and become passionate supporters, evangelistic campaigns are fruitful. To make this possible, they must know and trust the evangelist wholeheartedly and endorse his or her ministry to their congregations.

Third, as Scott Bauer has pointed out, once local church leaders have developed conviction and commitment, "The entire congregation's life must be directed towards the efforts of the crusade."[815] Evangelistic campaigns cannot bear fruit without successful mobilization of the laity. Local Christians must be passionate about evangelism and be willing to serve in various capacities during the campaign.

Fourth, campaign evangelism provides a tremendous opportunity for local Christians to be trained in evangelism and to bring their own families and friends to the Lord. Utilizing already established relationships is key in this regard.

Fifth, the success of evangelistic campaigns also depends on the unity and cooperation of local Christians who represent different denominational backgrounds. For this, they have to leave behind secondary denominational issues, while refusing to compromise the integrity of the gospel.

Finally, local churches must strive to preserve the decision-makers from the campaign and assimilate them into their own churches. They must remember that the primary responsibility for follow-up rests with them, not with the evangelist or his or her team. When local churches apply these insights to the evangelistic campaigns, they will see qualitative results in their churches and community.

Following this extensive research on Luis Palau, one important question must be answered: Is mass evangelism still viable and effective for the evangelization of the world? As Win Arn once noted, the answer is both yes and no.[816] If mass evangelism is done in the same traditional way, it inevitably will become outdated and fail to effectively reach people with the gospel. But if mass evangelism is open to changing its approaches properly, in accordance with rapidly changing cultures, it will be not only viable but one of the most powerful strategies for winning multitudes to Christ.

Without a doubt mass evangelism has its limitations. There is no method of evangelization without shortcomings. While some criticisms are persuasive and valid, the strategic role of mass evangelism for the evangelization of the world cannot be overshadowed. As Edward F. Murphy aptly observes, "We cannot reject mass evangelism without violating the Scriptures. We cannot deny its effectiveness without ignoring church history."[817]

Alvin Reid's list of great evangelists includes George Whitefield, John Wesley, Jonathan Edwards, Charles Finney, D. L. Moody, and Billy Graham.[818] It is the conviction of this writer that at the end of the list the name of Luis Palau deserves to be added. From the time he first preached the gospel on the streets of Argentina as a teenager to his success as a renowned global evangelist, Palau's passion for the gospel and compassion for the lost have never flagged. Even at the age of seventy-two his ministry is still growing.[819] Today he is a much-sought evangelist, preacher, conference speaker, author, apologist, broadcaster, counselor, and mentor. Palau's global impact on evangelism will be evaluated properly only when he finishes his course on Earth.

Palau's successful ministry in the past and the growing ministry today are compelling enough to prove mass evangelism's validity for the evangelization of the world. Despite inherent limitations, mass evangelism can still serve as an effective and strategic method of evangelism, when utilized relevantly and creatively. Perhaps Palau's own words will be adequate to finish this study: "Years ago I wrote in my Bible, alongside Matthew 28:18–20, 'God has not lost His enthusiasm for the Great Commission. Have I?' May that never be true in your life and in mine! I can honestly say evangelism is more exciting the longer I keep at it!"[820]

Endnotes

814 Luis Palau, "The Evangelist Has a Strategy for Harvest," in *The Mission of an Evangelist*, ed. J. D. Douglas (Minneapolis, MN: World Wide Publications, 2001), 233.

815 Scott Bauer, "Crusade Evangelism" (D.Min. project, Oral Roberts University, 1995), 80.

816 Win Arn, "Mass Evangelism: The Bottom Line" in *Pastor's Church Growth Handbook* (Pasadena, CA: Church Growth Press, 1979), 105.

817 Edward F. Murphy, "Mass Evangelism Is Not Obsolete," *Christianity Today*, 28 February 1975, 6.

818 Alvin Reid, *Introduction to Evangelism* (Nashville, TN: Broadman & Holman Publishers), 266.

819 Cf. Luis Palau and Timothy Robnett, *Telling the Story: Evangelism for the Next Generation* (Ventura, CA: Regal Books, 2006), 32. Palau expresses his wish to be faithful to his calling to the end, just as Whitefield, Moody, and Graham did. Cf. The following statement that Palau made at Amsterdam '86 shows his passion for the gospel: "If I'm remembered for anything when I die, I want it to be this: that I had a heart and life which burned with the love and power of the Holy Spirit. A heart afire with love for God and for people. A message aflame with power to convict the souls of men and win them to Christ. That is my reason for living. That is my purpose in being an evangelist." Luis Palau, "The Evangelist and the Ministry of the Holy Spirit," in *The Calling of an Evangelist*, ed. J. D. Douglas (Minneapolis, MN: World Wide Publications, 1987), 135.

820 Luis Palau and David Sanford, *Luis Palau: Calling America and the Nations to Christ* (Nashville, TN: Thomas Nelson, Inc., 1994; rev. 2000), 207.

APPENDIX 1

LPA STATEMENT OF FAITH*

1. We believe that the Bible is the verbally inspired Word of God, without error in the original writing, and the supreme and final authority in doctrine and practice.
2. We believe in one God, eternally existent in three Persons: Father, Son, and Holy Spirit.
3. We believe in the deity of our Lord Jesus Christ, in His virgin birth, in His sinless life, in His miracles, in His vicarious death and atonement through His shed blood, in His bodily resurrection, and in His personal return in power and glory.
4. We believe that for the salvation of lost and sinful man, faith in the Lord Jesus Christ and regeneration by the Spirit are essential.
5. We believe in the present ministry of the Holy Spirit, by Whose indwelling the Christian is enabled to live a godly life.
6. We believe in the forgiveness of sins, the resurrection of the body, and life eternal.
7. We believe in the spiritual unity of the Church, which is the Body of Christ, composed of all who are regenerated through faith in the Lord Jesus Christ.

*This section was taken from: "Statement of Faith," LPA, 8 September 2008 [online]; accessed 8 September 2008; available from http://www.palau.org/about/mission; Internet.

APPENDIX 2

LPA MISSION STATEMENT*

1. **Proclaim the Gospel** In dependence upon God, we want to win as many people as possible to Jesus Christ throughout the world, proclaiming His Good News by all available means to the millions of people who have yet to respond to the Gospel.

2. **Mobilize the Church** In dependence upon God, we want to emphasize with the Church the principles of victorious Christian living (Galatians 2:20), so as to stimulate, revive, train, and mobilize the Church to continuous, effective evangelism, follow-up, and church growth.

3. **Equip the Next Generation** In dependence upon God, we want to hold high the banner of biblical evangelism, influencing Christianity worldwide and raising up a new generation of godly leaders, so that the Church's commitment to evangelism will never die.

*This section was taken from: "Mission Statement," LPA, 8 September 2008 [online]; accessed 8 September 2008; available from http://www.palau.org/about/mission; Internet.

APPENDIX 3

CHRONOLOGICAL ARRANGEMENT OF LUIS PALAU'S CAMPAIGNS*

Year	Location	Length	Attendance	Inquirers
2008				
	Celebrate Freedom '08 Atlanta	1 day	47,000	200
	Portland CityFest, Portland, Oregon	2 days	185,000	2,316
	BeachFest, Myrtle Beach	2 days	19,000	540
	BucurestiFest	2 days	14,522	1,958
	Best Dressed 50Fest, Kingston, Mandeville, and Montego Bay	2 days	350,798	21,207
	Buenos Aires Festival '08	2 days	850,000	19,463
	Rolling Hills Men's Retreat	2 days	2,200	162
	Mission ConneXion	2 days	742	102
2007				
	Hangchou, China	1 day	8,000	300
	Cairo Festival, Cairo, Egypt	2 days	13,815	5,152
	Festival Hispanos '07, Portland, Oregon	2 days	11,500	373
	Buenos Aires pre-event (Vision de Futuro)	1 day	15,000	950
	Keswick, England EC	2 days	2,000	64
	Edinburgh, Scotland Youth Program	1 day	400	70
	Celebrate Freedom 2007, Atlanta	1 day	42,000	500

Year	Location	Length	Attendance	Inquirers
	Orange County Festival (Andrew Palau)	1 day	5,000	29
	Heartland Festival, Omaha	2 days	108,900	5,462
	Celebrate Freedom 2007, Dallas	2 days	100,000	268
	Nashville CityFest	2 days	90,000	1,681
	Monterrey Festival, Mexico	2 days	401,950	15,741
	Tampa Bay Festival, Florida	2 days	140,000	3,471
2006				
	RiverFest pre-event	1 day	420	27
	CityFest Houston	2 days	225,000	3,875
	London (Savoy – Business Leaders Event)	1 day	350	40
	Costa Rica Festival	2 days	410,000	17,405
	Orlando Festival	2 days	85,000	3,143
2005				
	Guatemala (Counsel by mail: 210 & Internet: 3,060)			3,270
	Washington, D.C.	2 days	103,075	3,970
	Bend, Oregon	1 day	12,000	546
	Madrid, Spain	2 days	85,675	4,266
	Mendoza, Argentina	2 days	120,000	4,314
	Costa Rica (pastors event)	2 days	7,300	104
2004				
	Lima, Peru	2 days	667,000	42,200
	Cardiff, Wales	2 days	9,000	184
	FijiFest, Fiji Islands	10 days	52,200	4,321
	Minneapolis, St. Paul, Minnesota	2 days	200,000	9,819
	Reno, Nevada	2 days	30,000	3,282
	Beijing, China	9 days	9,663	322
	Mar de Plata, Argentina	2 days	311,300	9,800
2003				
	Manchester, England	2 days	55,000	2,204
	Fort Lauderdale, Florida (and USA parties)	2 days	340,375	7,968
	Buenos Aires, Argentina	2 days	851,942	28,153
2002				
	Los Angeles Promise Keepers (rally)	1 day	8,300	344
	England/Scotland	7 days	2,766	500
	Puget Sound Region	2 days	151,700	4,021
	Cleveland Promise Keepers (rally)	1 day	11,500	566

Year	Location	Length	Attendance	Inquirers
	Syracuse, New York	2 days	53,500	3,496
	Woodbridge, Virginia	1 day	5,100	117
	Myrtle Beach, South Carolina	2 days	93,000	2,439
2001				
	Córdoba, Argentina	2 days	211,480	6,284
	Garden Grove, California	1 day	2,880	604
	Santa Cruz, California	2 days	55,887	1,940
	Boise, Idaho	2 days	102,160	1,966
	Managua, Nicaragua	1 day	300,000	3,800
	Connecticut/Massachusetts	6 weeks	120,000	8,222
	Mexico City Promise Keepers (rally)	1 day	1,500	150
2000				
	Rosario, Argentina	4 days	130,000	2,900
	Evansville, Indiana	5 days	31,063	1,696
	Los Angeles Promise Keepers (rally)	1 day	12,000	600
	Tucson, Arizona	4 days	52,215	1,945
	Portland, Oregon	2 days	140,000	1,250
	Garden Grove, California	2 days	6,146	374
	North Dakota/Minnesota	1 month	72,477	4,617
	Sheffield, England	7 days	26,858	2,962
	Monterrey, Mexico	6 days	94,872	7,047
1999				
	Santiago and Viña del Mar, Chile	5 days	38,764	2,783
	Formosa/Corrientes, Argentina	9 days	43,735	4,274
	Riga, Latvia (and 2 other cities)	6 days	34,935	1,385
	Portland, Oregon	2 days	93,000	1,226
	Garden Grove, California	3 days	11,000	300
	Strasbourg and Nice, France	4 days	8,245	507
	North West England	2 weeks	26,270	3,841
	Mission Maine	1 month	77,615	5,688
	Villahermosa, Mexico	7 days	117,200	4,236
	Istanbul, Turkey	3 days	1,625	84
1998				
	Camas/Washougal, Washington	3 days	2,750	260
	Montevideo, Uruguay	6 days	67,800	4,047

Year	Location	Length	Attendance	Inquirers
	East Midlands, England (7 cities)	3 weeks	33,955	3,588
	Tucson Promise Keepers (rally)	1 day	9,962	109
	Nogales, Laredo, Nuevo Laredo	10 days	54,898	3,200
	Garden Grove, California	4 days	14,550	1,194
	Philadelphia Promise Keepers (rally)	1 day	41,200	850
	Koror, Republic of Palau	5 days	14,060	1,362
	Guam	3 days	2,354	386
	Knoxville Promise Keepers (rally)	1 day	19,000	183
	Toronto (Chinese)	3 days	12,000	397
	Rapid City, South Dakota	4 days	36,988	1,544
	Olympia, Washington	6 days	18,065	733
	Woodburn, Oregon	3 days	3,011	156
	Cairo, Egypt	4 days	13,800	1,329
	Egypt (by video in 585 churches)	5 days	555,000	30,900
	Patagonia (5 cities)	15 days	52,600	3,500
1997				
	Lincoln City, Oregon	3 days	2,765	353
	The Dalles, Oregon	3 days	3,826	374
	Kansas City, Missouri	7 days	40,995	3,136
	Helsinki, Finland, (rallies)	2 days	3,690	56
	Vancouver Promise Keepers (rally)	1 day	6,000	150
	Seaside, Oregon	3 days	4,534	302
	Maracaibo, Venezuela	4 days	63,500	3,101
	Parkdale, Oregon	3 days	1,420	101
	Bristol and West England	11 days	35,716	2,929
	El Paso, Texas	7 days	46,545	3,834
	Ciudad Juárez, Mexico	5 days	95,635	4,447
	Bogotá, Colombia	2 rallies	35,000	1,300
	Macao	2 rallies	3,800	310
	Hong Kong	6 days	127,740	12,350
	Guatemala City (affinity events)	2 days	3,650	385
	Hillsboro, Oregon	3 days	6,008	445
	Chiang Mai, Thailand	5 days	18,250	704
1996				
	El Salvador (3 cities)	8 days	149,000	4,850
	Hasselt, Flanders, Belgium	2 days	2,450	89

Year	Location	Length	Attendance	Inquirers
	New York Promise Keepers (rally)	1 day	34,600	1,500
	Chicago Promise Keepers (rally)	1 day	68,972	1,565
	Greater Chicago	57 days	129,615	10,112
	Tegucigalpa, Honduras	6 days	103,700	5,364
1995				
	Bolivia (3 cities)	11 days	184,037	22,011
	Tyler, Texas	11 days	51,969	1,522
	Washington Promise Keepers (rally)	1 day	50,440	5,200
	Londonderry, Northern Ireland	6 days	18,000	450
	Detroit Promise Keepers (rally)	1 day	72,280	6,000
	Kathmandu, Nepal	4 days	26,000	1,440
	Miami, Florida	9 days	78,904	3,269
1994				
	Asunción, Paraguay	9 days	74,387	6,702
	Barcelona and L'Escala, Spain	5 days	10,250	374
	Stillwater and Tulsa, Oklahoma	11 days	41,510	1,110
	Grand Rapids and Holland, Michigan	10 days	68,089	3,662
	Willow Creek Community Church	3 services	12,600	
	Pusan, South Korea (rally)	1 day	20,000	
	World Cup rally, Washington	1 day	6,000	60
	World Cup rally, Chicago	1 day	3,000	276
	San Fernando Valley	6 days	54,105	2,184
	Gdansk, Poland	3 days	6,100	1,160
	Luton, England	4 days	8,000	296
	Guatemala (3 cities)	2 weeks	386,030	17,158
1993				
	Taiwan (3 cities)	15 days	118,000	8,600
	Fort Worth, Texas	9 days	44,290	1,425
	Chile (2 cities)	5 days	15,671	295
	Jamaica (11 cities)	15 days	245,000	17,500
1992				
	Panama	9 days	41,670	1,596
	Phoenix, Arizona	8 days	72,000	2,346
	Porto, Portugal	3 days	17,000	431
	McAllen, Texas / Reynosa, Mexico	10 days	106,430	5,405

Year	Location	Length	Attendance	Inquirers
	Boulder Promise Keepers (rally)	1 day	22,000	650
	Peoria, Illinois	6 days	38,750	1,809
	Dublin, Ireland	3 days	17,400	1,367
	Mexico City	3 weeks	142,000	10,500
1991				
	Davao City and Manila, Philippines	8 days	256,000	8,459
	San Antonio, Texas	8 days	55,600	3,070
	Fortaleza, Brazil	7 days	52,200	2,690
	Tri-Cities, Washington	6 days	16,437	561
	Sofia, Bulgaria	3 days	16,200	5,900
	Romania (5 cities)	11 days	125,900	39,446
	Stuttgart, Germany (rally)	1 day	5,500	400
	Palm Springs, California	6 days	10,800	404
	Mexico City (rallies)	4 days	11,400	155
	San José, Costa Rica	4 days	233,100	3,722
1990				
	Stockholm, Sweden (rallies)	3 days	13,000	120
	Okinawa and Osaka, Japan	10 days	60,900	7,199
	Des Moines, Iowa	10 days	35,500	1,606
	Jakarta and Surabaya, Indonesia	9 days	89,000	8,128
	Brno and Bratislava, Czechoslovakia	6 days	8,950	1,120
	Gothenburg, Sweden (rallies)	4 days	20,500	2,882
	Romania (3 cities)	9 days	215,000	46,172
	Bangkok, Thailand	4 days	27,700	1,940
	Acapulco, Mexico (rally)	1 day	6,000	250
	Quad Cities, Illinois / Iowa	10 days	19,500	1,750
	Toronto, Ontario (rally)	1 day	6,900	290
	Madras, India	6 days	63,000	5,100
1989				
	Spain (5 cities)	8 days	10,000	1,000
	Monterrey, Mexico	5 days	65,000	4,877
	U.S.S.R. (5 cities)	10 days	40,000	8,500
	Bogotá, Colombia	6 days	166,000	10,288
	Manila, Philippines	1 day	18,000	250
	Tell Wales (6 regions)	5 weeks	78,000	3,866

Year	Location	Length	Attendance	Inquirers
	Spokane, Washington	10 days	40,000	2,194
	Budapest, Hungary (rally)	1 day	12,000	997
	Guatemala City, Guatemala	8 days	224,000	8,200
	Lubbock, Texas (rallies)	4 days	7,000	52
1988				
	Cuttack, India	5 days	41,000	4,116
	Scottsdale, Arizona (rallies)	3 days	4,400	127
	Turin, Italy (rallies)	2 days	5,500	100
	Porto Alegre, Brazil	4 days	37,000	1,729
	Copenhagen, Denmark	6 days	41,300	792
	Torshavn, Faroe Islands	3 days	13,700	326
	Tuxtla Gutierrez, Mexico	5 days	56,400	2,998
	Mexico City (rallies)	1 day	5,600	
	Ciudad Victoria, Mexico	4 days	37,800	3,144
	Toronto, Ontario (rallies)	3 days	5,500	253
1987				
	Hong Kong	8 days	219,100	31,268
	Manhattan, Kansas	9 days	19,400	968
	Dziegielow, Poland (rallies)	8 days	27,600	564
	Skagit Valley, Washington	5 days	14,200	675
	Nairobi, Kenya (rally)	1 day	6,000	350
	Auckland, New Zealand	15 days	165,500	6,312
	New Zealand (4 areas)	7 days	103,000	2,618
	Suva, Fiji	4 days	50,100	2,501
1986				
	Sweden (4 cities)	6 days	10,500	
	Portland, Oregon (rally)	1 day	7,100	83
	Fresno, California	8 days	56,000	3,345
	Mount Union, Pennsylvania (rallies)	3 days	30,000	
	Singapore	7 days	337,500	11,902
	European Tour (4 countries)	10 days	34,900	700
	Argentina (6 cities)	25 days	333,000	12,322
1985				
	Salem, Oregon	5 days	18,000	709
	Mexico City (rallies)	4 days	8,000	800

Year	Location	Length	Attendance	Inquirers
	Portland, Oregon (rally)	1 day	12,800	307
	Mount Union, Pennsylvania (rallies)	3 days	25,000	
	European Tour (5 countries)	12 days	46,100	1,599
	Zurich, Switzerland	22 days	112,500	1,233
1984				
	Lima, Peru	9 days	240,750	15,640
	Arequipa, Peru	7 days	45,750	5,931
	Los Angeles, California (rallies)	3 days	15,000	400
	Albuquerque, New Mexico (rallies)	2 days	1,050	163
	Vancouver, British Columbia (rally)	1 day	25,000	
	Colorado Springs, Colorado	8 days	18,950	975
	London, England	41 days	318,000	20,000
	The Netherlands (4 cities)	4 days	4,000	
	San Juan, Puerto Rico (rally)	1 day	35,000	1,000
1983				
	Utrecht, Netherlands (rally)	1 day	20,000	1,000
	London, England	50 days	210,000	8,000
	Modesto, California	7 days	70,000	1,414
	Hermosillo, Mexico	8 days	36,000	3,458
	San Antonio, Texas (rallies)	2 days	31,000	600
	Aneby, Sweden	4 days	40,000	
1982				
	Guatemala City, Guatemala	8 days	827,000	3,800
	Leeds, England	10 days	35,000	938
	Paraguay (7 cities)	20 days	153,800	10,559
	Helsinki, Finland	7 days	63,000	1,400
	Bellingham, Washington	7 days	29,000	443
	Newcastle, Australia	17 days	52,000	1,400
	Madison, Wisconsin	9 days	8,550	300
1981				
	San Diego, California	12 days	40,000	1,204
	Glasgow, Scotland	36 days	198,000	5,326
1980				
	Argentina (4 cities)		26,100	733
	Ascunción, Paraguay		4,000	140

Year	Location	Length	Attendance	Inquirers
	Guayaquil, Ecuador	14 days	76,000	2,850
	Los Angeles, California	9 days	51,000	1,945
	Scotland (6 cities)	4 weeks	62,500	2,000
	England (10 cities)	10 days	30,000	2,700
1979				
	Caracas, Venezuela	6 days	65,500	1,343
	Aberdeen, Scotland	10 days	27,900	538
	Northeast Scotland (rallies)	19 days	38,000	826
	Newcastle, Australia	4 days	22,500	450
	Veracruz, Mexico	7 days	38,000	3,098
1978				
	Acapulco, Mexico	5 days	26,000	2,266
	Bolivia (3 cities)	15 days	180,000	18,916
	Uruguay (6 cities)	19 days	101,000	8,104
1977				
	Guatemala (2 cities)	9 days	64,000	1,300
	Montevideo, Uruguay (rally)	1 day	12,000	500
	Santo Domingo, Dominican Republic	14 days	105,400	3,962
	Cardiff, Wales	21 days	60,000	1,585
	Buenos Aires, Argentina	5 days	81,500	3,074
	Germany (2 cities)	10 days	66,150	539
	Boise, Idaho	2 days	5,000	
1976				
	Rosario, Argentina	21 days	77,100	5,183
	Asunción, Paraguay	16 days	100,300	4,936
	Montreat, North Carolina (rallies)	6 days	10,000	
	European Tour (5 countries)	4 weeks	20,000	189
	Bogotá, Colombia	3 days	31,500	1,150
	Chiclayo, Peru	4 days	14,000	810
	Mexico (8 cities)	14 days	111,100	5,337
1975				
	Managua, Nicaragua	22 days	187,000	5,711
	South American Tour (3 countries)	12 days	38,300	1,295
	Iguala, Mexico	16 days	17,100	1,013
	Central American Tour	6 days	14,100	446

Year	Location	Length	Attendance	Inquirers
	United States (various rallies)		7,000	50
	Europe (various rallies)		18,000	422
1974				
	San Juan, Puerto Rico (rally)	1 day	500	65
	Bolivia (3 cities)	20 days	82,400	9,210
	Grants Pass, Oregon	10 days	31,400	624
	Spain (5 cities)	9 days	8,100	224
	Quito, Ecuador	21 days	79,900	3,120
	Netzahualcoytl, Mexico	8 days	43,000	1,432
	United States (various rallies)		4,500	65
1973				
	Quito, Ecuador (rally)	1 day	300	10
	Cochabamba, Bolivia (rally)	1 day	1,500	50
	Spain (5 cities)	9 days	5,000	350
	United States (various rallies)		15,200	130
	Ciudad Obregon, Mexico	6 days	15,800	488
	Santo Domingo, Dominican Republic	12 days	71,600	2,373
	Reynosa, Mexico / McAllen, Texas	11 days	30,000	1,144
1972				
	Spokane, Washington	8 days	5,000	236
	Puebla, Mexico	3 days	3,200	233
	Guatemala (3 cities)	22 days	115,000	3,197
	Costa Rica	21 days	62,500	3,205
	United States (various rallies)	3 days	2,300	31
1971				
	Costa Rica	3 days	2,500	84
	Mexico	12 days	9,600	724
	Lima, Peru	17 days	108,400	5,010
	Honduras	17 days	57,000	2,434
	Guatemala	22 days	128,800	3,158
	United States (various rallies)		5,900	236
1970				
	Costa Rica (rally)	1 day	1,000	91
	Honduras	9 days	7,300	248
	Guatemala	10 days	13,900	771

Year	Location	Length	Attendance	Inquirers
	Arena Mexico, Mexico City	10 days	106,000	6,670
	El Salvador	10 days	16,600	1,550
	Mexico (4 cities)	35 days	35,800	2,716
	United States (various rallies)		7,600	118
1969				
	Quito, Ecuador	8 days	10,200	461
	Guatemala and El Salvador		8,700	120
	Mexico (7 cities)	104 days	104,500	7,360
1968				
	San Cristobal, Venezuela	15 days	11,200	672
	Colombia (3 cities)	19 days	41,300	1,596
	Buen Pastor Church, Mexico	12 days	2,350	192
1967				
	Huancayo, Peru	8 days	18,400	346
	Arequipa, Peru	7 days	11,900	658
1966				
	Mexico	13 days	2,650	240
	Bogotá, Colombia	4 days	42,000	865
	Quito, Ecuador	9 days	1,200	89
	Colombia (4 cities)	70 days	29,600	1,796
1965				
	Quito, Ecuador		3,000	130
	Cerro de Pasco, Peru	9 days	4,750	255
	Colombia (3 cities)	32 days	8,450	464
	Colombia, Costa Rica, and Guatemala		20,000	575

*This section was taken from: LPA, "Ministry Impact Statistics," September 2008. These statistics were arranged and provided by Kathy Chastain, media coordinator of LPA. It begins with a statement as follows: "Luis Palau and his team have spoken in person to more than 25 million people in 72 nations. During the past four decades, Palau has held 460 evangelistic festivals, crusades, and rallies in Central and South America, North America, Europe, the South Pacific, Asia, and Africa. 1,080,079 people (inquirers) have made documented decisions for Jesus Christ at these festivals, crusades and rallies."

BIBLIOGRAPHY

Primary Sources*

Books

Palau, Luis. *Walk on Water, Pete!* Ventura, CA: Regal, 1974; Portland, OR: Multnomah Press, 1981.

____________. *The Schemer and the Dreamer: God's Way to the Top*. Portland, OR: Multnomah Press, 1976.

____________. *The Moment to Shout: God's Way to Face Walls*. Portland, OR: Multnomah Press, 1977; Grand Rapids: Discovery House Publishers, 1977.

____________. *Sex and Youth*. Nashville, TN: Editorial Caribe, 1978.

____________. *Whom Shall I Marry?* Nashville, TN: Editorial Caribe, 1978.

____________. *Heart after God: Running with David*. Portland, OR: Multnomah Press, 1978, renamed as *A Man After God's Heart: Running with David*. Grand Rapids: Discovery House, 1978.

____________. *Our God Reigns: Scotland Messages*. Compiled and Edited by David L. Jones. London: Luis Palau Team (UK) Trust, 1981.

____________. *Personal Promises of the Bible*. Colorado Springs, CO: Shaw Books, 1982.

____________. *So You Want to Grow*. UK: Kingsway Publications, 1984; reprint, Eugene, OR: Harvest House Publishers, 1986.

____________. *Tough Questions*. London: Hodder & Stoughton, 1984.

____________. *What Is a Real Christian?* Portland, OR: Multnomah Press, 1985.

____________. *Steps Along the Way*. UK: Kingsway Publications, 1985.

*Luis Palau's books and booklets in this list are arranged chronologically.

____________. *My Response*. Chicago, IL: Moody Press, 1985.

____________. *Liberating Disciplines*. Miami, FL: Editorial Unilit, 1986.

____________. *Que Quieres Que Haga Por Ti?* Miami, FL: Editorial Unilit, 1986.

____________. *Love, Sex, and Marriage*. Miami, FL: Editorial Unilit, 1987.

____________. *Occultism and Witchcraft*. Miami, FL: Editorial Unilit, 1987.

____________. *Grande Entre Los Grandes*. Grand Rapids: Vida Publishers, 1987.

____________. *Commentary on the Gospel of John*. Miami, FL: Editorial Unilit, 1990.

____________. *La Prosperidad: Un Tema Para Tratar*. Miami, FL: Editorial Unilit, 1990.

____________. *I Have Everything … Almost Everything*. Miami, FL: Editorial Unilit, 1991.

____________. *Radical Renewal*. Downers Grove, IL: Inter-Varsity Press, 1991; Eastbourne, England: Crossway Books, 1991.

____________. *Say Yes! How to Renew Your Spiritual Passion*. Portland, OR: Multnomah Press, 1991; Grand Rapids: Discovery House Publishers, 1994.

____________. *Who Will Win This War?* Miami, FL: Editorial Unilit, 1992.

____________. *When Loneliness Hurts*. Nashville, TN: Grupo Nelson, 1993.

____________. *Healthy Habits for Spiritual Growth: 52 Principles for Personal Change*. Grand Rapids: Discovery House Publishers, 1994.

____________. *Your New Life with Christ*. Wheaton, IL: Crossway Books, 1996.

____________. *Building a Happy Home*. Nashville, TN: Grupo Nelson, 1998.

____________. *A Man After God's Heart: Running with David*. Grand Rapids: Discovery House Publishers, 1998.

Coauthored Books

Jenkins, Jerry B., and Luis Palau. *Luis Palau: Calling the Nations to Christ*. Old Tappan, NJ: Revell, 1978; Chicago, IL: Moody Press, 1980.

____________. *The Luis Palau Story*. Old Tappan, NJ: Revell, 1980; London: Pickering & Inglis, 1980.

Jones, David L., and Luis Palau. *Scottish Fires of Revival*. Cupertino, CA: D.I.M.E. Publishers, 1980.

Palau, Luis, Stephen Sorenson, and Amanda Sorenson. *Time to Stop Pretending*. Wheaton, IL: Victor Books, 1985; Wheaton, IL: SP Publications, 1985; rev. ed. *Stop Pretending*. Colorado Springs, CO: Victor Books, 2003.

Calcada, Leticia, and Luis Palau. *Cristo a Las Naciones: La Historia de Luis Palau y Su Equipo*. Miami, FL: Editorial Unilit, 1988.

Palau, Luis, and Pat Palau. *How to Lead Your Child to Christ*. Portland, OR: Multnomah Press, 1991.

Palau, Luis, and David Sanford. *Luis Palau: Calling America and the Nations to Christ.* Nashville, TN: Thomas Nelson, Inc., 1994; rev. 2000.

Palau, Luis, and Mike Umlandt. *The Only Hope for America: The Transforming Power of the Gospel of Jesus Christ.* Wheaton, IL: Crossway Books, 1996.

Bascuti, Ellen, and Luis Palau. *The Peter Promise: Powerful Principles from the Life of Peter*, rev. ed. of *Walk on Water, Pete!* Grand Rapids: Discovery House, 1996.

Palau, Luis, and David Sanford. *God Is Relevant: Finding Strength and Peace in Today's World.* New York: Doubleday, 1997; Renamed as *Is God Relevant?* London: Hodder & Stoughton, 1997.

Halliday, Steve, and Luis Palau. *Where Is God When Bad Things Happen? Finding Solace in Times of Trouble.* New York: Doubleday, 1999; Thorndike, ME: G.K. Hall, 1999; Cambridge: Lutterworth Press, 1999.

Palau, Luis, and Mike Yorkey. *It's a God Thing: Pictures and Portraits of True Miracles.* Rockland, MA: Wheeler Pub., 2001; New York: Doubleday, 2001.

Halliday, Steve, and Luis Palau. *High Definition Life: Trading Life's Good for God's Best.* Grand Rapids: Revell, 2005.

____________. *High Definition Life: Going Full Throttle for Life's Best*, student edition. Old Tappan, NJ: Revell, 2005; Grand Rapids: Fleming H. Revell, 2005.

Palau, Luis, and Timothy Robnett. *Telling the Story: Evangelism for the Next Generation.* Ventura, CA: Regal Books, 2006.

Palau, Luis, and Zhao Qizheng. *A Friendly Dialogue Between an Atheist and a Christian.* Grand Rapids: Zondervan, 2008.

Booklets

Palau, Luis. *Dream Great Dreams: Enlarge Your Vision of God.* Portland, OR: Multnomah Press, 1984.

____________. *Experiencing God's Forgiveness: Being Freed from Sin and Guilt.* Portland, OR: Multnomah, 1984.

____________. *Quieres Un Hogar Feliz?* Miami, FL: Editorial Unilit, 1989.

____________. *Going Forward with Jesus Christ.* Portland, OR: LPEA, 1989.

____________. *Por La Senda del Perdon.* Miami, FL: Editorial Unilit, 1991.

____________. *Papa, Mam Quiero Ir Al Cielo.* Miami, FL: Editorial Unilit, 1992.

____________. *Una Mirada Biblica a la Familia.* Miami, FL: Editorial Unilit, 1992.

____________. *Experiencing Personal Renewal.* Portland, OR: Multnomah Press, 1992.

____________. *Dios Esta A Mi Lado.* Nashville, TN: Grupo Nelson, 1993.

Articles and Essays

Palau, Luis. "Luis Palau." In *Billy Graham: A Tribute from Friends*, ed. Vernon McLellan, 137–139. New York: Faithwords, 2002.

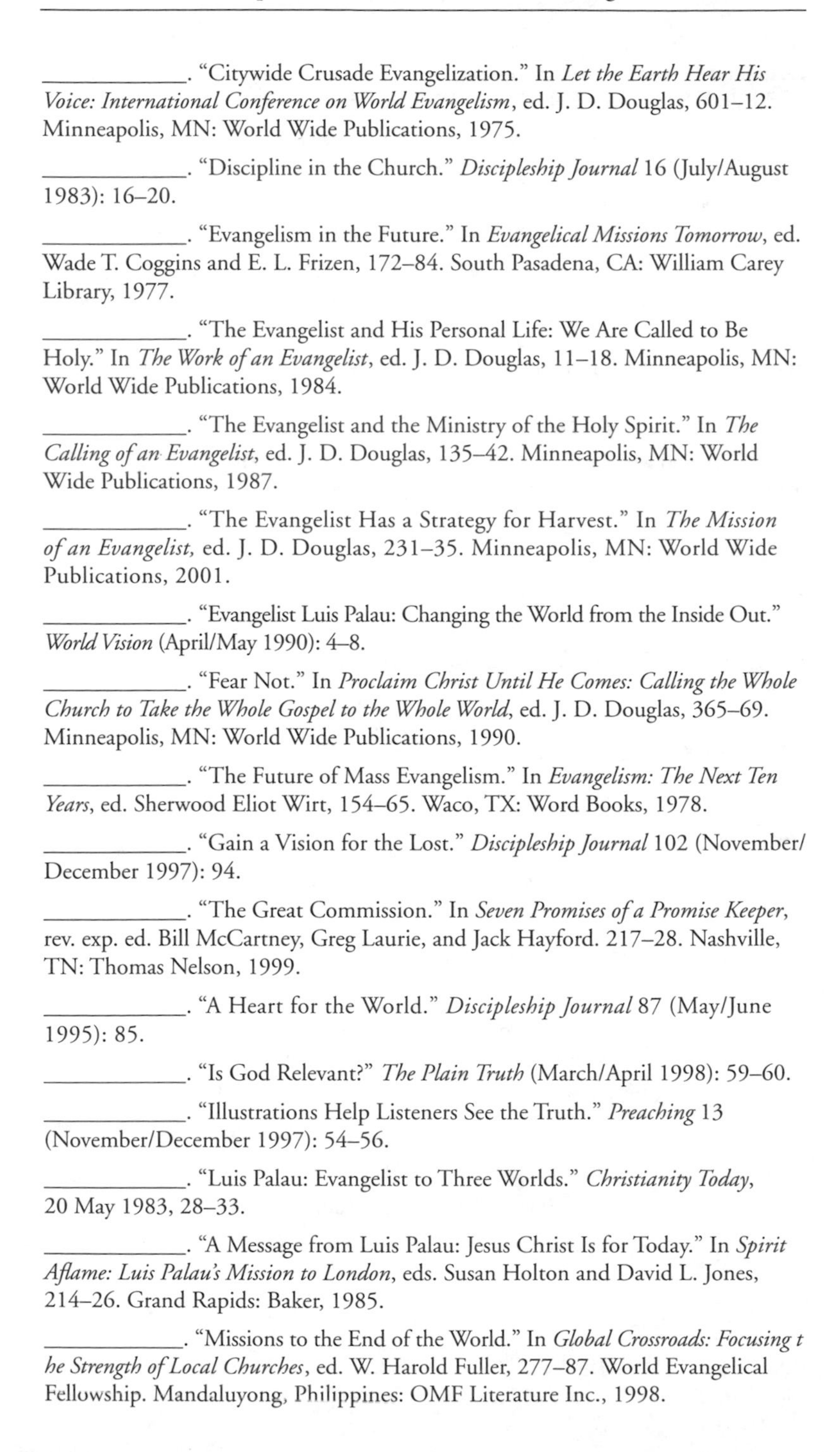

____________. "Citywide Crusade Evangelization." In *Let the Earth Hear His Voice: International Conference on World Evangelism*, ed. J. D. Douglas, 601–12. Minneapolis, MN: World Wide Publications, 1975.

____________. "Discipline in the Church." *Discipleship Journal* 16 (July/August 1983): 16–20.

____________. "Evangelism in the Future." In *Evangelical Missions Tomorrow*, ed. Wade T. Coggins and E. L. Frizen, 172–84. South Pasadena, CA: William Carey Library, 1977.

____________. "The Evangelist and His Personal Life: We Are Called to Be Holy." In *The Work of an Evangelist*, ed. J. D. Douglas, 11–18. Minneapolis, MN: World Wide Publications, 1984.

____________. "The Evangelist and the Ministry of the Holy Spirit." In *The Calling of an Evangelist*, ed. J. D. Douglas, 135–42. Minneapolis, MN: World Wide Publications, 1987.

____________. "The Evangelist Has a Strategy for Harvest." In *The Mission of an Evangelist,* ed. J. D. Douglas, 231–35. Minneapolis, MN: World Wide Publications, 2001.

____________. "Evangelist Luis Palau: Changing the World from the Inside Out." *World Vision* (April/May 1990): 4–8.

____________. "Fear Not." In *Proclaim Christ Until He Comes: Calling the Whole Church to Take the Whole Gospel to the Whole World*, ed. J. D. Douglas, 365–69. Minneapolis, MN: World Wide Publications, 1990.

____________. "The Future of Mass Evangelism." In *Evangelism: The Next Ten Years*, ed. Sherwood Eliot Wirt, 154–65. Waco, TX: Word Books, 1978.

____________. "Gain a Vision for the Lost." *Discipleship Journal* 102 (November/ December 1997): 94.

____________. "The Great Commission." In *Seven Promises of a Promise Keeper*, rev. exp. ed. Bill McCartney, Greg Laurie, and Jack Hayford. 217–28. Nashville, TN: Thomas Nelson, 1999.

____________. "A Heart for the World." *Discipleship Journal* 87 (May/June 1995): 85.

____________. "Is God Relevant?" *The Plain Truth* (March/April 1998): 59–60.

____________. "Illustrations Help Listeners See the Truth." *Preaching* 13 (November/December 1997): 54–56.

____________. "Luis Palau: Evangelist to Three Worlds." *Christianity Today*, 20 May 1983, 28–33.

____________. "A Message from Luis Palau: Jesus Christ Is for Today." In *Spirit Aflame: Luis Palau's Mission to London*, eds. Susan Holton and David L. Jones, 214–26. Grand Rapids: Baker, 1985.

____________. "Missions to the End of the World." In *Global Crossroads: Focusing t he Strength of Local Churches*, ed. W. Harold Fuller, 277–87. World Evangelical Fellowship. Mandaluyong, Philippines: OMF Literature Inc., 1998.

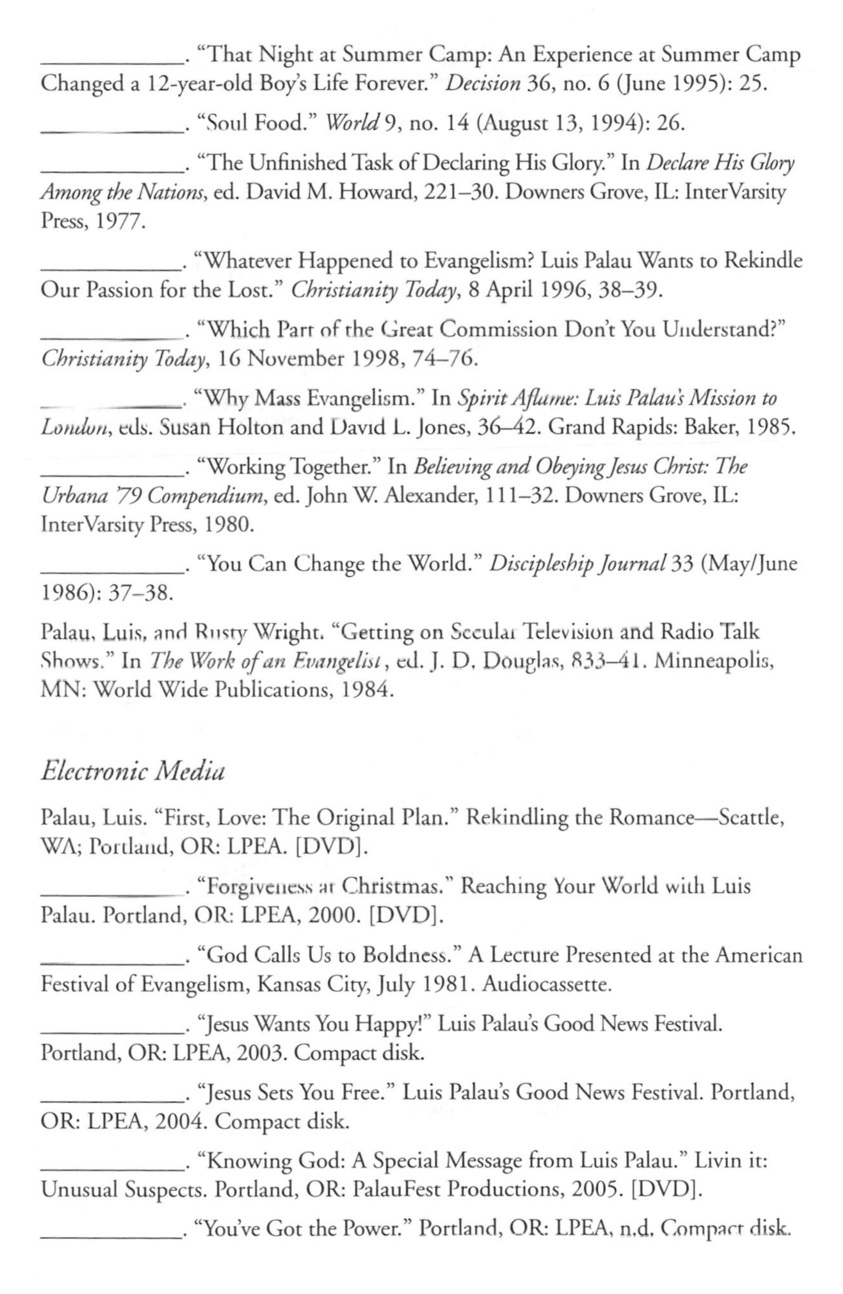

____________. "That Night at Summer Camp: An Experience at Summer Camp Changed a 12-year-old Boy's Life Forever." *Decision* 36, no. 6 (June 1995): 25.

____________. "Soul Food." *World* 9, no. 14 (August 13, 1994): 26.

____________. "The Unfinished Task of Declaring His Glory." In *Declare His Glory Among the Nations*, ed. David M. Howard, 221–30. Downers Grove, IL: InterVarsity Press, 1977.

____________. "Whatever Happened to Evangelism? Luis Palau Wants to Rekindle Our Passion for the Lost." *Christianity Today*, 8 April 1996, 38–39.

____________. "Which Part of the Great Commission Don't You Understand?" *Christianity Today*, 16 November 1998, 74–76.

____________. "Why Mass Evangelism." In *Spirit Aflame: Luis Palau's Mission to London*, eds. Susan Holton and David L. Jones, 36–42. Grand Rapids: Baker, 1985.

____________. "Working Together." In *Believing and Obeying Jesus Christ: The Urbana '79 Compendium*, ed. John W. Alexander, 111–32. Downers Grove, IL: InterVarsity Press, 1980.

____________. "You Can Change the World." *Discipleship Journal* 33 (May/June 1986): 37–38.

Palau, Luis, and Rusty Wright. "Getting on Secular Television and Radio Talk Shows." In *The Work of an Evangelist*, ed. J. D. Douglas, 833–41. Minneapolis, MN: World Wide Publications, 1984.

Electronic Media

Palau, Luis. "First, Love: The Original Plan." Rekindling the Romance—Seattle, WA; Portland, OR: LPEA. [DVD].

____________. "Forgiveness at Christmas." Reaching Your World with Luis Palau. Portland, OR: LPEA, 2000. [DVD].

____________. "God Calls Us to Boldness." A Lecture Presented at the American Festival of Evangelism, Kansas City, July 1981. Audiocassette.

____________. "Jesus Wants You Happy!" Luis Palau's Good News Festival. Portland, OR: LPEA, 2003. Compact disk.

____________. "Jesus Sets You Free." Luis Palau's Good News Festival. Portland, OR: LPEA, 2004. Compact disk.

____________. "Knowing God: A Special Message from Luis Palau." Livin it: Unusual Suspects. Portland, OR: PalauFest Productions, 2005. [DVD].

____________. "You've Got the Power." Portland, OR: LPEA, n.d. Compact disk.

Internet Websites

Palau, Luis. "Call to Evangelize America." LPA [online]. Accessed 14 October 2007. Available from http://www.palau.org/articles/index.php; Internet.

____________. "How Big Is Your Vision?" LPA [online]. Accessed 14 October 2007. Available from http://www.palau.org/articles/index.php; Internet.

____________. "My Cloud of Witnesses." LPA [online]. Accessed 14 October 2007. Available from http://www.palau.org/articles/index.php; Internet.

____________. "The Only Hope for America." LPA [online]. Accessed 14 March 2008. Available from http://www.palau.org/articles/index.php; Internet.

____________. "Persuading Others to Follow Christ." LPA [online]. Accessed 14 October 2007. Available from http://www.palau.org/articles/index.php; Internet.

____________. "What Did You Say?" LPA [online]. Accessed 14 October 2007. Available from http://www.palau.org/articles/index.php; Internet.

____________. "When You Don't Feel Like Sharing Your Faith." LPA [online]. Accessed 14 October 2007. Available from http://www.palau.org/articles/index.php; Internet.

Secondary Sources

Books

Aldrich, Joe. *Gentle Persuasion: Creative Ways to Introduce Your Friends to Christ.* Portland, OR: Multnomah Press, 1988.

____________. *Life-Style Evangelism: Crossing Traditional Boundaries to Reach the Unbelieving World.* Portland, OR: Multnomah Press, 1981.

Allen, Roland. *Missionary Methods: St. Paul's or Ours; A Study of the Church in the Four Provinces.* New York; Chicago, IL: Fleming H. Revell Company, 1913.

Allison, Lon, and Mark Anderson. *Going Public with the Gospel.* Downers Grove, IL: InterVarsity Press, 2004.

Archibald, Arthur C. *Establishing the Converts.* Philadelphia, PA: The Judson Press, 1952.

____________. *New Testament Evangelism.* Philadelphia, PA: The Judson Press, 1946.

Arias, Mortimer, and Alan Johnson. *The Great Commission: Biblical Models for Evangelism.* Nashville, TN: Abingdon Press, 1992.

Arn, Win, ed. *The Pastor's Church Growth Handbook.* Pasadena: Church Growth Press, 1979.

____________. *The Pastor's Manual for Effective Ministry.* Monrovia, CA: Church Growth, 1988.

Atkinson, Donald A., and Charles L. Roesel. *Meeting Needs Sharing Christ: Ministry Evangelism in Today's New Testament Church.* Nashville, LifeWay, 1995.

Barna, George. *Evangelism That Works: How to Reach Changing Generations with the Unchanging Gospel.* Ventura, CA: Regal Books, 1995.

Barna, George and Mark Hatch. *Boiling Point: It Only Takes One Degree*. Ventura, CA: Regal, 2001.

Barrett, David B. *Evangelize! A Historical Survey of the Concept*. Birmingham, AL: New Hope, 1987.

Barton, R. *Beggar to Beggar: A Basic Handbook for Beginning Evangelists*. 1993. (This is available from the author's website: rickbartonministries.org.)

Bascuti, Ellen. *Luis Palau: Evangelist to the World*. Uhrichsville, OH: Barbour Publishing, 2000.

Boyd, Malcolm. *Crisis in Communication: A Christian Examination of Mass Media*. Garden City, NY: Doubleday, 1957.

Brierley, Peter. *Future Church: A Global Analysis of the Christian Community to the Year 2010*. London: Monarch Books, 1998.

____________. *Mission to London: Phase 1, Who Responded?* London: MARC Europe, 1984.

____________. *Mission to London: Phase 2, Who Went Forward?* London: MARC Europe, 1984.

Bruce, F. F. *The Spreading Flame: The Rise and Progress of Christianity*. Vol. 1, *The Dawn of Christianity: The Story of the Infant Church to the Fall of Jerusalem, A.D. 70*. Grand Rapids: William B. Eerdmans, 1956.

Bryant, David. *How Christians Can Join Together in Concerts of Prayer for Spiritual Awakening and World Evangelization*, rev. ed. Foreword by Luis Palau. Ventura, CA: Regal Books, 1988.

Cairns, Earle E. *An Endless Line of Splendor: Revivals and Their Leaders from the Great Awakening to the Present*. Wheaton, IL: Tyndale House Publishers Inc., 1986.

Carson, Donald A., ed. *Telling the Truth: Evangelizing Postmoderns*. Grand Rapids: Zondervan, 2000.

Carson, Donald A., and John D. Woodbridge, eds. *Scripture and Truth*. Grand Rapids: Zondervan, 1983.

Coggins, Wade T., and E. L. Frizen. *Evangelical Missions Tomorrow*. Pasadena, CA: William Carey Library, 1977.

Coleman, Robert E. *The Master Plan of Evangelism*, 2nd ed. Grand Rapids: Spire, 1994.

Conn, Harvie M. *Planting and Growing Urban Churches*. Grand Rapids: Baker, 1997.

Cornish, Rick. *5 Minute Apologist*. Colorado Springs: NavPress, 2005.

Cupit, Tony, ed. *Five Till Midnight: Church Planting for A.D. 2000 and Beyond*. Atlanta, GA: Home Mission Board of the Southern Baptist Convention, 1994.

Davis, J. *The Pastor's Best Friend: The New Testament Evangelist*. Springfield, MI: Gospel Publishing House, 1997.

Dawson, Scott, ed. *The Complete Evangelism Guidebook: Expert Advice on Reaching Others for Christ*. Foreword by Luis Palau. Grand Rapids: Baker Books, 2006.

Dodd, C. H. *The Apostolic Preaching and Its Development.* London, England: Hodder and Stoughton, 1936.

Douglas, J. D., ed. *The Calling of an Evangelist.* Minneapolis, MN: World Wide Publications, 1987.

____________. *Equipping for Evangelism.* Minneapolis, MN: World Wide Publications, 1994.

____________. *Let the Earth Hear His Voice: International Conference on World Evangelism.* Minneapolis, MN: World Wide Publications, 1975.

____________. *The Mission of an Evangelist.* Minneapolis, MN: World Wide Publications, 2001.

____________. *Proclaim Christ Until He Comes: Calling the Whole Church to Take the Whole Gospel to the Whole World.* Minneapolis, MN: World Wide Publications, 1990.

____________. *The Work of an Evangelist.* Minneapolis, MN: World Wide Publications, 1984.

Dozier, Edwin B. *Christian Evangelism: Its Principles and Techniques.* Tokyo, Japan: The Jordan Press, 1963.

Drane, John. *Evangelism for a New Age.* London, England: Harper Collins Publishers, 1994.

____________. *The Evangelist.* Nashville, TN: Word Publishing, 2001.

____________. *The Impact of Billy Graham Crusades: Are They Effective?* Minneapolis, MN: World Wide Publications, 1982.

Drummond, Lewis A. *Leading Your Church in Evangelism.* Nashville, TN: Broadman Press, 1972.

____________. *The Life and Ministry of Charles G. Finney.* Minneapolis, MN: Bethany House, 1983.

____________. *Reaching Generation Next: Effective Evangelism in Today's Culture.* Grand Rapids: Baker Books, 2002.

____________. *The Word of the Cross: A Contemporary Theology of Evangelism.* Nashville, TN: Broadman, 1992.

Drummond, Lewis A., Thom S. Rainer, and T. V. Thomas, eds. *Biblical Affirmations for Evangelism.* Minneapolis, MN: World Wide Publications, 1996.

Ellis, E. Earle. *Prophecy & Hermeneutic in Early Christianity.* Grand Rapids: Baker Books, 1993.

Evans, William Glyn. *Profiles of Revival Leaders.* Nashville, TN: Broadman Press, 1976.

Feeney, J. H. *Church Planting by the Team Method.* International Bible Society. Anchorage, AK: Abbott Loop Christian Center, 1988.

Ferm, Robert O., and Caroline M. Whiting. *Billy Graham: Do the Conversions Last?* Minneapolis, MN: World Wide Publications, 1988.

Ferm, Robert Oscar. *Cooperative Evangelism.* Grand Rapids: Zondervan Publishing House, 1958.

____________. *The Psychology of Christian Conversion.* Westwood, NJ: Revell, 1959.

Finney, Charles Grandison. *Lectures on Revivals of Religion.* New York/Chicago/Toronto/London/Edinburgh: Fleming H. Revell Company, 1868.

Fish, Roy. J. *Giving a Good Invitation.* Nashville, TN: Broadman, 1974.

Ford, Leighton. *The Christian Persuader.* New York: Harper and Row Publishers, 1966.

Fordham, Keith. *The Evangelist: The Heart of God.* Fayetteville, GA: KFEA Publications, 2002.

Fuller, W. Harold, *People of the Mandate: the Story of the World Evangelical Fellowship.* Foreword by Luis Palau. Grand Rapids: Baker Book House, 1996.

Garrison, David. *Church Planting Movements: How God Is Redeeming a Lost World.* Midlothian, VA: WIG Take Resources, 2004.

Geisler, Norman L. *Christian Apologetics.* Grand Rapids: Baker, 1976.

Gibbs, Eddie. *Church Next: Quantum Changes in How We Do Ministry.* Downers Grove, IL: InterVarsity Press, 2000.

Gibbs, Nancy, and Michael Duffy. *The Preacher and the Presidents: Billy Graham in the White House.* New York: Center Street, 2007.

Goodall, Norman. *The Ecumenical Movement: What It Is and What It Does.* London: Oxford University Press, 1961.

Graham, Billy. *A Biblical Standard for Evangelists.* Minneapolis, MN: World Wide Publications, 1984.

____________. *Choose Ye This Day.* Minneapolis, MN: World Wide Publications, 1989.

____________. *Just As I Am: The Autobiography of Billy Graham.* Grand Rapids: Zondervan, 1997.

____________. *Revival in Our Time: The Story of the Billy Graham Evangelistic Crusades.* Wheaton, IL: Van Kampen Press, 1950.

Green, Bryan. *The Practice of Evangelism.* London: Hodder and Stoughton, 1951.

Green, Hollis. *Why Churches Die.* Minneapolis, MN: Bethany Fellowship, 1972.

Green, Michael. *Evangelism in the Early Church.* Grand Rapids: Wm. B. Eerdmans Publishing Company, 1970.

Hadaway, Kirk. *Church Growth Principles: Separating Fact from Fiction.* Nashville, TN: Broadman Press, 1991.

Hadden, Jeffrey K. and Charles E. Swann. *Prime Time Preachers.* Reading, MA: Addison-Wesley Publishing Co., 1981.

Hanegraaf, Hank. *Counterfeit Revival.* Dallas, TX: Word, 1997.

Hangen, Tona J. *Redeeming the Dial: Radio, Religion, & Popular Culture in America.* Chapel Hill, NC: The University of North Carolina Press, 2002.

Hardman, Keith. *Seasons of Refreshing: Evangelism and Revivals in America.* Foreword by Luis Palau. Grand Rapids: Baker Books, 1994.

____________. *The Spiritual Awakeners*. Chicago, IL: Moody Press, 1983.

Hartt, Julian N. *Toward a Theology of Evangelism*. New York: Abingdon, 1955.

Henry, Carl F. H., and W. Stanley Mooneyham, eds. *One Race, One Gospel, One Task*. 2 vols. Minneapolis, MN: World Wide Publications, 1967. A Compendium of the World Congress on Evangelism, Berlin 1966.

Hinson, E. Glenn. *The Evangelization of the Roman Empire*. Macon, GA: Mercer University, 1981.

Holton, Susan, and David L. Jones. *Spirit Aflame: Luis Palau's Mission to London*. Grand Rapids: Baker Book House, 1985.

Hudson, Winthrop S. *Religion in America: An Historical Account of the Development of American Religious Life*, 2nd ed. New York: Charles Scribner's Sons, 1973.

Hunter, George G. III. *How to Reach Secular People*. Nashville, TN: Abingdon, 1992.

Huston, Sterling W. *Crusade Evangelism and the Local Church*, rev. ed. Minneaspolis, MN: World Wide Publications, 1996.

Kilgore, James E. *Billy Graham the Preacher*. New York: Exposition Press, 1968.

Legrand, Lucien. *Unity and Plurality: Mission in the Bible*. Translated by Robert R. Barr. Maryknoll, NY: Orbis Books, 1990.

Lewis, Larry L., *The Church Planter's Handbook*. Nashville, TN: Broadman Press, 1993.

Lindsell, Harold. *Battle for the Bible*. Grand Rapids: Zondervan, 1976.

Little, Paul E. *How to Give Away Your Faith*. Downers Grove, IL: InterVarsity, 1966.

Lloyd-Jones, Martyn. *Preaching and Preachers*. Grand Rapids: Zondervan, 1972.

____________. *Revival*. Wheaton, IL: Crossway Books, 1987.

Lochte, Bob. *Christian Radio: The Growth of a Mainstream Broadcasting Force*. Jefferson, NC: McFarland & Company, Inc., 2006.

Longenecker, Richard N., ed. *Patterns of Discipleship in the New Testament*. Grand Rapids: William. B. Eerdmans, 1996.

Loscalzo, Craig A. *Evangelistic Preaching That Connects*. Downers Grove, IL: InterVarsity, 1995.

Malphurs, Aubrey. *Planting Growing Churches for the 21st Century*, 2nd ed. Grand Rapids: Baker Books, 1998.

Martin, William. *A Prophet with Honor: The Billy Graham Story*. New York: William Morrow and Company, Inc., 1991.

McDow, Malcolm, and Alvin L. Reid. *FireFall: How God Has Shaped History Through Revivals*. Nashville, TN: Broadman & Holman Publishers, 1997.

McGavran, Donald, ed. *Church Growth and Christian Mission*. New York: Harper and Row Publishers, 1965.

____________. *Effective Evangelism: A Theological Mandate*. Phillipsburg, NJ: Presbyterian and Reformed Publishing, 1988.

_____________. *Understanding Church Growth*, rev. ed. Grand Rapids: Eerdmans, 1970.

McLoughlin, William G. *Modern Revivalism: Charles Grandison Finney to Billy Graham*. New York: Ronald Press, 1959.

_____________. *Revivals, Awakening, and Reform*. Chicago, IL: The University of Chicago Press, 1978.

McPhee, Arthur. *Friendship Evangelism: The Caring Way to Share Your Faith*. Grand Rapids: Zondervan, 1979.

Melton, J. Gordon, Phillip Charles Lucas, and Jon R. Stone. *Prime-Time Religion: An Encyclopedia of Religious Broadcasting*. Phoenix, AZ: Oryx Press, 1997.

Miles, Delos. *Introduction to Evangelism*. Nashville, TN: Braodman Press, 1983.

Mitchell, Curtis. *Billy Graham: Saint or Sinner*. Old Tappan, NJ: Fleming H. Revell Company, 1979.

Moberg, David O. *The Great Reversal*. Philadelphia, PA: J. B. Lippencott, 1977.

Morris, James. *The Preachers* [Billy Graham, A. A. Allen, Oral Roberts, C. W. Burpo, and others]. New York: St. Martin's Press, 1973.

Mott, John R. *Cooperation and the World Mission*. New York: International Missionary Council, 1935.

Nichols, Alan, ed., and Richard Crabbe, asst. ed. *The Whole Gospel to the Whole World*. Charlotte, NC: Lausanne Committee for World Evangelization and Regal Books, 1989.

Orr, J. Edwin. *The Flaming Tongue: The Impact of Twentieth Century Revivals*. Chicago, IL: Moody Press, 1973.

_____________. *The Re-Study of Revival and Revivalism*. Pasadena, CA: School of World Mission, 1981.

Packard, William. *Evangelism in America: From Tents to TV*. New York: Paragon House, 1988.

Packer, J. I. *Beyond the Battle for the Bible*. Westchester, IL: Cornerstone Books, 1980.

_____________. *Evangelism and the Sovereignty of God*. London: InterVarsity Fellowship, 1961.

Padilla, C. René, ed. *The New Face of Evangelicalism: An International Symposium on the Lausanne Covenant*. London: Hodder and Stoughton, 1976.

Perry, Lloyd M., and John R. Strubhar. *Evangelistic Preaching*. Chicago, IL: Moody Press, 1979.

Peters, George W. *Saturation Evangelism*. Grand Rapids: Zondervan Publishing House, 1970.

Pickering, Ernest D. *The Theology of Evangelism*. Clarks Summit, PA: Baptist Bible College Press, 1974.

Pippert, Rebecca Manley. *Out of the Saltshaker & Into the World*. Downers Grove, IL: InterVarsity, 1979.

Pointer, Roy. *Crusade Evangelism: The Fruit That Remained; A Discussion Arising from Mission to London*. Bromley, Kent (England): MARC Europe, 1988.

Pollock, John. *Billy Graham: Evangelist to the World.* San Francisco: Harper and Row, Publishers, 1979.

____________. *Crusades, 20 Years with Billy Graham*. Minneapolis, MN: World Wide Publications, 1966.

____________. *Moody: A Biography Portrait of the Pacesetter in Modern Mass Evangelism.* New York: The Macmillan Company, 1963.

Rainer, Thom S. *The Book of Church Growth: History, Theology, and Principles.* Nashville, TN: Broadman and Holman, 1993.

____________. ed. *Evangelism in the Twenty-First Century: the Critical Issues.* Wheaton, IL: Harold Shaw Publishers, 1989.

Richardson, Rick. *Evangelism Outside the Box: New Ways to Help People Experience the Good News.* Downers Grove, IL: InterVarsity, 2000.

Reid, Alvin. *Introduction to Evangelism*. Nashville, TN: Broadman & Holman Publishers, 1998.

Roberts, W. Dayton. *Revolution in Evangelism: The Story to Evangelism-in-Depth in Latin America.* Chicago, IL: Moody, 1967.

Sanchez, Daniel R., ed. *Church Planting Movements in North America*. Fort Worth, TX: Church Starting Network, 2007.

Schultze, Quentin J., ed. *American Evangelicals and the Mass Media*. Grand Rapids: Academie Books, 1990.

____________. *Televangelism and American Culture*. Grand Rapids, MI: Baker, 1991.

Schwarz, Christian A., *Natural Church Development: A Guide to Eight Essential Qualities of Healthy Churches.* Carol Stream, IL: ChurchSmart Resources, 1998.

Sjogren, Steve. *Conspiracy of Kindness: A Refreshing New Approach to Sharing the Love of Jesus with Others.* Ann Arbor: Servant Publications, 1993.

Smith, Timothy L. *Revivalism and Social Reform: American Protestantism on the Eve of the Civil War.* Gloucester, MA: Peter Smith, 1976.

Soards, Marion L. *The Apostle Paul: An Introduction to His Writings and Teaching.* New York: Paulist Press, 1987.

Stebbins, Tom H. *Friendship Evangelism by the Book*. Camp Hill, PA: Christian Publications, 1995.

Stiller, Brian. *A Generation Under Siege.* Foreword by Luis Palau. Wheaton, IL: Victor Books, 1983.

Stoll, David. *Is Latin America Turning Protestant? The Politics of Evangelical Growth*. Berkeley and Los Angeles, CA: University of California Press, 1990.

Stott, John R. W. *Between Two Worlds.* Grand Rapids: Eerdmans, 1982.

____________. *Christian Mission in the Modern World.* Downers Grove, IL: InterVarsity, 1975.

____________. *The Lausanne Covenant: An Exposition and Commentary.* Minneapolis, MN: World Wide Publications, 1975.

Streett, R. Alan. *The Effective Invitation.* Old Tappan, NJ: Fleming H. Revell Company, 1984.

Sweazey, George E. *Effective Evangelism: The Greatest Work in the World.* New York: Harper & Row Publishers, Inc., 1953.

Sweet, William Warren. *Revivalism in America.* Nashville, TN: Abingdon Press, 1944.

Terry, John Mark. *Church Evangelism: Creating a Culture for Growth in Your Congregation.* Nashville, TN: Broadman & Holman Publishers, 1997.

____________. *Evangelism: A Concise History.* Nashville, TN: Broadman & Holman Publishers, 1994.

Towns, Elmer, and Douglas Porter. *The Ten Greatest Revivals Ever: From Pentecost to the Present.* Ann Arbor, MI: Servant Publications, 2000.

Wagner, C. Peter. *Church Growth and the Whole Gospel: A Biblical Mandate.* New York: Harper & Row Publishers, Inc., 1981.

____________. *Church Planting for a Greater Harvest.* Ventura, CA: Regal Books, 1990.

Warren, Rick. *The Purpose Driven Church.* Grand Rapids: Zondervan Publishing House, 1995.

Watson, David. *I Believe in Evangelism.* Grand Rapids: William B. Eerdmans Publishing Co., 1976.

Webber, Robert E. *Ancient-Future Faith.* Grand Rapids: Baker, 1999.

Wells, David F. *God the Evangelist: How the Holy Spirit Works to Bring Men to Christ.* Grand Rapids: Eerdmans, 1987.

____________. *Turning to God: Biblical Conversion in the Modern World.* Exeter, United Kingdom: The Paternoster Press, 1989.

Whalin, W. Terry. *Luis Palau.* Minneapolis, MN: Bethany House Publishers. 1996.

Wirt, Sherwood Eliot, ed. *Evangelism: The Next Ten Years.* Waco, TX: Word Books, 1978.

Wood, A. Skevington. *Evangelism: Its Theology and Practice.* Grand Rapids: Zondervan Publishing House, 1965.

Articles and Essays

"Andrew Palau Festivals." *Proclaim!* 2008, 22–23.

Arn, Charles. "A Response to Dr. Rainer: What Is the Key to Effective Evangelism?" *Journal of the American Society for Church Growth* 6 (1995): 75.

Arn, Win. "Mass Evangelism: The Bottom Line." In *Pastor's Church Growth Handbook.* Pasadena, CA: Church Growth Press, 1979.

Autrey, C. E. "A Theology of Evangelism." In *Evangelism Today and Tomorrow*, ed. Charles L. Chaney and Granville Watson, 47–54. Nashville, TN: Broadman Press, 1993.

Barrett, Sandra. "Arise Uganda!" *Proclaim!* Vol. 1. 2004, 20.

Beougher, Timothy. "The Great Commission and Personal Evangelism." In *The Challenge of the Great Commission.* Naples, FL: Pinnacle Publishers, 2005.

Bessenecker, Scott. "Paul's Short-term Church Planting: Can It Happen Again?" *Evangelical Missions Quarterly* 33 (1977): 326–32.

Blunt, Sheryl Henderson. "Palau Pulls Back." *Christianity Today*, 6 February 2006, 22.

Boyd, Forrest. "Luis Palau in Aberdeen: Melting Scottish." *Christianity Today*, 20 July 1979, 42–43.

Boyd, Malcolm. "Crossroads in Mass Evangelism?" *The Christian Century*, 20 March 1957, 359–61.

Capon, John. "Billy Graham and Luis Palau: Fanning Revival Fires in England—Events and Strategies Behind a Remarkable Summer of Evangelism." *Christianity Today*, 13 July 1984, 27–31, 52–53.

Carson, Donald A. "Evangelicals, Ecumenism and the Church." In *Evangelical Affirmation*, ed. Kenneth S. Kantzer and Carl F. H. Henry. Grand Rapids: Zondervan, 1990.

Cassidy, Michael. "Limitations of Mass Evangelism and Its Potentialities." *International Review of Mission* 65 (April 1976): 202–15.

Chastain, Craig. "Livin It: Taking the Good News to the Core Sports Culture and Beyond." *Wireless Age*, January/February/March 2004, 24–26.

Clapp, Rodney. "Luis Palau Invades the University of Wisconsin: Is the Time Ripe for More Campus Evangelism?" *Christianity Today*, 19 March 1982, 38–40.

Claassen, Kimberly. "Luis Palau Beachfest: Taking the Good News to the People." *Wireless Age*, January/February 2003, 28–30.

____________. "Reviving the Nations." *The Plain Truth* (March/April 1998): 10–13.

Clelland, Donald, Thomas C. Hood, C. M. Lipsey, and Ronald Wimberly. "In the Company of the Converted: Characteristics of a Billy Graham Crusade Audience." *Sociological Analysis Journal* 35 (Spring 1974): 45–56.

Coleman, Calmetta Y. "Luis Palau: The Next Billy Graham of Everywhere?" *Wall Street Journal* 77, no. 16 1995, sec. B, p.1, 9.

Conard, William W. "Principles Behind the Rosario Plan." *Latin America Pulse* XIII, no. 3 (October 1978): 2–8.

Conard, William and David L. Jones. "Uniting for Evangelization in Booming Caracas." *Christianity Today*, 4 January 1980, 56–57, 59–60.

Craston, Richard Colin. "Crusade Evangelism." *Churchman* 85 (Winter 1971): 263–73.

Daniels, E. J. "Organizing for the Evangelistic Crusade." In *Evangelism Today and Tomorrow*, ed. Charles L. Chaney and Granville Watson, 154–71. Nashville, TN: Broadman Press, 1993.

DeMoss, Nancy. "Reaching Business and Political Leaders." In *The Work of an Evangelist*, ed. J. D. Douglas, 647–59. Minneapolis, MN: World Wide, Publications, 1984.

Douglas, James D. "God's Good Gaucho and Roundup Time in Glasgow." *Christianity Today*, 17 July 1981, 90.

____________. "Luis Palau Returns for Glasgow Crusade." *Christianity Today*, 29 May 1981, 34–35.

"Evangelism in the New Millennium." *Proclaim!* September 1999, 4.

"Evangelism: The Best Form of Social Action." *Christianity Today*, 17 February 1989, 51–52.

Fear, John. "Strategy Report Mass Media." In *Let the Earth Hear His Voice: International Conference on World Evangelism*, ed. J. D. Douglas, 598–600. Minneapolis, MN: World Wide Publications, 1975.

"The 50 Most Influential Christians in America." *The Church Report* (January 2005): 14–16.

Firebaugh, Glenn. "How Effective Are City-wide Crusades?" *Christianity Today*, 27 March 1981, 24–29.

Ford, Leighton. "The Strategic Role of Mass Evangelism." *Christianity Today*, 24 November 1961, 31–32.

Frame, Randy. "Palau Holds Mass Crusades Throughout Paraguay: Encouraging Results are Reported in This Emerging South American Nation." *Christianity Today*, 12 November 1982, 72, 76.

Gerber, Vergil. "Let's Anticipate the Harvest." *Church Growth Bulletin* 12 (April 1976): 516–19.

Gilling, Bryan. "Mass Evangelistic Theology and Methodology and the 1987 Luis Palau Mission to Auckland." *Transformation* 8, no. 1 (January-March 1991): 9–14.

Graham, Billy. "Church Growth and Multiplied Evangelism." *Church Growth Bulletin* 3 (1967): 1.

____________. "The Gifts and Calling of the Evangelist." In *Evangelism Today and Tomorrow*, ed. Charles L. Chaney and Granville Watson, 36–40. Nashville, TN: Broadman Press, 1993.

Green, Kelly. "Mass Evangelism for the 90s: A New Look at an Old Approach." In *Evangelism for a Changing World*, eds. Timothy Beougher & Alvin Reid, 141–51. Wheaton, IL: Harold Shaw Publishers, 1995.

Hamblin, Robert A. "The Message of Evangelism." In *Evangelism Today and Tomorrow*, ed. Charles L. Chaney and Granville Watson, 88–96. Nashville, TN: Broadman Press, 1993.

Hardaway, Gary. "Bolivia: Prayer in a Time of Trouble." *Christianity Today*, 15 March 1974, 56–57.

Hardy, David. "A Season of Service." *Multnomah*, Spring 2008, 4–7.

Hayford, Jack. "Let's Learn from Billy Graham. What Is This Man's Secret? Billy Graham's Ministry Values Are Worth Studying." *Ministries Today* 13, no. 2 (March/April 1995): 24–25.

"The Heart of a Singer/Songwriter: Matt Redman." *Proclaim!* 2008, 10.

Hefley, James C. "In Bogotá, a Banquet of Hope and Caribbean Crusade." *Christianity Today*, 18 November 1977, 44–47.

Hertz, Todd. "Beach Blanket Rebirth: Luis Palau to Take Fort Lauderdale Spring Break Festival Nationwide." *Christianity Today*, 2 February 2003, 25.

Hesselgrave, David J. "Essential Elements of Church Planting and Growing in the 21st Century." *Evangelical Missions Quarterly* 36, no. 1 (January 2000): 24–32.

Holloway, Stewart. "Hit the Trail! The Life and Ministry of Billy Sunday." Seminar paper, EVANG 7642—The History of Spiritual Awakening, Spring 2003. Photocopy.

Horton, Michael S. "Evangelicals and Catholics Together: The Christian Mission and the Third Millenium—A Critical Review." *Modern Reformation*, January 1994, 22–33.

Hunter, George G. III. "Informing Apostolic Ministry: Research and Writing for Effective Evangelism." *Journal of the Academy for Evangelism in Theological Education* 15 (1999-2000): 18–29.

Huston, Sterling W. "Methods of Attracting a Larger Audience: Countries and Areas with Sophisticated Media." In *The Work of an Evangelist*, ed. J. D. Douglas, 503–13. Minneapolis, MN: World Wide Publications, 1984.

"Is TV Appropriate for Mass Evangelism?" *Christianity Today*, 16 October 1987, 50.

James, Rob. "Extreme Orthodoxy." *Christianity Today*, 1 January 2005, 22.

Johnson, Heddon T. "The Religious Crusade: Revival or Ritual?" *American Journal of Sociology* 77 (March 1971): 4–6.

Johnson, James E. "Charles Grandison Finney: Father of American Revivalism." *Christian History* 20: 6–9.

Jones, David L. "A Response from the Luis Palau Evangelistic Association." *Transformation* 8 (January–March 1991): 14.

"Just As We Were: Is Mass Evangelism Dead?" *Christianity Today*, 5 July 2007, 54.

Kantzer, Kenneth S., ed. "Candid Conversation with the Evangelist." *Christianity Today*, 17 July 1981, 18–24.

Kennedy, John W., and Bradley Baurain. "Palau Preaches to a Preoccupied Metropolis." *Christianity Today*, 16 July 1996, 68–69.

Knight, Walker. "Dialogue Favors Cooperation in Evangelism, Not Structures." *Home Missions*, October 1968, 15–16.

____________. "Televangelism, Pro and Con." *Home Missions*, June 1973, 8–9.

Kuyvenhoven, Andrew. "Evangelism and Evangelists." *Ecumenism* 85 (March 1987): 20–21.

"Luis Palau: Evangelist to Three Worlds." *Christianity Today*, 20 May 1983, 28–33.

"Luis Palau Legacy Campaign." *Proclaim!* 2008, 29.

Mathews, Ed. "Mass Evangelism: Problems and Potentials." *Journal of Applied Missiology* 4 (1993): 441.

Maust, John. "Palau Spanish-Language Crusade Pulls L.A. Hispanics Together for First Time." *Christianity Today*, 8 August 1980, 38–40.

____________. "Terrorist Death Threat Fails to Force Palau Out of Peru." *Christianity Today*, 18 January 1985, 51.

McGavran, Donald A. "New Methods for a New Age in Missions." *International Review of Missions* 44 (1955): 394–403.

McWilliam, John. "Mass Evangelism: Reaching Your City in the Eighties." *Urban Mission* 3 (September 1985): 7–14.

Mills, Jim. "An Interview with Luis Palau." *Discipleship Journal* 12 (November/December 1982): 39–42.

Miranda, Juan Carlos. "Rosario Came Just in Time." *Church Growth Bulletin* 14 (September 1977): 150–51.

Moreau, Scott A., and Mike O'Rear. "Doing Evangelism on the Internet." *Evangelical Missions Quarterly* 36 (2000): 218–22.

Muck, Terry C. "An Open-air Crusade in the Soviet Union? Believe It!" *Christianity Today*, 20 October 1989, 36–37.

____________. "Under the Eye of the Big, Red Machine." *Christianity Today*, 15 December 1989, 20–25.

Murphy, Edward F. "Continente '75: Evangelism in Ripened Fields." *Church Growth Bulletin* 12 (January 1976): 507–9.

____________. "Mass Evangelism Is Not Obsolete." *Christianity Today*, 28 February 1975, 6–9.

Neff, David. "Billy Graham in Germany: 'Personal Evangelism on a Mass Scale.'" *Christianity Today*, 8 March 1993, 64, 66.

Northcott, Cecil. "The Graham Crusade: Abdication of Evangelism." *The Christian Century* 83 (1966): 673–74.

Ogawa, Matthew S., and Vern Rossman. "Evangelism Through Mass Media and Audio Visual Materials." *International Review of Missions* 50 (1961): 417–29.

Palau, Kevin. "Cooperative Evangelism." In *The Mission of an Evangelist*, ed. J. D. Douglas, 319–20. Minneapolis, MN: World Wide Publications, 2001.

Park, Leland M. "Radio, TV and the Evangelist: The Mass Media at Work." *The Christian Century*, 15 August 1973, 804–7.

Perez, Pablo E. "Latin America: Hope and Reality." In *Serving Our Generation: Evangelical Strategies for the Eighties*, ed. Waldron Scott, 57–76. Colorado Springs, CO: World Evangelical Fellowship, 1980. (Papers presented in preparation for the 7th General Assembly of the World Evangelical Fellowship, London, March 24–28, 1980.)

Peters, George. "Great-Campaign Evangelism." In *Crucial Issues in Missions Tomorrow*, ed. Donald A. McGavran, 202–26. Chicago, IL: Moody Press, 1972.

Pierard, Richard V. "From Evangelical Exclusivism to Ecumenical Openness: Billy Graham and Sociopolitical Issues," *Journal of Ecumenical Studies* 20, no. 3 (Summer 1983): 425–46.

Piotrowski, William K. "Evangelism in a Chilly Climate." *Religion in the News* 4, no. 2 (Summer 2001): 26, 29.

Plowman, Edward E. "Church Growth: A Plan That Worked." *Christianity Today*, 17 December 1976, 33–34.

____________. "Continente '75: From Managua to the Masses." *Christianity Today*, 19 December 1975, 31–33.

Riggs, Charles. "Follow-up in Crusade and Church Evangelism." In *Let the Earth Hear His Voice: International Conference on World Evangelism,* ed. J. D. Douglas, 614–19. Minneapolis, MN: World Wide Publications, 1975.

Rubenstein, Sura. "Preacher to the World: Oregon's Luis Palau." *Northwest*, 15 September 1985, 6–12.

Sanderson, Leonard. "The Role of the Vocational Evangelist." In *Evangelism Today and Tomorrow*, ed. Charles L. Chaney and Granville Watson, 146–53. Nashville, TN: Broadman Press, 1993.

Sanford, David. "Luis Palau: Calling America and the Nations to Christ." *Life Wise* (December/January 2002): 8–11.

Scherer, James A. "Prospects and Problems in Global Evangelization." *Word and World* 1 (1981): 9–19.

Schmidt, Henry J. "Crusade Decisions: Counting and Accounting for Lost Sheep," *Church Growth Journal of the North American Society for Church Growth*, 1 (1990): 14–40.

Scott, Waldron. "Discipleship Evangelism." In *Evangelism: The Next Ten Years*, ed. Sherwood Eliot Wirt, 103–14. Waco, TX: Word Books, 1978.

Shackleford, Al. "The Crusade on TV: A National Response." *Home Missions*, June 1969, 28.

Silvoso, Edgardo. "In Rosario It Was Different—Crusade Converts Are in the Churches," *Evangelical Missions Quarterly* 14, no. 2 (April 1978): 83–87.

____________. "The Naranjo People Movement in Argentina." *Church Growth Bulletin* 11 (November 1974): 452–59.

Sosa, Pablo. "The Witness of the Church Through Mass Media." *International Review of Missions* 69 (1980): 205–10.

Stoll, David. "A Protestant Reformation in Latin America?" *The Christian Century* 107, no. 2 (17 January 1990): 46.

Swatos, William H., Jr. "Getting the Word Around: A Research Note on Communicating an Evangelistic Crusade." *Review of Religious Research* 33, no. 2 (December 1991): 176–85.

Tapia, Andres T. "Evangelist Sets Sights on U.S. Latinos." *Christianity Today*, 15 July 1996, 68.

"Television and Radio Made the Greatest Impact During Evangelist Luis Palau's Recent Two-week Crusade in Guayaquil, Ecuador." *Christianity Today*, 24 October 1980, 74.

"To Reach a Nation, Reach the Leaders!" *Proclaim!* 2006, 7.

Todd, Hertz. "Evangelistic Circus in a Box." *Christianity Today*, 7 October 2002, 18.

Umlandt, Mike. "A Father's Passion." *New Man: Proclaiming Life to Men* (June 1997). Reprinted from LPA.

Wagner, C. Peter. "Concepts of Evangelism Have Changed over the Years." *Evangelical Missions Quarterly* 10 (January 1974): 41–47.

____________. "Evangelism and Social Action in Latin America." *Christianity Today*, 7 January 1966, 10–12.

____________. "Plan Rosario: Milepost for Saturation Evangelism." *Church Growth Bulletin* 14 (September 1977): 145–49.

Williams, James. "Specialized Counseling During Evangelistic Campaigns." In *Work of an Evangelist*, ed. J. D. Douglas, 495–98. Minneapolis, MN: World Wide Publications, 1984.

Woehr, Chris. "Palau Crusade Tests New Religious Freedoms." *Christianity Today*, 27 April 1992, 50–51.

Wright, Rusty. "'Credibility' Gap Worries Evangelists." *Christianity Today*, 15 August 1994, 53.

____________. "Downtown Evangelism Makes a Comeback." *Christianity Today*, 8 January 2001, 24.

____________. "Palau Brings Reconciliation Message to Ethnic Mix." *Christianity Today*, 24 April 1995, 40.

Dissertations and Theses

Asa, Robert Lynn. "The Theology and Methodology of Charles G. Finney as a Prototype for Modern Mass Evangelism." Ph.D. diss., Southern Baptist Theological Seminary, 1983.

Bauer, Scott. "Crusade Evangelism." D.Min. project, Oral Roberts University, 1995.

Fleming, Travis Dean. "An Analysis of Bill Bright's Theology and Methodology of Evangelism and Discipleship." Ph.D. diss., Southern Baptist Theological Seminary, 2003.

Giovannetti, William A. "A Strategy for Linking Crusade Evangelism with Church Planting." D.Min. project, Fuller Theological Seminary, 1996.

Johnston, Thomas Paul. "The Work of an Evangelist: The Evangelistic Theology and Methodology of Billy Graham." Ph.D. diss., Southern Baptist Theological Seminary, 2001.

Kang, Sung Ho. "Major Vocational Evangelists from Charles Finney to Billy Sunday and Their Development of Methods for Urban Mass Evangelism." Th.M. thesis, Southwestern Baptist Theological Seminary, 1997.

McBride, Kevin T. "Retaking the Village Green: Building Strategic Partnerships for Evangelism That Work in New England." D.Min. thesis, Gordon-Conwell Theological Seminary, 2001.

McGinnis, Michael Lee. "A Church Growth Analysis of Mass-cooperative Evangelism." Th.D. diss., Mid-America Baptist Theological Seminary, 1985.

Morrow, William Brad. "Mass Evangelism and Its Effect on Church Planting: A Filipino Case Study." Ph.D. diss., Southern Baptist Theological Seminary, 2003.

Thompson, William Oscar, Jr. "The Public Invitation as a Method of Evangelism: Its Origin and Development." Ph.D. diss., Southwestern Baptist Theological Seminary, 1979.

Electronic Media

"Livin It." Portland, OR: PalauFest Productions, 2004. [DVD].

"Livin It LA." Portland, OR: Livin It Productions, 2006. [DVD].

"Livin It: Unusual Suspects." Portland, OR: PalauFest Productions, 2005. [DVD].

"Luis Palau Festival: Live from Fort Lauderdale, FL." Portland, OR: PalauFest Productions, 2003. [DVD].

"Luis Palau Festivals: Friends of the Festival Counselor Training." Portland, OR: LPA, n.d. [DVD].

"Matt Redman: Modern Psalmist." Portland, OR: LPA, n.d. [DVD].

"Portland Cityfest Luis Palau: Love, Serve, Celebrate." Portland, OR: LPA, 2008. [DVD].

Unpublished Material

Palau, Kevin. "A New Look for Mass Evangelism." n.d.

LPA. "Ministry Impact Statistics." September 2008.

LPA. "An Overview of Luis Palau's Life and Ministry." October 2007.

LPA. "Festival Counseling and Follow-up," n.d. [Microsoft PowerPoint File].

Internet

Chismar, Janet. "Luis Palau Heats Up New England." *Religion Today*, 6 June 2001 [online]. Accessed 12 July 2008. Available from http://www.crosswalk.com/news/religiontoday/525940/; Internet.

Sedensky, Matt. "Luis Who? Man Could Be Nation's Next Top Evangelist." *The Associated Press*, 29 April 2007 [online]. Accessed 27 September 2007. Available from http://www.ocala.com/apps/pbcs.dll/article?AID=/20070429/NEWS/204290362/1368/googlesitemapnews; Internet.

"Luis Palau Association Statement of Faith" [online]. Accessed 8 September 2008. Available from http://www.palau.org/about/mission; Internet.

"Luis Palau Association Mission Statement" [online]. Accessed 8 September 2008. Available from http://www.palau.org/about/mission; Internet.

"William (Billy) F. Graham" [online]. Accessed 25 November 2007. Available from http://www.billygraham.org/mediaRelations/bios.asp?p=1; Internet.

Websites

www.bgea.org
www.festivalvolunteer.com
www.godtube.com/luispalau
www.livinit.com
www.Palau.blip.tv
www.palau.org
www.reachingyourworld.org

Interviews

Palau, Kevin. Interview by author via telephone. August 8, 2008.

Palau, Luis. Interview by author via telephone. May 9, 2008.

____________. Second interview by author. Frisco, Texas. June 27, 2008.

Robnett, Timothy. Interview by author via telephone. August 6, 2008.

Williams, James. Interview by author via telephone. May 10, 2008.

____________. Second interview by author via telephone. August 8, 2008.